The Moncks and Charleville

House

The Moncks and Charleville House

House

by

Elisabeth Batt

BLACKWATER DUBLIN

I.S.B.N. 0 905471 08 3

The Blackwater Press
Folens Publishers
Airton Road
Tallaght
Co. Dublin.

Typeset and printed in the Republic of Ireland, by Folens Printing Co. Ltd.

Acknowledgments

I would like to thank all those who have given me valuable help; especially Mr. Michael Meaney who supplied most of the material on which the book is based, Canon Stokes who kindly read and corrected the manuscript, Professor W. L. Morton for valuable help with research, and Mrs. Kate Atterton who typed and retyped the manuscript, corrected the proofs and compiled the index.

I am also extremely grateful to Mr. McClelland of McClelland and Stewart, Toronto, for giving me permission to include material from "Monck, Governor General."

Genealogical Table

WILLIAM LE MOYNE (b. 14th - 15th century)

JOHN MONCKE
ancestor of
George Monck,
Duke of Albemarle

ROBERT MONCKE m. Elizabeth Eure

RICHARD m. Blanche Ansham

HENRY MONCK m. Johan Heathcock

CHARLES MONCK m. Elizabeth Blennerhassett
b. 15th century
General-Surveyor of
Customs in Ireland,
1617 and 1628
M.P. Strabane 1634-9
M.P. Coleraine 1639

HENRY MONCK m. 1673 Sarah Stanley

GEORGE MONCK m. Hon. Mary Molesworth
bp. 1705
barrister
M.P. Philipstown
(see page 4)

REBECCA MONCK m. John Forster

SARAH m. George
Berkeley,
Bishop of Cloyne

CHARLES MONCK m. 1695
bp. 1678   Agneta
barrister   Hitchcock
M.P. Newcastle,
Co. Durham 1711
M.P. Innistiogue
1713

WILLIAM MONCK m. Dorothy
bp. 1692   Bligh
(see page 4)

THOMAS MONCK m. 1753 Judith
Mason
(see page 2)

ANNE MONCK m. Henry
Quin, M.D.

HENRY MONCK m. 1739 Lady
Isabella
Bentinck

ELIZABETH m. Earl of
Tyrone
(1st Marquess
of Waterford)

1

THOMAS MONCK m. 1753 Judith Mason
barrister

WILLIAM MONCK m. Penelope Monck-Mason
b. 1763

Revd. THOMAS MONCK m. Jane Staples

CHARLES STANLEY MONCK m. 1784 Anne Quin
1st Viscount Monck
M.P. 1790 - 7
Gorey C. Waterford
d. 1802

ANNE ISABELLA MONCK m. 1777 Viscount Hawarden

HENRY STANLEY MONCK m. 1806 Lady Frances Le Poer Trench
1785 - 1848
2nd Viscount Monck
cr. 1st Earl of Rathdowne 1822

CHARLES JOSEPH m. 1817 Bridget Willington
KELLY MONCK
1791 - 1849
3rd Viscount Monck

ANNE WILHELMINA MONCK m. 1812 Daniel James Webb
b. 1786

ISABELLA MONCK m. 1805 Thomas Wilson
b. 1790

EMILY m. 1837 William Smythe
b. 1818
d. 1837
and had issue

LOUISA
b. 1820
d. 1870

GEORGINA m. 1841 Edward Croker
b. 1821
d. 1870
(and had issue)

CAROLINE
b. 1823
d. 1890

HARRIETTE (Henrietta)
b. 1825
d. 1899

MARY
b. 1828
d. 1881

ELIZABETH m. 1844 CHARLES STANLEY MONCK
LOUISE MARY
b. 1814
d. 1892
(see page 3)

WILLIAM MONCK

RICHARD m. Frances "Feo" Cole
MONCK

ANNE m. 1841 James Napier Wevv
MONCK

ISABELLA MONCK

HENRIETTA m. 1848 Francis Brooke
MONCK

ELIZABETH MONCK

(see page 5)

2 sons & 2 daughters d. in infancy

ANNE d. 1876

FRANCIS m. 1834 Owen Cole
b. 1809
d. 1871

FRANCES "FEO" b. 1835   FRANK b. 1837

CHARLES STANLEY MONCK
b. 1819; d. 1894
4th Viscount Monck m. 1844 Lady ELIZABETH LOUISE MARY MONCK

JOHN MONCK

2

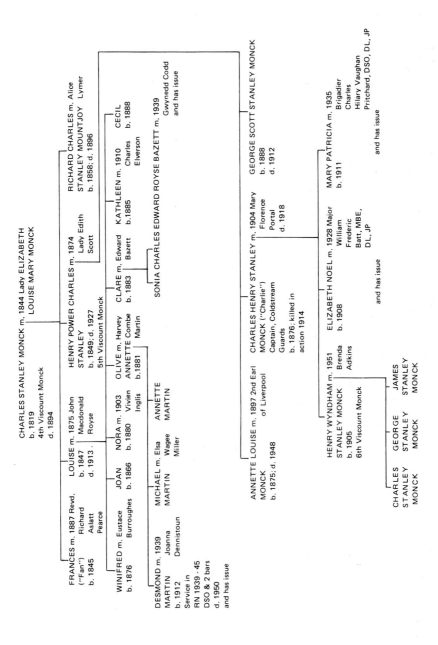

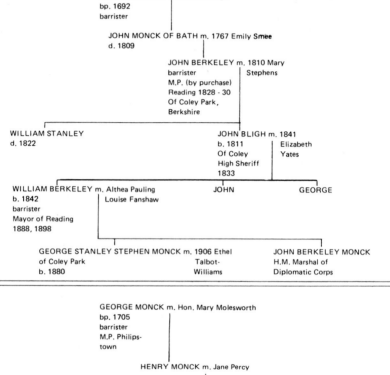

WILLIAM MONCK m. Dorothy Bligh
bp. 1692
barrister

JOHN MONCK OF BATH m. 1767 Emily Smee
d. 1809

JOHN BERKELEY m. 1810 Mary
barrister   Stephens
M.P. (by purchase)
Reading 1828 - 30
Of Coley Park,
Berkshire

WILLIAM STANLEY   JOHN BLIGH m. 1841
d. 1822   b. 1811   Elizabeth
                                         Of Coley   Yates
                                         High Sheriff
                                         1833

WILLIAM BERKELEY m. Althea Pauling   JOHN   GEORGE
b. 1842   Louise Fanshaw
barrister
Mayor of Reading
1888, 1898

GEORGE STANLEY STEPHEN MONCK m. 1906 Ethel   JOHN BERKELEY MONCK
of Coley Park   Talbot-   H.M. Marshal of
b. 1880   Williams   Diplomatic Corps

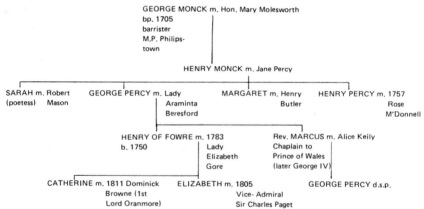

GEORGE MONCK m. Hon. Mary Molesworth
bp. 1705
barrister
M.P. Philips-
town

HENRY MONCK m. Jane Percy

SARAH m. Robert   GEORGE PERCY m. Lady   MARGARET m. Henry   HENRY PERCY m. 1757
(poetess) Mason   Araminta   Butler   Rose
                                 Beresford   M'Donnell

HENRY OF FOWRE m. 1783   Rev. MARCUS m. Alice Keily
b. 1750   Lady   Chaplain to
                  Elizabeth   Prince of Wales
                  Gore   (later George IV)

CATHERINE m. 1811 Dominick   ELIZABETH m. 1805   GEORGE PERCY d.s.p.
Browne (1st   Vice- Admiral
Lord Oranmore)   Sir Charles Paget

4

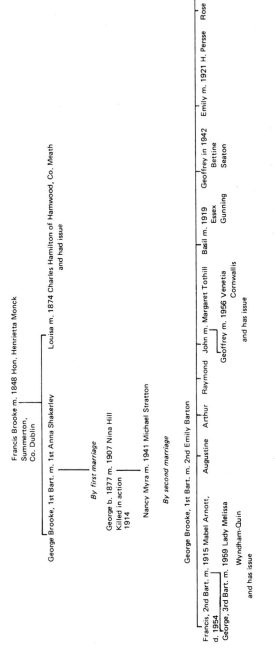

Francis Brooke m. 1848 Hon. Henrietta Monck
Summerton,
Co. Dublin

George Brooke, 1st Bart. m. 1st Anna Shakerley

Louisa m. 1874 Charles Hamilton of Hamwood, Co. Meath
and had issue

By first marriage

George b. 1877 m. 1907 Nina Hill
Killed in action
1914

Nancy Myra m. 1941 Michael Stratton

By second marriage

George Brooke, 1st Bart. m. 2nd Emily Barton

Francis, 2nd Bart. m. 1915 Mabel Arnott,
d. 1954
George, 3rd Bart. m. 1959 Lady Melissa
Wyndham-Quin
and has issue

Augustine   Arthur   Raymond   John m. Margaret Tothill

Geoffrey m. 1956 Venetia
Cornwallis
and has issue

Basil m. 1919
Essex
Gunning

Geoffrey in 1942
Bettine
Seaton

Emily m. 1921 H. Persse   Rose

5

Contents

PART I

IRELAND: 1819-1861

1

'No finer driver'

On the evening of 17 September 1828, Henry Rathdowne was sitting in his library waiting to be told the outcome of his wife's twelfth lying-in. If a shade of anxiety clouded the usual serenity of his handsome face, it was not solely on account of his wife Frances, dearly as he loved her; but because genealogically so much depended on the gender of the new baby. Of the eleven children born during the sixteen years of their marriage, three had died in infancy, including the only two boys. If the new arrival should be a girl, Henry Rathdowne's estates in counties Wicklow, Meath, Wexford, Dublin, Westmeath and Kilkenny, would pass to his soldier brother, Charles Joseph, who would also become the 3rd Viscount Monck. In this case there were circumstances which would make such a break in the direct line particularly unfortunate. The earldom of Rathdowne, bestowed by George IV six years earlier, would become extinct because, as a new creation, it could not pass to a brother or nephew.

Henry had no intention of allowing his wife to follow the example of her own mother, Anne Countess of Clancarty, who had borne nineteen children. Frances was now forty-one, only two years younger than himself; this must positively be her last performance, and she seemed to be taking her time over it.

It was getting on for midnight when the library door opened and a terrified manservant was pushed into the room. 'My lord,' he quavered, 'the doctor has desired me to inform you that her ladyship has had a little daughter.' Henry raised his blue eyes from the book he had been pretending to read and looked calmly at the nervous messenger. 'Please thank the doctor,' he said pleasantly, 'and say that I hope her ladyship and the little daughter are both very well.'

Presumably the doctor had expressed a wish that his patient be left undisturbed till morning, for Henry now retired for the night.

Never having been one to fret himself over what could not be helped, he was soon sleeping peacefully. But not for long. He was roused by a timid knock on the door, followed by the reluctant entrance of the same unfortunate servant. 'My lord,' he stammered, 'the doctor has asked me to say that her ladyship has just had – another little daughter.' Again Henry betrayed no emotion. 'I hope,' he said, 'that her ladyship and both little daughters are very well,' adding, as the man was leaving the room: 'If her ladyship should have any more little daughters, you needn't call me till eight.'

Neither then, nor at any time during the next fifteen years, did he refer to the sad fact that he had no direct heir, preferring to treat the situation as if it did not exist. Charles Joseph's eldest son, 'young' Charles, passed a happy childhood and adolescence in the peaceful obscurity of his father's modest home in County Tipperary, ignorant of the fact that the birth of two girl-cousins in 1828 had held any special significance for himself. For the time being, family letters and journals ignored his existence, dealing exclusively with the senior branch of the Monck family.

'Young' Charles' uncle, Henry Rathdowne, was often asked if he were descended from George Monck, the first Duke of Albemarle, of Restoration fame; and like the present generation, he grew tired of pointing out that there were no direct descendants of the great general whose son, the second Duke, had been childless. To those who were so ignorant as to suggest that the Moncks of Charleville obtained their Irish estates as the result of the general's good offices to Charles II, Henry retorted that, in 1660, his own ancestors had long been settled in Ireland and were already doing very nicely for themselves.

In actual fact, the Moncks owed a good proportion of their estates to their habit of making prudent marriages; it could almost be said that when they were not marrying their own first cousins, they were marrying heiresses. Henry Rathdowne's great-great-grandfather, Charles Monck*, a cousin of the Duke's father, was joint surveyor-general of customs in Ireland in 1627, and a survey of the northern ports, written in his own hand, is in the British Museum.

---

* Henry's great-great-grandfather, Charles Monck of St. Stephen's Green, Dublin, a cousin of the Duke's father, was admitted to King's Inn in 1617; Surveyor-general of all the customs in Ireland in 1618 and 1627; M.P. for Strabane in 1634; and subsequently M.P. for Coleraine.

Twelve years later he had a seat in parliament as member for Coleraine, and had acquired land in County Westmeath. He married the daughter of Sir John Blennerhassett, the Lord Chief Baron of the Exchequer.

His son Henry owned a house and large garden on the east side of St. Stephen's Green in Dublin. His marriage to Sarah Stanley brought him the estate of Grangegorman in County Dublin, in acknowledgment of which her surname was given as an extra baptismal name to the eldest son in every succeeding generation. In 1705 Henry and Sarah's son, Charles, married the less romantically named Agneta Hitchcock. She inherited a house and lands in County Wicklow, which had been granted to her great-uncle, Sir William Flower, by Charles II. From this time, the Monck family made the Wicklow house, Charleville, their home; which gave rise to the remark made early in the present century by one of their descendants: 'The Moncks are such snobs! They all call their sons Stanley, but not one single Monck has ever been christened Hitchcock.' Agneta's inheritance was the last addition made to the Moncks' landed property. It had been acquired by them by purchase or through marriage, but had originally been wrested from the Irish owners during successive invasions of that country.

Charles and Agneta had three children – Henry, Thomas and Anne. After his father's death, Henry commissioned the building of three houses in Upper Merrion Street, keeping Number 21 for his own use. Number 24 was sold to Lord Mornington and subsequently became the birthplace of the future Duke of Wellington. Henry's marriage to Isabella ('Bell') Bentinck, daughter of the first Duke of Portland, put his family on the social-political map, if only in a modest corner of it. He was the last to marry an heiress; thereafter the Moncks married for love, with a strong bias towards their own cousins.

Before the second half of the eighteenth century the history of the Monck family consists of a list of faceless names, a succession of Charleses alternating with Henrys – politicians, soldiers or barristers – and a list of the names of their wives and of the properties, if any, brought into the family by the said wives. Halfway through the century, however, some of them begin to 'get up off the page', headed by one who brought a new strain into the Monck ancestry, and a strain of true Irish blood at that. This was a certain

5

Doctor Henry Quin, an M.B. of Trinity College, Dublin, as well as
an M.D. of Padua, who had in Dublin what has been described as 'a
fashionable and well-rewarded practice'.[1] Appointed as King's
Professor of the Practice of Medicine and successively Censor,
Registrar, Treasurer and six times President of The Royal College of
Physicians, it is hard to know how he found time for his patients;
especially as, besides 'uncommon ability' in the art of copying
ancient cameos and intaglios in glass paste, polished and coloured
with metallic pigments, learnt while studying in Italy, he was also
particularly noted as an outstanding harpsichord player. He had a
private theatre in his house in St. Stephen's Green (now St. Patrick's
Nurses' Home) and private concerts were performed there.

He is best remembered, however, for being among the select few
to perform in Lord Mornington's celebrated 'Musical Academy for
Amateurs' in Fishamble Street. The name 'Academy' is misleading
as no music was taught there; in fact no professional musicians were
allowed inside what was an extremely snobbish and exclusive
musical club, the membership of which was confined to 'persons
moving in the highest sphere of society'. In spite of this a high
standard was maintained and it was a distinction to be asked to
perform at the monthly private concerts, for which the performers
rehearsed weekly, and also at the annual public concert by means of
which enough money was raised to provide £4 for each of nearly
13,000 poor families.

Anne Monck, younger sister of Henry Monck of Charleville, was
among the performers who included among others the Archbishop
of Tuam, the Earl of Lucan, the Earl of Bellamont and the Provost
of Trinity College. Anne Monck's brother Henry had become dis-
agreeably pompous since connecting himself with the politically
powerful Bentinck family, but even he could not object to his sister
making music in such distinguished company. However he was soon
to regret his leniency. By her regular attendance at the rehearsals,
Anne was thrown weekly into the company of the charming and
talented Doctor Quin who, as a star performer and liked by
everyone, was seen to his best advantage at the 'Academy'.

Anne was no weakling and she defied her brother whose anger
was terrible when he heard that *his* sister wished to marry a man who
earned his living by applying leeches and prescribing pills and
purges. 'Harry Monck's sister is to marry Dr. Quin, a very ingenious

man who is in great vogue,' wrote Mrs. Delany, the Madame de Sévigné of Ireland. 'Mr. Monck told his sister that he could not ask the Duke of Portland's sister to *sit in the room* with the son of an apothecary. To this Miss Monck retorted: "Brother, I am sorry for your pride." When I told the Duchess of this, she laughed much and said: "Why, I know him well. He has visited us and dined with us."'[2] Throughout the controversy, Anne Monck stood firm. She and her doctor married and raised a family of little Quins, only one of whom is relevant to this story: a daughter who was given her mother's name, Anne.

'Harry' Monck had some excuse for his jaundiced outlook on life. His fourteen years of marriage had produced only one child, a daughter Elizabeth*, while his brother Thomas had three sons and a daughter**. Thomas Monck, who had married his cousin, Judith Mason, was M.P. for Old Leighlin. A barrister by profession, he is chiefly remembered for having been one of the quartet to draw up the complicated will of the actress, Peg Woffington. When he died in 1772, his eldest son, Charles Stanley, became his uncle's heir.

Charles Stanley, grandson of Charles and Agneta, and grandfather of 'Young' Charles, was sent to Eton when he was ten years old. During his third year in the school there took place 'the most serious rebellion that is ever known to have occurred at Eton' originating in a controversy between the Assistant Masters and the Sixth Form Praepostors.'[3]

In 1775, Charles Stanley was gazetted as a cornet in the 14th Light Dragoons, and became a captain four years later. Three troops of his regiment were stationed at Carrick-on-Suir in 1782, and he was the Captain Monck referred to in 'Retrospection' by Dorothea Herbert. This daughter of a parson in the Established (Protestant) Church wrote that:

> The Right Boys attacked a party of our men who were out at night drawing Mountain Tythes. They beat them most desperately, left them for dead, and carried off the Tythe Corn. We sat up till four o'clock for them and sent a second party to

---

*   In 1769 Elizabeth Monck married Lord Tyrone, later created Marquis of Waterford.
** Thomas Monck's daughter, Anne Isabella, married in 1777, Cornwallis Maude, Baron de Montalt and 1st Viscount Hawarden.

reconnoitre. Them also they beat, and great was our horror to see them return mangled and covered with blood, without their Companions – whilst their Wives and Children came shrieking for their Husbands and parents. The Day following was the Fair Day of Carrick. Mr. Cox and Captain Monck of the 14th Light Dragoons with a party of Military scoured the Country, surrounded the Ringleaders in their Houses, and lodged them in gaol.

Charles Stanley, 1st Viscount Monck as a boy, painted circa 1768, by Robert Hunter.

This incident was one of numerous protests against the unjust tithe system which compelled Irish Catholics to support Protestant clergy. Many of those who had to pay tithes had barely enough to live on themselves, without contributing to the support of a church which they looked on as alien and heretical. In a lesser degree the system was hard on the Protestant clergy, who were victims of reprisals against a system which they had no power to abolish.

The young captain had no alternative other than to carry out his military duties, the chief of which was the suppression of violence and lawlessness. Eighty years later his grandson, 'young' Charles, was to protest strongly against the tithe system, and was among those who worked for its suppression. But the Charles of 1782 was a soldier, and thus bound by his oath of allegiance to King George III. Even when he left the army and entered the world of politics, he still remained a loyal subject of the English Crown, though he never thought of himself as anything but an Irishman.

It is not known whether Henry Monck made peace with his sister, Mrs. Quin, after her marriage, or whether he still refused to allow his wife to 'sit in the room' with Doctor Quin. While his sister had disappointed his social aspirations, in 1769 his only daughter, Elizabeth, made up for it by marrying Lord Tyrone, later to become the first Marquess of Waterford. If there had been a breach between the Monck and Quin families, it was bridged by young Lady Tyrone who joined the 'Musical Academy' as a harpsichordist. Whatever her relations may or may not have been with her uncle and aunt Quin, one member of the Monck family was on very intimate terms with them. This was Charles Stanley, old Henry Monck's nephew, heir and hope for the future. It must have been a bitter blow to the old man when Charles announced his intention of marrying his first cousin, Anne Quin, daughter of the man who was considered unfit to associate with Lady Isabella Monck. On the other hand, it was a happy day for Mrs. Quin when in 1784 she saw her daughter married to the future owner of her old home, which she herself had left under a cloud of disapproval at the time of her marriage to the doctor.

In 1787 old Henry Monck died and Charles Stanley and Anne went to live at Charleville when their son, Henry Stanley, was two years old. His birth was followed by that of two daughters, Anne Wilhelmina and Isabella; and in 1791 by a second son, Charles Joseph. Charles Stanley was thirty-six when he inherited Charleville

Left: Charles Stanley, 1st Viscount Monck (1754-1802). Miniature by Charles Robertson.
Below Left: Anne, Viscountess Monck (d. 1822). Miniature by Charles Robertson.
Below Right: Henry Stanley (1785-1848) and Anne Wilhelmina Monck. Miniature by Charles Robertson.

and the Moncks' Dublin house in Upper Merrion Street besides estates in five other counties. In 1790 he entered the Irish House of Commons as member for Gorey in County Wexford. If he was politically ambitious, he was fortunate in his family connections; his sister, Anne Isabella, was married to Lord de Montalt, the member for the borough of Roscommon, who had lately been created Viscount Hawarden; while the 3rd Duke of Portland, nephew of Charles's aunt-by-marriage, had been successively Lord Lieutenant of Ireland, Prime Minister, Chancellor of Oxford University and Home Secretary.

Charles was helped and influenced by this statesman who was one of the chief of those who worked for the union between the English and Irish parliaments, for, as has been truly said, the independent Irish Parliament 'contained the seeds of its own destruction'.[4] It was composed of many conflicting interests and its constitution was never, at any time, on a satisfactory basis. The longed-for legislative independence had been welcomed in 1782 with enthusiasm, and it seemed at first that the Golden Age had dawned. But although much that was good was achieved, so many wrongs of such long standing could not be put right within a few years, especially when there were differences of opinion as to priority and method. The two great leaders, Henry Flood and Henry Grattan, were not always in accord; independence meant different things to different people and was, to a certain extent, only nominal. In theory, the Irish Parliament was subordinate only to the English Crown; but the Crown was represented by the Lord Lieutenant of Ireland who, with his Chief Secretary and other officials, constituted the Executive, and were all appointed in England by the party then in power. '. . . The Attorney General of England, with a dash of his pen, can reverse, alter, or entirely do away the matured result of all the eloquence, and all the abilities of this whole assembly.'[5] Irish legislation was therefore influenced by the fluctuations of English party politics, and never had a fair chance.

The Catholics were not the only body who considered that the concessions made to them did not go far enough; there was widespread discontent, inflamed by the news of the French Revolution. One of the causes of the outbreak of war between England and France was the publication in 1792 of a decree by the French Convention, 'offering help to all those nations who desired to overthrow their kings.' In 1791 the Society of United Irishmen had been formed with the object of setting up an independent republic. Led by Wolfe Tone and Lord Edward Fitzgerald, the Society had originally consisted mainly of Presbyterians from the north who had been greatly influenced by the American War of Independence. They were soon joined by the Catholic leaders; an attempt to suppress the Society drove it underground and a yeomanry corps was raised to maintain. order. Resentment increased as parts of the country were placed under what was virtually military rule, which was sometimes extremely harsh. True to their promise, in 1797 the French sent an expeditionary force to assist the republicans; but the expedition, under General Hoche, was dispersed by a storm at sea and never landed in Ireland. In the Irish Commons, Grattan was still pressing for further reforms, which were now considered dangerous by those who supported the English Crown, while falling short of the demands of the republicans.

Meanwhile, in many parts of the Irish countryside, the ordinary business of life pursued its humdrum course as if no threat of civil war hung over the island. After listening to the thunder of Grattan's oratory during turbulent sessions in College Green, Charles Stanley Monck would return to peaceful Charleville where he had assumed certain responsibilities in local government. There exists a printed pamphlet recording resolutions of the Association of Local Inhabitants of the Parishes of Bray and Powerscourt, during three meetings in the year 1791, with Charles Stanley Monck in the chair. The Association included some magistrates, and the resolutions passed were chiefly concerned with 'regulating the issuing of Licences for the Sale of Spirituous Liquors by Retail, and for remedying the abuses arisen from the immoderate use of such Liquors', and 'the prosecution of such Persons as clandestinely sell Spirituous Liquors without Licences'. Other subjects of resolutions included sheep-stealing and 'stealing or unlawfully cutting down, lopping or barking Trees'; also that 'the Sale of Light Bread in the Town of Bray is a Grievance, and that we will all endeavour as much as is in our Power to remedy the Evil; that we will call on the proper Magistrate to punish such Persons who shall sell Bread not of proper Weight, or use false Weights. That a Constable be appointed for the immediate Service of the Association, be allowed Four Guineas annually, as a fixed salary, and be further awarded according to his Merits in the Discharge of his Duty.' The meeting ended with a resolution 'that our Secretary do provide a proper Book to enter the Resolutions of this Meeting, and the same be signed by Members present.'

The Moncks stayed at 21 Upper Merrion Street while parliament was sitting, and Anne thoroughly enjoyed the social life in what was then a gay and fashionable city. Forty years later, old Mrs. Martin of Ballynahinch Castle entertained Maria Edgeworth with 'anecdotes of people in the world with whom she had lived in her youth', including 'Lady Monk [*sic*] and her lovers among princes and emperors'.[6]

Even in the country Anne liked to follow the prevailing fashion, and the latest whim among Irish chatelaines was the building of a small cottage or pavilion, fitted up in 'rustic' style, in which they and their friends could drink tea on summer evenings. In the next generation, this Irish version of Marie Antoinette's *Petit Trianon* became, at Charleville, a play-house for the children of the family. Anne's grand-daughter refers, in her journal, to 'Our Cottage', near the ravine in the demesne* known as 'The Glen'. No trace of the building remains, but a copse adjoining the Glen is called 'Cottage Wood' to this day.

When Charles Stanley's son Henry was nine years old, he was sent to Eton, the headmaster then being Dr. Heath. The early age at which boys then entered the school accounts for the childish nature of some of their pastimes, such as 'Bandalores'. 'A bandalore was a disc of boxwood with a deep groove in its outer edge, round which a string was coiled. The art was to send it flying through the air, uncoiling the string as it went, and by giving a jerk at a particular moment to bring the disc back again to the hand, recoiling the string on its return journey.'[7] The bandalore reappeared during the nineteen-thirties as the 'yo-yo', and has lately made a come-back in boys' preparatory schools. It may have been Henry's enthusiasm for bandalores, or for more exacting sports, which caused his name to appear in the 1796 lists as 'almost at the bottom of the school, and not much higher up in 1799'. During the latter part of his time at Eton, he was one of the boys who broke the rule which forbade tandem driving. Dr. Heath was famous for being a strict disciplinarian, but even he 'entirely failed to suppress this activity. On

* In Ireland the word 'demesne' is used instead of 'park'.

13

every holiday or half-holiday in his time, three or four tandems might be seen leaving the yard at Windsor, driven by Eton boys.'[8]

His elder son's lack of academic distinction was a sad disappointment to Charles, and was perhaps the cause of his decision to send Charles Joseph to Rugby instead of to Eton. Dean Liddell, looking back on this period, wrote that: 'Except in the case of the Rugby boys, slovenliness of style and incorrectness in writing English were the characteristics of public schoolboys.'[9] Charles Joseph went to Rugby in January 1799, twenty years before Dr. Arnold became headmaster. The poor child was only seven-and-a-half; but Charles Stanley had good reason for wishing both his sons out of Ireland during the months following the national rising of 1798.

In his *Short History of Ireland,* J. C. Beckett briefly summarises two irreconcilable views: 'To the English, the outbreak of rebellion, at a critical time of the war with France, was another of the many instances of Irish treachery; to the Irish, the suppression of the rebels was another example of English ruthlessness.' The two conflicting points of view could be summed up by the use of the word 'rebels' to describe those patriots who sought to free their country from the tyranny of English ascendancy. Just as a private road can be recognised by law as a right-of-way, if used by the public over a certain length of time, so Ireland had been an occupied country for so long that the English tended to regard her as a rather troublesome extension of England. Any attempts at resistance were designated treacherous and disloyal; whereas the suppression of their language, the Penal Laws and the trade restrictions were only some of the many reminders to Irishmen that they were subject to enemy occupation. 'The Irish peasant was crushed by a land system which . . . rested on the expropriation of land which he considered, by right, to belong to him . . . He felt he had been robbed of his heritage.'[10] Although in the eighteenth century the dispossession of the Irish was ancient history, it was still remembered in Ireland, the more so since the Irish were kept in subjection, poverty and illiteracy through the injustices of British rule and through the harshness of the agents of absentee landlords.[11] It was also remembered during the next century by Charles Stanley's grandson, 'young' Charles, who devoted his life to trying to persuade the British government to

14

repair injustices, and to remember that Irish tenants and labourers had 'rights of their own' with regard to the land.

Occurring at the height of the struggle between England and France, the '98 Rebellion sealed the fate of the independent Irish Parliament. For some years past there had been members in both English and Irish governments who had discussed the union of the two parliaments as a probable necessity. The Irish Parliament was divided on this point but those in favour believed it to be the only solution to what had become an impossible situation; and many Irish Catholics were in favour of the union believing that they would thereby get a fairer deal than they had been given by the Irish Parliament. *The Oxford History of England* states that 'the terms of the Union were never laid down before the Irish people and the two houses of the Irish Parliament voted their own abolition only after a shameful distribution of money and titles.'

It could have been owing to the influence of wire-pulling friends and relatives that Charles Monck had been created Baron Monck of Ballytrammon (in the peerage of Ireland) in 1797; but the subsequent Viscountcy bestowed on him in 1801 is believed to have been the direct result of his having voted for the Act of Union which was passed in the year 1800. He was among those who believed political union with England to be the only way out of the troubles which beset the Irish Parliament.[12] By the time he arrived at that painful decision, the strain of divided loyalties had seriously affected his health.

The only surviving reference to his illness is in a postscript to a long and rambling letter to Anne from their cousin, John Berkeley Monck, of Marlborough Buildings, Bath. He refers to Charles' and Anne's recent stay in Bath, chiefly in order to complain of having seen so little of them while they were there, affecting to disclaim any right to their time and attention while they could 'pass their time so much more agreeably with other relations such as Lord and Lady Hawarden who . . . *move* in so *different* a *Sphere* as to belong (as it were) to quite another *System* . . . so that he [Lord Hawarden] is now not only among the Lords, but *almost* among the Gods.'

A fortnight after the above letter was written, Charles benefited by the 'shameful distribution of titles' and was created a Viscount in the peerage of Ireland. He did not long enjoy this distinction. Five months later he was dead and his son Henry became Viscount

Monck, just seven weeks before his seventeenth birthday.

At Easter 1802, Henry had left Eton, never to return. Since he had made so little use of his eight years at school, some intensive private tuition was necessary, even in those days, to prepare him to enter Christ Church, Oxford, in the Hilary Term of 1804. Judging by the few letters which survive, he was not illiterate though there is no evidence that he was ever an intellectual type. Apart from his love of horses, his chief enthusiasms were for music and amateur theatricals. These last were then very popular and, by all accounts, some of the productions reached a high standard. Large gatherings would assemble for rehearsals in a country house, such as Carton*, and other guests would join the house party in time for the performance. 'Viscount Monck was an amateur actor at the private theatre at Kilkenny at which, among others, Tommy Moore assisted. He excelled in such characters as 'Diggory', 'Tony Lumpkin' and the Jew in *The School for Scandal.'*[13] He also sang and played the 'cello and it was as an amateur musician that he became a member and eventually President of the Dublin Beefsteak Club.[14] This Club had been founded in the previous century by Thomas Sheridan, father of Richard Brinsley Sheridan, and in the nineteenth century it had become the leading musical club in Dublin.

He entered the university as a 'nobleman', which meant that he dined at a table set aside for peers, wore a gold-braided gown and a gold tassel on his mortar board. This tassel was known as a 'tuft' and gave rise to the word 'tuft-hunter', which was the current term used to describe a social climber. Officially the 'noblemen' were exempt from all examinations. However, when Henry went up to Oxford, the Dean of Christ Church was Dr. Cyril Jackson who was noted for getting work out of the undergraduates regardless of their rank. Henry was not allowed to waste his time, although his only distinction at Oxford was his having been the subject of these lines of doggerel in celebration of his prowess as a four-in-hand whip:

> There's my Lord Monck;
> Whether sober or drunk,
> There's no finer driver
> Than my Lord Monck.

* Carton, in County Meath, was the home of the Duke of Leinster.

The Christ Church records report that he 'went down in Hilary Term, 1806'; this was for no more sinister reason than that he was shortly to be married.

He showed good taste in his choice of a bride, Frances le Poer Trench being by far the most attractive personality in this gallery of family 'portraits'. Her family were originally French Huguenots, but one of her ancestors had married Frances Power, a descendant of Cormac Oge McCarty, thus bringing a strain of true Irish blood into the Trench family. Henry Monck could also claim Irish descent through his mother who had been Anne Quin. Frances' father, the 1st Earl of Clancarty, of Garbally Park, County Galway, had died in 1805. He has been described as 'an inveterate gambler who ran through two fortunes, leaving his wife and family mortgaged up to the hilt.'

Coming nearly at the end of a family of nineteen, Frances had been brought up in straitened circumstances. Luckily her mother was a woman of no mean spirit; somehow she managed to get all her children educated. Her sons rose high in their respective professions while her daughters made 'good' marriages from a material point of view. Rumour has it that her daughters, if not her sons, all spoke with strong Irish brogues. This did not prevent Lady Clancarty from running Garbally like a little court, exacting the strictest ceremony, the influence of which persisted long after her death.[15] Her eldest daughter, Anne, who married William Gregory of Coole Park, inspired the first couplet of a rhyming alphabet on the Trench family:

A's for Lady Anne, a mighty stiff party,
Who curtseyed each morn to her mother, Clancarty.

The 'stiffness' did not persist throughout this family of nineteen and there was no trace of it in Frances who was the youngest daughter but one. She was enchanting to look at, and Henry had to face keen competition. Since their early childhood they had had plenty of opportunities for meeting. The Ballinasloe Fair was one of Ireland's most popular social occasions, besides being the largest sheep and cattle fair in the country and the second largest horse fair in the world. It was held annually on the Garbally estate, and Lord Clancarty was its patron.

After his death, Anne Lady Clancarty had a house in Belvedere Place, Dublin, from where, according to the Reverend Robert Daly, Frances took part in 'the gaieties of the world'. Henry was determined to marry her daughter, Frances, before someone else carried her off, and their wedding took place in Dublin on 26 July 1806, when Henry was two days short of his twenty-first birthday. Soon afterwards, Henry's widowed mother married Sir John Carden of Templemore Priory in County Tipperary; she was his fourth wife. This now became the home of her two daughters and Charles Joseph. All three married neighbours of their stepfather, and settled in the same county; and this was why Charles Joseph's son, 'young' Charles, was born and brought up in County Tipperary.

Fanny's immediate task was to produce an heir for Henry, and she dutifully settled down to do so. Unfortunately, her first three children were all girls, the eldest, born in 1807, being baptised Anne after her two grandmothers. Fanny-the-second followed in 1809, and Harriet arrived in the January of 1811 but only lived for thirteen months. Her death in February 1812 came at a bad time for Frances who was expecting her fourth child. But sorrow was turned to triumphant joy when, in May, the long-awaited son was born. The Moncks' troubles, however, were not over. Charles Stanley Spencer Perceval was 'always delicate', and when he was eleven months old, Frances took him to stay at her mother's Dublin house in Belvedere Place in order to get 'medical advice'. The child and his nurse were accommodated in a 'very good airy room', usually occupied by Jane Masters who was lady's maid to Lady Clancarty's unmarried daughter, Louisa. But the medical advice, airy room and devoted nursing were of no avail, and little Charles died.[3]

The arrival, on 1 March 1814, of Elizabeth Louise Mary was not an occasion of unmixed rejoicing, although her parents had been growing accustomed to disappointment. There was nothing for it but to try again, and William Power Stanley was born less than two years later. When the baby was two months old, Frances took him with her on a visit to one of her elder sisters, Lady Elizabeth McClintock, who lived at Dunleer in County Louth. She travelled the forty-odd miles in her own carriage, changing horses at least three times at the post-houses which served much the same purpose as the filling-stations of to-day. The probable reason for taking so young a child on a journey was that she had determined to nurse him herself. Whether or not she usually followed the prevailing fashion of employing a wet-nurse for that purpose, this precious little son was to be entrusted to no-one but his mother. But the visit to Drumcar, the McClintocks' home, proved fatal to William, who caught 'the hooping-cough' there and died.

In contrast to the delicacy of her short-lived brothers and of some of her sisters, Elizabeth Louise Mary was almost indecently healthy. During the whole of her life, until a short time before she died at the age of seventy-eight, there is no record of her having had a day's illness. But the flourishing state of at least one of their daughters did not atone to Henry and Frances for the loss of their two little sons; nor was it any consolation to them to hear, between the births of Emily in 1818 and Georgina in 1820, that Charles Joseph's first child was a boy, 'young' Charles. This is very nearly where we came in, since it was the existence of 'young' Charles, with two young brothers thrown in, that aggravated the Rathdownes' disappointment when their twin daughters were born in 1828.

Charles Joseph, Henry Rathdowne's younger brother, had joined the 43rd Regiment in 1811 and been with Wellington's army in Spain. He was badly wounded during the Peninsular campaign but was able to return to his regiment in time to be present at the battle of Vittoria, when Wellington ran the French out of Spain, and at Toulouse, which was the last battle of the Peninsular War. After Napoleon's abdication, while the victorious allies assembled for the Congress of Vienna, Charles Joseph's regiment was sent to America. They took part in the battle of New Orleans, and sailed for Europe in May 1815. On arrival at Spithead they learnt that Napoleon had escaped from Elba and that the'peace' was at an end. The 43rd sailed for the Netherlands, but did not reach Ghent until 19 June – missing the battle of Waterloo by one day. They joined the other allied troops who were occupying Paris, and on 24 September, Charles Joseph wrote from there to his sister, Anne Wilhelmina. She had been married three years earlier to Daniel James Webb of County Tipperary, where her mother was now living as the wife of Sir John Carden. 'There is every possibility of our remaining in the neighbourhood of Paris for these many months to come,' wrote Charles Joseph –

The Prussians are not at all in favor of the King.* There was a Plot discovered a few days since by the Government, and ninety thousand stand of arms taken up, which were of course intended for the lovers of Buonaparte to act against the Loyalists. The Plot was, that on the day appointed for the signing of the Peace a number of the Buonapartists were to go into the Senate House armed with stilettos with the intention of putting to death all the Allied Sovereigns as also Louis 18th. They say that the army on the Loire is broken up and the greatest part of them are now larking about Paris, and it is supposed the arms which were taken were intended for them.

The whole of the British force were reviewed about two miles from Paris last week, it must have been a very grand sight for the spectators, but very disagreeable I assure you for the Performers, as we were the whole time in a Cloud of Dust.

The Allies have taken away almost all the Pictures out of the Gallery of the Louvre, and as they still continue carrying them off I suppose by the end of next week they will all be gone.

I saw very little of Henry Carden** while he was near Paris, as his Regt only remained a short time, and they were some miles at the opposite side of Paris to what we are. We are only about a mile and half from the Town in Camp.

I saw young Lalor of Cranagh the other evening, who told me you were all well . . . I heard from a Friend of mine yesterday who had seen a Dublin paper, that Isabella's marriage was in it, but shall not write to congratulate her on it until it is officially notified. At any rate I sincerely wish her all happiness. Pray apologise to my Mother for my being so infamously idle in not writing to her, and tell her that when we get into winter quarters I shall write constantly.

Is the *beautiful* and *amiable* Miss Darby married yet? I have not forgotten her tho' so long away. I do not mean in the sentimental way of talking as at present I have no thoughts of it. Remember me kindly to Mr. Webb who I hope shortly to have the pleasure of being acquainted with. I suppose you see my Mother almost every day. Remember me affectionately to her and Sir John, etc., and all my friends in your neighbourhood . . .

* Louis XVIII, brother of Louis XVI who had been guillotined in the Revolution.
** Henry Carden was the son of Charles' step-father by a former marriage.

20

Charles Joseph's familiarity with the neighbourhood of
Templemore suggests that his mother had married and settled there
before he joined his regiment in 1811. Evidently he had not been
home on leave since that date, as he had still to make the acquaintance of his brother-in-law, Daniel Webb, and of Thomas Wilson,
also of Tipperary, whose marriage to Isabella Monck had just taken
place. Charles Joseph also made his home in Tipperary when he left
the army, having married in 1817 – not the beautiful and amiable
Miss Darby, but Bridget Willington of Killeskehane in the same
county.

Notes to Chapter One

1   J. D. H. Widdess, *History of the Royal College of Physicians in Ireland* (Edinburgh, 1963).
2   Llanover, Lady (ed.), *The autobiography and correspondence of Mary Granville, Mrs. Delany* (London, 1861).
3   H. C. Maxwell Lyte, *A history of Eton College 1440-1875* (London, 1875).
4   M. Hayden and J. A. Moonan, *A short history of the Irish People* (Dublin, 1922).
5   Arthur Young, *A tour in Ireland . . .* (Dublin, 1780).
6   Edgeworth, Maria, *Tour in Connemara and the Martins of Ballinahinch* (London 1950).
7   Sir H. Maxwell Lyte, *op. cit.*
8   Ibid.
9   Gregory, Lady Augusta (ed.), *Sir William Gregory: an autobiography* (London, 1894).
10 Sir Winston Churchill, *A history of the English-speaking peoples* (Blenheim).
11 'Probably on your property and (on) mine is living in a cabin the man whose forefathers possessed them, and every feeling of whose nature . . . induces him, and those who sympathise with him, to wish for our downfall.' John Robert Godley to William Monsell, 1847.
12 'Corrupt, unrepresentative, unable to control the executive, its very laws still subject to a royal veto exercised by the British Government of the day, the glorified colonial assembly which was snuffed out by the Act of Union . . . was far from the ideal Parliament.' F. S. L. Lyons, *Ireland Since the Famine*, (London, 1972).
13 O. B. Cole to W. E. Gladstone, 11 October 1848. Gladstone Papers. B.M.
14 In 1823 the members of the Beefsteak Club presented a jewelled, gold snuffbox to their President. Set with diamonds and emeralds, the lid was bordered by an assortment of musical instruments surrounding the initial 'R' beneath an earl's coronet. The interior is

engraved with Henry's arms, and the jewelled underside with the presentation inscription: 'By the Members of the Beef Steak Club of Dublin to the Earl of Rathdowne. In testimony of their high respect for him, and as a mark of their unanimous approbation of His Lordship's conduct during the many years he has been President of their Society.' (Sotheby)

15 Thackeray remarked on the courtly manners in Irish houses he visited, while in other ways there was less formality between parents and children than in England. W. M. Thackeray. *My Irish Sketchbook* (London, 1843).

2

Henry and Frances

When Henry took his nineteen-year-old bride to Charleville, it was still called 'the new house' and described in contemporary guide-books as 'a handsome modern mansion of granite'. It had been built by Henry's father, Charles Stanley, to replace the old house which was destroyed by fire in 1792.[1] He had commissioned the building of an austerely dignified house, the front of which is in Palladian style

Charleville House, County Wicklow.

and described as 'a close copy of the front of Lucan House, County Dublin. The beautiful silvery-grey local limestone of which the front and sides of Charleville are built makes the house particularly attractive in its setting of parkland and mountain,'[2] four miles inland from the Irish Sea and guarded from the north, south and west by the Wicklow Mountains.

The well-proportioned rooms, with their magnificent ceilings and cornices and solid mahogany doors, were exactly as they are today. Fanny brought with her a handsome gilt clock to stand on the marble chimney-piece in the 'large drawing room'. Though made in London, it has always been called 'the Sèvres clock' and is ornamented by a curious group consisting of a young mother seated on a bench and clasping the upraised foreleg of a nanny-goat, who gazes enquiringly into her face; while a naked child lies on the ground sucking at the goat's teat. It is still in the possession of the Monck family, as is the pianoforte which, in those days, stood in the barrel-ceilinged 'small drawing room'. Opinions differ as to who was the original owner of the beautiful little mahogany 'square', ornamented with gilt rosettes and inlay; but very likely it had belonged to Doctor Henry Quin, and was brought to Charleville by his daughter when she married Charles Monck.*

After the union of the English and Irish Parliaments, Dublin ceased to be a centre of fashion, but at no period of his life did Henry join the ranks of the absentee landlords who spent most of their time, and their Irish rents, in London. Unlike his father, he appears to have been totally devoid of ambition, political or otherwise, though it does not necessarily follow that he was without occupation. As the Irish equivalent of 'provincial squire', he held various posts in local government such as Justice of the Peace and Deputy Lieutenant in County Wicklow, and served on charitable committees in Dublin; in addition to which, his far larger estates in other parts of Ireland involved local commitments in those counties. His land in County Wicklow was more or less surrounded by the large Powerscourt estate which was constantly being added to. Powerscourt House stood high and was a well-known landmark in the countryside; while Charleville can only be seen, from a distance,

---

* According to Dr. Burney, the square painoforte was introduced into England in 1762 by Johann Christian Bach. It was the first keyboard instrument with a 'hammer' action, instead of the 'plucking' action of the harpsichord which it resembles in appearance.

by climbing one of the hills which surround the Glencree valley. Approaching it by either the front or the back avenue, one comes upon it unawares, wherein lies part of its charm.

The Powerscourts were more fashionable than the Moncks, whose interests and activities were almost entirely confined to Ireland, whereas successive Viscounts Powerscourt are mentioned in eighteenth- and early nineteenth-century memoirs of social and political circles in London. Yet, although they never intermarried, there was such a close association between the two families that it is impossible to write about one without including the other. Their houses, built on opposite sides of the river Dargle which ran between the two properties, were divided from each other by three miles of carriage-drive and road, but were only a mile apart by way of the private footpath and footbridge. The relations between them were friendly, apart from an occasional scuffle over boundaries or 'grass rights', inevitable when the said boundaries zig-zagged in and out of each other and were never very clearly defined.

The Topographical History of Ireland describes the 'abundance [in Glencree] of highly-cultivated demesnes, luxuriant plantations and wooded eminences, finely contrasting with the rude grandeur of rugged masses of rock rising majestically from the narrow glens, and the loftier elevation of the surrounding mountains.' The village nearest to both Charleville and Powerscourt is Enniskerry, and guide-books of the last century never mention it without alluding to the 'salubrious' mountain and sea air which made the district popular.

Besides the large 'demesnes' such as Powerscourt, there were many smaller properties and the Moncks had plenty of neighbours, the nearest to Charleville being the Grattans of Tinnehinch and the Howards of Bushey Park. Henry Grattan, the Irish statesman, had built a house at Tinnehinch; part of the site had been leased to him by the 3rd Lord Powerscourt, while part was 'leased in 1790 by Charles Stanley Monck . . . for three lives.' Even without these and many other neighbours, Fanny could not have been lonely. Her elder brothers and sisters with their families were often staying at Charleville; she and Henry visited their homes which were scattered all over Ireland, and she was in close touch with her mother, Anne Lady Clancarty, who had a house in Dublin.

Henry was very gregarious and enjoyed seeing his friends; but because of his great love for Charleville, he preferred them to come to his home rather than that he should go to theirs. This intense devotion to Charleville and its surroundings has been shared by all members of the family in every generation, as if the place cast a spell of happy enchantment over its children.

Fanny, who had been brought up in the flat countryside of east Galway, was captivated by the wild loveliness of her new home. Riding or driving with Henry, and often on foot, she soon became familiar with the countryside; not only the demesne with its lush meadows and woods where the stately trees grew to an immense height in the rich, moist soil of the valleys, but with the wilder regions beyond. There were narrow, twisting *boreens** sunk deep between walls where ferns, Herb Robert and the little purple *Linaria cymbalaria* – or ivy-leaved toad-flax – grew between the loosely-piled grey stones; in the spring, the gorse turned the banks and hills into a sheet of gold, scenting the air on sunny days. Later in the year, the higher mountain slopes would be glorious with heather, and the low *frochaun*** bushes would yield a plentiful crop of their tiny grape-like fruit. So many fern-bordered streams flow down the mountains, that one is never far from the sound of water leaping from rock to rock in miniature cataracts. Some of these were on their way to join the golden-brown waters of the river Dargle, thus linking Charleville with the distant mountains.

Charleville is in the parish of Powerscourt and in 1814, the year in which Elizabeth Monck was born, the Reverend Robert Daly was appointed to that living. He had known both Henry and Frances since they were children, and they loved and revered him. A native of Galway, he was on extremely friendly terms with Frances's elder brother, Power Trench (later Archbishop of Tuam), and it is possible that strings had been pulled in order to get him to Powerscourt. There were at that time at least 2,000 Protestants in the parish though that number was afterwards greatly decreased by emigration. Daly was a man of strong personality and forceful character, and his influence over his parishioners was great. Of Frances Monck, Daly's biographer wrote that she was –

*   Lanes
**   Bilberry.

. . . one whose heart the Lord had already opened to attend to divine things, and she highly valued Mr. Daly's teaching, both for herself and for her children. He was, during the remainder of her life, her spiritual guide and counsellor in every difficulty; whilst she, on her part, gave him her assistance, in every way in her power, in carrying out his views for the good of his people.[4]

After her death, Daly himself described his relationship with her as 'a long course of most intimate acquaintance and friendship, and the free-est expression of thought and feeling on both sides,' and said that there had not been one among his parishioners whom he 'knew so intimately and valued so highly.' Yet it is doubtful whether either his intimacy with her or his influence over her was so great as in the case of those whom he, personally, had 'led into the fold' – such as

This is a photograph of the water-colour which used to hang in the present house, with 'The old house which was burnt in 1792' written on the back. The old house was more than once altered, and there is some evidence to suggest that Whitmore Davies (believed to have done the present house) had been commissioned to do some work on the old house a few years before it was destroyed by fire.

Theodosia, daughter of Colonel Howard of Bushey Park, and also young Richard Powerscourt whose second wife Theodosia was to become.

Doctrinally, Daly was what now would be called a conservative evangelical and a fundamentalist; and though his views were much the same as those in which Frances had been reared, she seems always to have preserved a kind of independence and an immunity from the changing religious fashions. With her family she faithfully attended Robert Daly's Sunday services and weekday 'lectures'; she supported and took an active part in all the work of the parish, both religious and secular; but she did not yield him the enthusiastic discipleship which he received from his many 'converts'.

The seventeenth-century church, built to hold seven hundred people, stood in the grounds of Powerscourt House. On Sundays the stableyard was filled with carriages, while horses were picketed to the trees all along the avenue. In 1814 there was no rectory and no glebe land on which to build one. Daly had private means and was quite prepared to build a house at his own expense. That Richard Powerscourt refused to allow him to build on his estate is difficult to understand when he was so tolerant as to allow his grounds to be invaded every Sunday by church-goers. Daly's biographer suggests that his brusque, downright manner may have prejudiced Lord Powerscourt against him. Henry Monck came to the rescue and offered a site on his own land, further from the church than Daly would have wished, but better than nothing. He also allowed the Rector to live in Dargle Cottage while the house was under construction, though Daly eventually moved to Coolekay (variously spelt Coolekeigh or Coolequay) so as to be in a better position to supervise the building of the new rectory – or glebe-house, as it was called.

In a cottage near the glebe-house, Frances started a day-school and a Sunday school, and Daly himself established other small schools throughout the parish. The day-schools existed mainly to teach reading, writing and 'cyphering' and, in the case of the girls, needlework, the object being to train the children to earn their own living.

In 1813, Richard Powerscourt married Lady Frances Jocelyn who died in 1820, after a long illness which was said to have brought about the reconciliation between her husband and Robert Daly. At

Frances, daughter of 1st Earl of Clancarty, wife of Earl of Rathdowne (1787-1843)

Old Powerscourt Church (1620-1863). Drawing by David Moore after a sketch at
Powerscourt House.

the time of her death, Powerscourt was already co-operating with
the Rector, and had even taken over one of the Sunday school
classes. This was the more creditable since he was fully occupied
during that year in preparing for George IV's first and only visit to
Ireland. His lavish preparations included the further embellishment
of Powerscourt House where the King was entertained at a great
banquet, and the making of a new road to connect the house with
Powerscourt Waterfall, one of the famous beauty spots of Ireland.*
Henry Monck is not mentioned, in public records, as having played
any significant part during the royal visit, although J. W. Croker[5]
noted that he had been among the guests at a dinner following the
levée which had been attended by 'the finest array of noblemen and
gentlemen ever to be seen at Dublin Castle.'[6]

There is no record that he entertained the King at Charleville, nor
did he contribute, either financially or otherwise, to any political
party. Yet four months later, the King created him Earl of

---

* Powerscourt Waterfall is formed by the river Dargle which, flowing from its source on
the heights of Djouce, here descends a steep cliff.

Rathdowne. The reason for this has never been discovered, but not all the incidents of the King's four-week visit were recorded, and this must have been the outcome of one of them.

One story, handed down by word of mouth in the Powerscourt family, concerns the King's failure to visit the waterfall. In honour of the occasion, Lord Powerscourt had decided to improve on nature by an ingenious device; the water was dammed above the cliff, to be released by a cord pulled by His Majesty who would be ensconced in some kind of an erection or stand built specially for him. *The Topographical History of Ireland* stated that 'unfortunately time did not allow the King to use the new road, nor did he ever see the waterfall.' It was generally believed that the banquet lasted longer than the time scheduled for it, thus throwing out the programme. The facts, as related by a descendant of his host, are that by the time the banquet ended the King was in no fit state to appear in public, and had to be privately conveyed to the royal yacht by Lord Powers-court and his friends. It was an embarrassing situation, but it saved the King's life. The engineers who constructed the dam had mis-calculated; when the waters were released, they inundated the pavilion and had the King been there he would have been drowned.

At least four of Henry's daughters are known to have inherited his love for music. These were Anne, Fanny, Elizabeth and Emily. There is no record of their mother having been especially gifted in that respect; she would, in any case, have had little time left over from bearing and rearing her large family of daughters, and super-vising their education. The four elder girls were taught by a Miss Royce, referred to affectionately as 'Roycey'. Judging by results, she was an exceptionally good teacher, even allowing for supplementary lessons from Dublin masters.

The girls' religious instruction was undertaken by Frances herself. Her life was entirely God-centred, and it says much for the charm of her personality that not one of her daughters was put off by her religious zeal, and that dozens of nephews and nieces, some of them the same age as herself, paid frequent visits to Charleville, undeterred by the 'other worldly' atmosphere. In addition to morning and evening family prayers, the private devotions of each member of the family included reading the daily portions of scripture prescribed by the Church Calendar, the psalms for the day and the study of a biblical commentary. As soon as the girls were old enough, they taught in the Sunday school classes and helped their mother with her day-school and with her many charitable concerns. In these activities they were joined by Theodosia, Lady Powerscourt, widow of the 5th Lord Powerscourt. He had died in August 1823, a few months after his second marriage; and, during the minority of her stepson, Theodosia made her home at Powerscourt.

Frances Rathdowne and Theodosia Powerscourt, with Robert Daly, inaugurated in September 1827, the first of the Waterfall Dinners which became an annual event. From the various schools in the parish, attended by Catholics as well as by Protestants, over five hundred children were conveyed to the famous waterfall on the Powerscourt estate. On a level stretch of grass, within sight of the waterfall, the children sat at long tables and ate roast beef and plum pudding provided by Daly, Frances and Theodosia, who also waited on their young guests. Their assistants included Anne and Fanny Monck, now aged respectively twenty and eighteen; while at thirteen, Elizabeth was quite old enough to act as a waitress. The staple diet of the majority of Irish peasants was potatoes, with milk for those who could afford it; so it is no wonder that the substantial Waterfall Dinners were memorable occasions.

It was taken for granted by Frances and her daughters that they should provide food and warm clothing for the poorer families in the district, especially where there was sickness. In later years it became the fashion to deride this practice and 'the thin soup of charity' became a catch-phrase to describe the extreme of niggardliness. Those who adopt this attitude can never have visited a home in which an entire family is laid low by an epidemic, and where ready-cooked food suitable for invalids is gladly welcomed. As for the 'thin soup', old recipes for broth include a strong meat stock with the addition of chicken, ham, vegetables, yolks of egg and cream, the whole laced with a pint of home-brewed ale and three noggins of brandy – a nourishing meal in itself. This potent brew made a very practical substitute for the 'meals on wheels' of a later age. The Moncks knew every man, woman and child on the estate, and did what they could to help the poorer families without feeling either ashamed or complacent for doing so. They had never heard of do-gooders nor of Lady Bountifuls, and paternalism had not yet become a dirty word. This was simply something that had to be done, and in those days it was really necessary.

In these secular activities, Theodosia and Frances worked together harmoniously; with regard to theological matters, however, their views became increasingly divergent. Powerscourt House had become a centre for those evangelicals who specialised in the study of prophecy, and Theodosia came under the influence of Edward Irving, the leader of a movement which was called after his name, and of John Darby, the founder of the Plymouth Brethren. Theodosia eventually left the Church of Ireland and joined the Plymouth Brethren whose first conference was held at Powerscourt.

Undeterred by these new cults, Frances Rathdowne continued to practise and teach what was called 'simple Bible Christianity' without being drawn into ecclesiastical party politics. These were greatly agitated by the passing, in 1829, of the Emancipation Bill which opened parliament to Roman Catholics. This measure, so long overdue, caused consternation among the more militant Irish Protestants. In February of that year, one of Frances's elder brothers, the Reverend Charles le Poer Trench, Archdeacon of Armagh, gave vent to his indignation in a letter to Henry Rathdowne:

> Upon politics I am dumb and dumbfounded. *'Put not your trust in princes nor in any child of Man.'* Hoodwinked – cheated – decoyed – sold – betrayed by friends and foes. There is nothing left to us of all that our *forebears* bought for us with their blood . . . Be assured that there is no circumstance so calculated to poison her vigor, to emaciate her strength – and to reduce her in the scale of Nations – as Popery! Adieu Adnum – I am sick of it.
>
> most affectly yrs, C. le P. T.

Five months after this letter was written, Anne Lady Clancarty died and was buried in the Moncks' burial-ground beside their family vault. Her son, the Archdeacon, may have preferred to forget that she had been the sister of Lord Mountjoy who, as Luke Gardiner, had sponsored the Catholic Relief Bills of 1778 and 1782.

The tone of his letter suggests that the Archdeacon considered his brother-in-law Rathdowne to be not sufficiently aggressive in the cause of belligerent Protestantism. Yet Henry had been roped into

33

the Brunswick League, of which his wife's nephew, Lord Dunlo, was also a member. The Brunswick League or Club was composed of those ardent Tories who supported the claim of the Duke of Cumberland as next heir to the throne after William IV. This sinister-looking brother of the King was considered by his adherents to be a stauncher champion of the Tory-Protestant faction than the young Princess Victoria with her Whig associations. The assumption that Henry Rathdowne supported the Duke of Cumberland, is based on Thomas Moore's satirical verse in which Henry's name is mentioned, though thinly disguised:

The Brunswick Club
A letter having been addressed to a very distinguished personage, requesting him to become the Patron of this Orange Club, a polite answer was forthwith returned, of which we have been fortunate enough to obtain a copy.

Private   Brimstone Hall, September 21st, 1828
          Lord Belzeebub presents
To the Brunswick Club his compliments
And much regrets to say that he
Cannot, at present, their Patron be.
    In stating this Lord Belzeebub
Assures on his honour the Brunswick Club
That 'tisn't from any lukewarm lack
Of zeal or fire he thus holds back –
As even Lord Coal himself is not   [Cole]
For the Orange party more red-hot
But the truth is, till their Club affords
A somewhat decenter show of Lords
And on its list of members gets
A few less rubbishy Baronets
Lord Belzeebub must beg to be
Excus'd from keeping such company.
Who the devil, he humbly begs to know
Are Lord Gl-nd-ne and Lord D-nlo?
Or who, with a grain of sense, would go
To sit and be bored by Lord M-yo?

       . . .   .

Breathes there a man in Dublin town,
Who'd give but half of half-a-crown
To save from drowning my Lord R-thd-ne?
Or who wouldn't also gladly hustle in
Lords R-d-n, B-n-d-n, C-le, and J-c-l-n?
In short, though from his tenderest years
Accustom'd to all sorts of 'Peers,
Lord Belzeebub must question whether
He ever yet saw mix't together
As 'twere in one capacious tub,
Such a mess of noble silly-bub
As the twenty Peers of the Brunswick Club.

. . .   .

But he begs to propose, in the interim
(Till they find some prop'rer Peers for him)
His Highness of C-mb-d as sub,
To take his place at the Brunswick Club –
Begging, meanwhile, himself to dub
Their obedient servant,
                    Belzeebub.
It luckily happens, the R-y-l Duke
Resembles so much in air and look
The head of the Belzeebub family
That few can any difference see;
Which makes him, of course, the better suit
To serve as Lord B's substitute.

Moore's satire was published in the September of 1828, four days after the birth of the Rathdownes' twin daughters. During the following year, a fourth son was born to Henry's brother, Charles Joseph, whose eldest child, 'young' Charles Stanley, was now ten years old.

Henry Rathdowne's brother, Charles Joseph Monck, never recovered from the severe wound he had received during the Peninsular War. In 1816 he left the army, on half-pay, and made his home at Belleville, Templemore in County Tipperary, near to his wife's family and to the home of his mother and stepfather, Sir John

35

and Lady Carden. His children – young Charles, John, William and Richard, Anne, Henrietta, Isabella and Elizabeth – were born and spent their childhood there. In the Templemore church records of 1826, Charles Joseph is named as one of five officers of health appointed annually by the vestry – to raise money locally 'amongst all creeds and classes towards the payment of the doctor, clothing, flannel and blankets, and medical care of the poor, care of orphans and foundlings, and payment of fares of foundlings to the Foundling Hospital in Dublin, costs of burial ot unknown poor people, as well as sometimes contributing towards the cost of fares for those emigrating to America.'[7] For the majority of the Irish population, the standard of living was then seldom higher than near-starvation level, and the small tenant-farmers – subject to the abuses caused by absenteeism – had no resources with which to meet the periodical bad harvest or failures in the potato crop. In 'caring for the poor', the officers of health were literally saving the destitute from dying of starvation; and through their father's involvement in this work, Charles Joseph's sons and daughters grew up with a greater awareness of the misery around them than was usual in children of the 'landlord class'. Unlike their father and uncle, the four boys were educated in Ireland instead of being sent to English schools; and the eldest son, young Charles, entered Trinity College, Dublin, in 1835 when he was sixteen. There he came under the influence of the Professor of Political Economy, Isaac Butt, who later was to found the Irish Home Rule Party.

At about the same time, Charles Joseph came to live in Dublin at a house in Merrion Square. He was now partly, if not entirely paralysed, and his crippled condition prevented him from visiting Charleville, the home of his childhood. Young Charles, however, spent a great deal of his time there, and was on familiar terms with his uncle and aunt Rathdowne, and with his nine girl cousins.

Henry and Frances

Notes to Chapter Two

1   In common with other Irish houses of its period, the fireplaces had defective flues, being built with hollow walls, 'and the smoke finding its way out in the best way it could.' Viscount Powerscourt, *A Description and History of Powerscourt* (London, 1903).
2   From a description of Charleville House by Mark Bence-Jones.
3   From *Various Peerage Cases, 1812-1851*. National Library of Ireland.
4   Madden, Mrs. Hamilton, *Memoir of the late Rt. Revd. Robert Daly* (London, 1875).
5   *The Croker Papers*, Vol. I, pp. 95-97.
6   *Account of a Visit to Ireland by H.M. King George IV in 1821* by Hubert Burke. British Museum.
7   *A History of the Parish of Templemore* by the Reverend Harden Johnstone, M.A., Rector of Templemore, County Tipperary.

3

The Sisters at Charleville

'As nine of us sisters lived to grow up, there are of course Lovers and Love-stories attached to our Histories'; so wrote Louisa Monck, fifth of the nine daughters of Henry and Frances Rathdowne. Her *History of the Lovers,* scribbled in a paper-covered notebook, is the only given account of Charleville in the early eighteen-thirties. Fortunately she was precociously observant and had a retentive memory, as she was only fourteen when Fanny, the second daughter, married Owen Cole in 1834.

Louisa believed that her parents were 'not altogether happy' about the marriage, and none of Fanny's sisters liked Owen. Yet there was nothing tangible to which the Rathdownes could reasonably object, either in his character or in his situation. He was extremely well off, and owned houses in London and Dublin as well as the house and estate in County Monaghan; he was 'talented', wrote verses and knew artists and writers. The Moncks had heard of him before they actually met him. During their last visit to Ryde, some of the Trench relations had spoken of Owen Cole, saying he had 'been upset by Irving and the speaking with tongues'. If his having been 'upset' meant that he had been influenced by Irving, Frances Rathdowne would not have been predisposed in his favour. She herself had no use for such Evangelical gimmicks and found the faith in which she had been reared quite enough to be going on with. However, by the time of Owen's introduction to the Monck family he was, outwardly at least, a loyal member of the Protestant Church, though Louisa felt 'a sort of dislike to Owen because he spoke to Fanny in a kind of loose way about God, calling Him "The Deity"!'

At the time it was difficult to know just what was wrong with him, except that he was rather precious, perhaps a bit of a bore, and that everything he said and did was slightly off-key. It was not until after the marriage that his mental instability became apparent. 'And why,'

Fanny Cole *nee* Monck (1809-1971). Portrait by Sir Frederick Burton, 1840.

wrote Louisa, many years later, 'did not some kind hand stir to snatch Fanny from such misery?' Owen was certainly in love with Fanny, whom Louisa describes as 'very attractive' with 'dark curls, white skin, brilliant colour, warm heart and agreeable conversation.' He had been staying in the neighbourhood, his widowed mother having rented a house in or near Enniskerry, and he was introduced to the Moncks by one of their Trench cousins. After that, Owen and Fanny used to meet out riding – 'Papa being with them of course made it all right,' Louisa is careful to explain. During that summer, Fanny had been detailed to read history with Louisa and Georgina, who do not seem to have had the excellent education which had been given to their elder sisters. Owen Cole was believed to have been personally acquainted with Sir Walter Scott, and great was the amusement of the young pupils when Fanny elected to read them 'The Lay of the Last Minstrel' instead of the history lesson. They also managed to find out that Owen had asked their papa to give Fanny a poem he had written, in which he had declared his passion for her. Fanny was still wavering, so Lord Rathdowne returned the poem with a pleasantly non-committal remark.

However, on one wet day the children were playing in the wide gallery on the first floor when they saw Owen go up to 'Mama's dressingroom'. This was a sitting-room adjoining Frances' bedroom, which the girls called 'The Refuge', and was where Frances was in the habit of giving audience to her daughters' suitors. There was, as usual, a crowd of her relations staying in the house and this would be the only room in which she could be sure of privacy. 'Of course we thought this looked like the crisis,' wrote Louisa, 'and we all went upstairs to talk in mysteries in the schoolroom.' It was rather an anti-climax to find that they were to be told nothing till the next morning, and with much girlish giggling they planned how they should feign surprise when the news should be broken to them. This plan was spoilt by the irrepressible Emily who had to be ticked off by her eldest sister for flippantly remarking in front of Fanny that 'Owen looked blue with heat and excitement.'

At twenty-five, Fanny may have thought it high time she got married. She had had her admirers, but on being invited to the house they had a way of transferring their affections to the next sister, Elizabeth, known in the family as Lizzy. As the middle one of the three grown-up daughters, with Anne deputising for their mother and with Lizzy monopolising the men, there was no particular niche for poor Fanny. Marriage with Owen might have its draw-backs but at least she would be mistress of his house, Brandrum in County Monaghan and a house in London, and when next she visited her parents' home it would be in all the dignity of a married woman.

The wedding must have seemed a disappointing affair to the younger girls. The family was in mourning owing to the death of one of Frances' many nephews; so Fanny and Owen were married in the hall at Charleville and the ceremony was performed by 'Uncle Charles', Archdeacon of Armagh, the least lovable of their le Poer Trench uncles. Owen wrote an account of the wedding to his greatest friend who had been at Christ Church, Oxford, with him and who was one of the trustees for the marriage settlement – the young member for Newark, William Ewart Gladstone:

> The ceremony . . . was performed with great solemnity by Lady F.'s uncle, one of the most striking-looking men in the world, and though performed in a house was so numerously attended that I was unavoidably the cynosure of many eyes. Lady F. had 13 bridesmaids, all dressed alike. The numbers were greatly thinned by the catastrophe which preceded it . . .

40

The promise of your future support and prayers is no less gratifying than your present.[1]

Anne, the eldest of the sisters, was now aged twenty-seven. Louisa knew from hearsay that at least three men had 'courted' Anne; William Pennefather had gone so far as to give her 'two or three things he had brought from Italy, and some dried plants'; but nothing had come of it and her present role in life was to be personal assistant to her mother and, to a certain extent, to her father. Both Henry and Frances Rathdowne were curiously passive and casual with regard to their daughters' futures, perhaps because their imaginations boggled at the thought of having to find nine sons-in-law. It was not due to any anxious planning on their part that the girls seem never to have had a dull moment. They were often at their Dublin house and we hear of them at balls and 'drawing rooms' at Dublin Castle. Also there were periodical visits to Ryde in the Isle of Wight, ostensibly for the sake of their health but actually because at that time Ryde was a fashionable watering-place and the Moncks met many of their friends and relations there.

The girls paid visits to their mother's large tribe of relations: to the Clancartys at Garbally and to the Gregorys at Coole Park in County Galway, the McClintocks in County Louth and the La Touches in County Kildare. At home they helped in the day-schools which their mother had started, and taught in Sunday school classes. There was always plenty of music-making at Charleville; Anne, Fanny, Elizabeth and Emily had inherited their father's love for music and Anne and Emily were fond of 'arranging chants' for the psalms sung at morning and evening family prayers at which the singing was accompanied by an instrument called 'the seraphim'. Anne did not confine her compositions to sacred music – 'Lady Anne Monck is writing the accompaniment to 'The Past',' Owen Cole told Gladstone.

They were all passionately devoted to their home and the surrounding countryside. When they went out riding with their father they were never out of sight of the Wicklow Mountains, and from the lower hills near the house they could see the Irish Sea. There were frequent dinner and tea visits in the neighbourhood, dinner then being the earlier of the two meals. There seem to have been few occasions when the house was not full of people staying with them, though these were often relations. At that time we never hear of dances being given at Charleville nor at any other house in the neighbourhood. The rigid views of their Rector, Robert Daly, may have had something to do with this.

> Sweet Vale of polyglots and pony-carriages;
> Barren, alas! in concerts, balls and marriages!
> Sweet Vale! Where prophecy and tea abound,
> But dulcimer and fiddle never sound.

In her biography, *Robert Daly, Bishop of Cashel,* Mrs. Madden quotes these lines which her father had written to describe the sedate way of life in the Glencree Valley during the time when Daly was Rector of Powerscourt; 'prophecy' being an allusion to the activities of Theodosia Lady Powerscourt. The puritanical restrictions did not, at Charleville, exclude card-playing and other games of chance. An inventory taken when Rathdowne died mentions eight card-tables, including two loo-tables and a backgammon table.

Henry Rathdowne was a fine horseman and a famous whip, but there is no mention of a pack of hounds in the district nor of any organised shooting at Charleville until after his death. If there really were no field sports, it says much for the girls' powers of attraction that there was no shortage of young men at Charleville. Their male cousins, and the friends introduced by those cousins, were continually coming and going. The 'goings' were often dramatic, especially if Elizabeth had been their object which was usually the case. In Louisa's words: 'Love, Lovers and Lizzy belonged to one another, from the time she knew what they meant, to the time she married .. not very early.' We have to make allowances for the fact that Louisa's *History of the Lovers* was written many years later when she had long been under the influence of William Smythe who disapproved of Elizabeth. But there is no denying that 'Lizzy was a sad flirt'. Without actively encouraging her admirers, she was not, in Louisa's opinion, nearly firm enough in discouraging them. Cousins, acquaintances, young men who came to study with Mr. McGee, the curate, all fell in love with her. 'I am afraid she led them on,' complains Louisa. Then she would discover that she did not care for them after all and the disconsolate suitors left the house, never to return. To do Elizabeth justice, it is hard to know how she

42

Anne Monck (1807-1876).

could have been expected to judge of the true state of her feelings towards any man without spending at least a little time alone in his company; and that, in itself, was considered as encouragement.

Just as her parents took no positive steps to provide any of their daughters with a 'Mister Right', so they seem to have been equally casual and undiscerning with regard to undesirable suitors. However, there was one strict rule: no girl was allowed to go out-of-doors alone with a man, even to walk round the 'pleasure-grounds', without one of her sisters making a third. It is one of the many black marks chalked up by Louisa against Elizabeth that she more than once broke this rule. She 'very improperly' allowed one of the McClintock cousins to walk with her down the back avenue and to stay while she read aloud to an old man in one of the cottages. And she actually went down the Glen alone with Mr. Jessop, an extremely wealthy young land-owner who was known to be in love with her. The Glen, mentioned earlier as being near the site of the eighteenth-century 'Cottage', is formed by a stream running between steep wooded banks on its way to join the river Dargle, and it has long been a favourite walk with every generation of the family. A footpath has been cut along one of the miniature cliffs, and children walking down this path have always stopped to drink from the spring of pure water which gushes from the bank.

It was in this romantic spot that Elizabeth walked alone with Jessop. 'Happily he did not kiss her; why I do not know.' Poor Louisa probably imagined that such a disaster would result in immediate pregnancy; anyway, she only had her sister's word for it that it did not happen. She describes how, coming from her piano practice in the small drawing-room, she found Elizabeth in the hall helping herself to 'a glass of wine and water from the luncheon-table' – which would seem to imply that luncheon was still a buffet affair at Charleville in those days and not a formal meal in the dining-room. Perhaps there had been more wine than water in the mixture; usually Elizabeth was uncommunicative about her love affairs and it was uncharacteristic of her to remark, as she did to Louisa: "Do you know what I am just going to do? I am going to tell Mr. Jessop I will marry him. But do not speak of it." 'Of course I went direct upstairs and told the schoolroom party. We were all in the greatest excitement,' wrote Louisa.

But there was a disappointment in store for the schoolroom party, as also for Jessop. Later in that same day Elizabeth went to Mama and confessed that she had been mistaken in her feelings. Jessop was then staying in the house, but Frances decided to say nothing to him till the next day. She herself had been greatly taken with the young man and perhaps hoped that her daughter was merely in a girlish panic and would think better of her decision. However, when Elizabeth did not appear at dinner that evening nor at breakfast next morning, Jessop must have been suspicious. He looked 'much put out' when Anne told him after breakfast that her mother wished to speak to him in private. And when the painful interview was over, he would not wait for his clothes to be packed but set out to walk the twenty miles to Dublin. Louisa admits to feeling very blank at the excitement being over. 'Mama suffered terribly about Lizzy's conduct, and the house was quite shut up.' As if that were not enough, Jessop had left what he thought was a sovereign for the footman; but in his agitation he left a new farthing instead and the house steward told the children that 'the footman complained greatly of the harm Lizzy had done him.'

The house cannot have been quite shut up for long for we soon hear of other young men pursuing Elizabeth. More than one of the McClintock cousins were in love with her at one time or another, and a friend of Owen Cole's had to be told by Owen that his attentions were unwelcome. Owen was also deputed to return some books of poetry that his friend had sent to Elizabeth. In general, the giving of presents seems not to have been discouraged; or perhaps Elizabeth's parents were not told of the books of poetry and books of prints given to her, nor of the many presents given to the younger children. This last was 'to make a shade for him and Lizzy', Louisa comments on one of these occasions.

Elizabeth's love of music was her vulnerable point and her more talented admirers wrote music for her or copied out music; if unable to do this, they sat at the piano with her or turned over the pages. Her instrument may still have been the pretty 'square' pianoforte, but unfortunately we have no description of what she wore during these musical sessions. Louisa's reference to her everyday morning dress – 'a plaid apron over that check we were all so fond of' – does not sound a happy combination.

The earliest picture we have of her is a water-colour portrait by Sir Frederick Burton. The picture is not dated but as her mother and her sister, Fanny Cole, were both painted by the same artist in 1840, it seems probable that Elizabeth sat for him during the same year or thereabouts.[2] In this portrait Elizabeth's dress is of a silvery-white, satin-like material; leaving her shoulders bare, the long narrow bodice is cut in one together with the voluminous skirt which completely envelops the chair on which she sits. The ends of a wide silk stole are draped over her arms at elbow level, its deep golden-brown colour exactly matching her hair which is parted in the centre and arranged in ringlets. The portraits show both sisters to have been extremely decorative and, judging from looks alone, it is diffi-cult to understand why Fanny had so often been cut out by her younger sister. It could have been because Fanny tried too hard; there is a fidgety restlessness in her expression and one can imagine her making desperate efforts to please, putting everything into the shop window. In contrast to this, Elizabeth looks calm and relaxed, making no demands. thinking her own thoughts which she feels no particular urge to share with anyone else. Her very blue eyes are like her father's, and she has the same half-amused, enigmatic expression. It is not surprising that the men who loved her were driven frantic, as they vainly tried to discover what made her tick. Most probably she did not know herself. The quotations which she copied into her 'commonplace book' give the impression that she

Elizabeth Monck (1814-1892). Portrait by Sir Frederick Burton *c.* 1840.

was searching for something to which she could dedicate herself;
some objective to which she could devote all the power and energy of
mind and body. She was less easily pleased than were her sisters
who, like a flock of pretty birds, enjoyed doing everything together
and had no secrets from each other. The daily round of trivial duties,
shared out among so many sisters, and the still more trivial pleasures
could not in themselves satisfy her; and if there was nothing which
really needed to be done, she saw no reason why she should not go
upstairs and read in her bedroom. One cannot blame Louisa for
being irritated by this rather tiresome and anti-social habit,
especially when it was doen to escape from a too-persistent admirer.

The gentlemen of that period were not ashamed of showing their
feelings and Elizabeth's swains made no attempt at assumed non-
chalance and stiff-upper-lipping when she turned them down.
Jonathan Woodward was by no means the only one who was found
shedding tears of despair. It was he who complained to the younger

girls that he had been awake all night owing to 'perturbation'. There may have been some excuse for him as this appears to have been one of the occasions when Elizabeth was slow in making up her mind. She can hardly have been unaware of his intentions though he did not actually declare himself till one evening, two days before his visit was due to end, when there was a dinner party in the house. Considering the many excellent opportunities he must have had during his visit, it seems an odd time to have chosen. Louisa merely noted that he was refused and we are left uncertain as to whether the proposal was made in public, whispered between courses, or if the pair rudely absented themselves from the general company. Although dinner would not have been much later than five o'clock, this was the end of October and they could not have escaped into the garden without attracting attention. At dinner the children came in for dessert and sat at a side-table; and if Louisa was still counted as one of them, her sharp eyes may for once have failed to see what was going on. But she makes up for her vagueness by her description of the last day of Jonathan's visit. He had stayed on, trying to persuade Elizabeth to change her mind, strolling with her up and down the Dark Walk, with Louisa following behind like a resentful little policewoman – 'It was a damp bad day and I had a *very* bad cough'. The Dark Walk is a wide path between an avenue of great yew trees and it had already witnessed many such scenes. In spite of this suggestive setting, Elizabeth remained firm, and Louisa gives us a touching picture of her sister administering sal volatile and water to the distraught Jonathan who was 'quite uncontrolled' when the time came for him to leave the house.

Another violent departure on a later occasion was that of Charles Hamilton. He had been one of several people staying in the house and he remained after the party broke up. Frances Rathdowne and two of her younger daughters went to pass a few days in Dublin leaving her sister, Lady Harriet Osborne, to look after the girls who remained at Charleville. Louisa was not feeling well and stayed in her bedroom until Elizabeth came upstairs and asked if she was well enough to come out as Mr. Hamilton wanted to walk round the grounds. 'If you are not, do not mind,' added Lizzy, 'for he is such a safe kind of man, there can be no harm in my going alone with him.' Sacrificing her own health to her sister's honour, Louisa replied that she would certainly get ready immediately. 'I cannot help thinking that Lizzy was making a fool of me, or else trying to deceive herself,' she remarks parenthetically. Before she had finished her elaborate preparations for a stroll round the gardens her sister appeared again, saying: 'Lou, you need not mind now, for Charles Hamilton is gone. He proposed for me and I refused him.' The scene of this proposal was the small drawing-room and Aunt Harriet, who had been in the hall all the time, overheard everything. With all the running up and down to Louisa, Elizabeth must have omitted to shut the massive mahogany door which would have been sound-proof if closed, unless Charles Hamilton had been shouting. Seeing his retreat cut off, he jumped out of the window and made off without even fetching his hat.

In spite of this crowded love life, or perhaps because of it, Elizabeth did not marry until she was thirty. Louisa glosses over the next few years, merely noting that Lizzy had several affairs going on, 'some happening more or less at the same time'. The spotlight is now turned on to Emily and, after her, on to Georgina, and also, though Louisa is unaware of the fact, on to Anne. For in 1836 the stage is set for the entrance of William Smythe, who was to play such a prominent part in the life of each member of the Monck family.

In 1836 Emily was eighteen and, by all accounts, the one who was most like her mother in character. It has been suggested that Frances Rathdowne was lacking in perception, at least where her daughters' suitors were concerned. This would imply that she did not see people as they really were; but it would perhaps be more accurate to say that she only saw them as they were while in her company. Louisa noticed that Owen Cole, for example, 'acted like a madman . . . everywhere but at Charleville.' The fact was that Frances was so thoroughly soaked in positive goodness of the very nicest sort that in her presence people really did behave differently from the way they did at other times; not from hypocrisy, but because they could not help themselves. It was not simply that she brought out the best in them; the qualities she saw in other people did not necessarily belong to them but were temporary reflections of her own. In this, as in other ways, Emily resembled her. Even allowing for the fact that her early death lent a halo to her sisters' memories of her, she must have been an enchanting creature. Brave and gay, with a great capacity for enjoying life, she was also deeply religious though without the least trace of priggishness. Not one of her sisters resented her being

48

her father's favourite child; indeed, she managed to get on well with everybody, even with her brother-in-law Owen, who wrote after her death: 'Lady E. [Emily] was certainly the sweetest creature I ever beheld.'[3] But there was a special closeness between her and Anne. Anne, at the age of eleven, had been god-mother at Emily's christening and Emily still called her 'my second mother'. Young Emily had been considered a sufficient chaperone when Anne and William Pennefather 'used to sit under the tree in the Dark Walk together a good deal.' According to Louisa, there had in the past been 'a boy and girl affection' between that same William Pennefather and Emily herself. Edward Pennefather, William's elder brother, 'also liked her, but behaved *so* well. All this happened at Ryde when she [Emily] was almost a child, but was always amongst the elder party in the boating excursions, when the mischief was done.' For all her prudery, Louisa had a suggestive way of putting things, leaving one curious to know the exact nature of the 'mischief' done; also in what way the younger Pennefather fell below the standards of his elder brother who 'behaved *so* well.'

Emily's drawing portfolio has recently come to light; among her own immature sketches are some exquisite pencil drawings of views in the Isle of Wight in the early eighteen-thirties, three of them signed 'W. Pennefather' and one signed 'E. Pennefather'. Presumably it was owing to Anne's partiality that Emily had been allowed to join in the activities of her elder sisters at an age when she should have been relegated to the school-room party. During Anne's mysterious illnesses, Emily was her chosen companion and in this Anne showed her usual good sense. Although we never learn the nature of Anne's illnesses, it is certain that they were not imaginary. During this summer of 1836 her condition was considered sufficiently serious for prayers to be said for her in church, and to bring Fanny and Elizabeth back to Ireland.

This is the first mention by Louisa of any of the family being in London though they must often have stayed there if only to break their frequent journeys to the Isle of Wight. Louisa only wrote of what she could describe as an eye-witness; but the diary of Owen's life-long friend, William Gladstone, describes musical evenings in the Coles' Knightsbridge house where he made social, political and literary contacts. Gladstone warmly praised his hostess but, when recording the still stronger impression made on him by her sister,

'Lady E.', he discreetly wrote in Italian. He still considered himself to be heart-broken as the result of his rejection by Caroline Farquhar, and excused his interest in Elizabeth by remarking on her striking resemblance to his lost love.[4] He made no further mention of her in his diary, but Owen's letters to him contain coy references to 'your friend Lady Elizabeth', later modifying the term to 'your former acquaintance'.

If Fanny Cole travelled in the same style as that of her parents, she would have taken her own carriage across to England; though she may not have followed the example of the Secretary to the Admiralty, J. W. Croker who, in 1821, sat in his own carriage on deck during a rough crossing and 'was not at all incommoded' though everyone else was 'deadly sick'.[5] Louisa does not tell us whether or not the sisters returned to London to resume their round of gaieties after Anne had recovered. She passed straight on to the events of that autumn when William Smythe was introduced into the family circle.

He was then just short of twenty-seven but already a grave young man with a stern sense of duty. Left fatherless at the age of five, at twenty-one he had been High Sheriff of his county, Westmeath, in a period when, in Ireland, that office was attended with a pomp and ceremony that was almost regal. In a miniature painted at the time of his betrothal, he has the face of a rather chubby Adonis, with fair hair, blue eyes and a pink and white complexion. He would look almost too good to be true but for the obstinate mouth and the slightly wooden cast of his undeniably handsome features.

He first saw Emily in church. Although the views of Mr. Daly may have acted as a slight damper on social activities in the neighbourhood, in some ways he was a social asset. His sermons were famous and during the summer months many people, like Owen Cole's mother, rented houses and even small cottages in and around Enniskerry in order to attend the Sunday services in Powerscourt Old Church, or Robert Daly's evening 'lectures' during the week. Some of these visitors came from England and Scotland, as well as from all over Ireland. It also became the fashion for serious-minded young men to drive out from Dublin, or from other parts of Ireland, to hear Robert Daly preach. Among these was a 'Mr. R. Plunket' who appeared in church one Sunday having brought his friend William Smythe of Barbavilla in County Westmeath. It would have been unlike William to admit to inattentiveness during a service, but on coming out of church that day he asked: 'Who is that pretty dark girl?' Plunket took the hint and asked Lady Rathdowne's permission to introduce his friend. From that day William never looked back. He came often to Charleville and shortly before Christmas he got himself invited to stay.

Perhaps the Rathdownes had at last woken up to the fact that they had three grown-up, unmarried daughters, that Louisa and Georgina could not be kept in the school-room much longer, and that there were still Caroline, Harriet and Mary to come. This could be why Emily was so often allowed to 'sit talking to William alone in the drawing room', though it is true that Frances had other things to keep her mind occupied just then. Fanny and Owen were at Charleville awaiting Fanny's second confinement and their baby, Nina, was born there in December. William was not one to rush his fences, at least where such a serious matter as his own marriage was concerned, and he took his time about coming to the point. Poor Emily became quite unhappy so the attraction may have been mutual. If so, it must have been the attraction of opposites; even Louisa, who thought William perfect, remarked that 'no one but Emily, with her playful, unreserved manner, could have got on with some one like him.' One morning Emily breakfasted upstairs; a tray was sent up to her from the dining-room and Louisa remembers that Emily 'wrote a little note to Mama, asking her to get William to cut her bread for her.' Anne began to be afraid that her darling Emily might be disappointed and tried to persuade her that 'there was nothing in it.'

Meanwhile the younger sisters were having an exciting time with the arrival of Fanny's baby and with William's cautious progress to watch and gossip over. Two of their mother's young nephews came to stay, also their uncle William, the boyish and jovial Admiral le Poer Trench. There had been an unusually heavy fall of snow followed by a hard frost, and young Lord Powerscourt came over to Charleville in his sleigh. The governess had gone away for Christmas, 'all the maids were sick', and the girls did very much as they pleased. Their two cousins used to come and visit them up in the school-room where they were sewing at their wedding clothes.

Their papa had gone to Belfast to attend 'a Protestant meeting', a political meeting of the Orange Lodges which supported the Duke of

51

Henry Stanley, 2nd Viscount Monck and Earl of Rathdowne (1785-1848).
(Artist unknown)

Cumberland's claim to the throne. William Smythe had not been
expected to stay at Charleville over Christmas and when Henry
Rathdowne returned home on that snowy Christmas Eve he was
unable to conceal his astonishment at finding his guest still in the
house. Even William had the grace to appear embarrassed; Louisa
remembered 'his look of agitation when Papa entered the room.' We
can picture the scene: Frances, frail but still beautiful, sitting very
upright in her high-backed chair, a lace shawl lightly covering her
head and falling to her waist; the bevy of daughters already dressed
for the evening, their ringlets falling over their bare shoulders; and
the boisterous welcome from the Admiral and his nephews as Henry
entered with snowflakes on his caped greatcoat. He would have
appeared very much the same as in the portrait which had been
painted for his married daughter, Fanny Cole: brown hair still thick

at the back and sides but receding from his forehead, his blue eyes as youthful-looking as ever. His genial hospitality would not have allowed his astonishment to be seen by anyone but his wife and daughters when he realised that the group included William Smythe.

But now Emily had become exasperated by William's caution; Louisa believed that they had actually had a quarrel. At dinner Emily refused to sit next to William; and as she took her place at the table, she muttered under her breath: 'I hate him!' Later in the evening, however, William persuaded her to join him in the small drawing-room. Her sisters went to sit with their father; and after a long time, Emily came in and announced: 'I am going to marry Mr. Smythe.' Her indulgent papa was merely 'amused' by the way she stated it as a fact, without first asking his leave. Thomas the footman brought in the tea-table, and Emily calmly proceeded to make the tea, though William was still too bashful to join them. He had gone upstairs to tell the good news to Owen Cole; rather tactlessly, as Fanny was nursing her baby and 'had to run away' when William burst in. After such a leisurely beginning, William showed what a fast worker he could be once his mind was made up. He and Emily were married two months later; and in the following November their child was born, a bare nine months after the wedding.

It is significant that, from the time of the betrothal till the day of the wedding, the prospective bridegroom occupies the central position in Louisa's narrative. During those weeks the foundation was laid for that relationship between William Smythe and his wife's family that was to have such important consequences for them all. Henry and Frances Rathdowne sincerely loved him and treated him, almost from the first, as if he really were their own son. In their eyes, he was a gentle, dignified man, serious-minded and with high principles. To Emily's sisters, with one exception, he was the wise and affectionate brother they must often have wished to have. They deferred to him in everything; confided in him, consulted him and invariably took his advice.

The exception in this chorus of adulation was, of course, Elizabeth. We have no means of knowing whether she excluded herself from the circle of William's yes-women because he disapproved of her, or if he judged her severely simply because she was not one of his fans. Louisa grieves over the 'lack of love' between them and dates it from a shocking occasion on which Elizabeth received and refused a proposal without telling mama of it. 'Although William spoke to her in a most Christian way, I fear the breach was never healed.' There is no doubt that William and Louisa enjoyed themselves, getting together over Elizabeth's unseemly conduct. Louisa could keep nothing from him and he soon knew all that she could tell him of her sisters and their doings. The wedding put only a temporary stop to these enthralling confidences, as William and Emily were again at Charleville in the September of that same year and stayed there till their baby was born.

They had come straight to Charleville from their wedding tour on the continent, which must have been a long one if they had started on their travels immediately after their marriage; but they may have postponed their tour until the summer. From about this time we have other sources of information in addition to Louisa's *History;* one of these describes a large chestnut tree in the garden at Barbavilla which Emily had named 'my summer parlour'. This shows that she must have spent at least some part of her married life in her husband's home before her death, which took place two weeks after the birth of her child.

Anne Monck wrote a moving account of Emily's death and of the days preceding it. The steadfast, burning faith of this nineteen-year-old girl made a lasting impression not only on her sisters, but also on their Rector, soon to become Bishop of Cashel. On the Sunday after her death he preached a sermon comparing Emily's passing with that of St. Stephen.[6] Robert Daly was outspoken to a fault and Emily was no hypocrite. Neither is there any false sentimentality in Anne's starkly realistic account. Emily had insisted on being told the true state of affairs and, on hearing that the doctors had given up hope, she said: 'I am afraid my death will not be a very triumphant one, because I am leaving so many I love behind.' But before the end her attitude increasingly became a steady 'looking forward' and it is impossible to doubt the sincerity of her perfect confidence. 'My darling little sisters, live to Christ. He only is worth living for,' she told Harriet and Mary when William brought them to her. Later she said to her mother: 'Now I am just like a little child going to sleep in my Father's arms.' Anne carefully noted that the time of her death – eleven in the morning on 22 November 1837 – was the very hour at which her child had been born a fortnight earlier; but she gave no hint as to the actual cause of death. She had seemed well and in her usual high spirits before the birth, looking over the baby-clothes – 'with all that thorough pleasure in her manner for which she was so remarkable. She was never *half*-pleased with anything,' wrote Anne. The delivery appears to have been a normal one, attended by a nurse and the family doctor. Normal, that is, for those days. Doctor Jason 'bled her from the arm' after labour had begun, which would hardly be done to-day. She was delighted with the baby girl, 'Little Emily', and all seemed to be going smoothly till the next day when she became 'very unwell'. Her symptoms were: pain in the neck, the left arm and the left side; 'an accumulation of Phlegm', later tinged with blood; a cough, and general weakness. Perhaps this last was the result of Doctor Jason's remedies. On the day following the birth he applied leeches to her stomach and subsequently bled her again and 'blistered' her. At one time she rallied sufficiently to begin feeding her child but soon became too weak to do so. She was given opium to relieve the pain, laudanum was rubbed on her neck and packs of hot salt, as well as hot bottles, were used to warm her. At first the doctor thought it unneccessary to call in another opinion, but eventually he agreed to send a messenger to a certain Sir Henry Marsh.

This Dublin physician was summoned by the family only in the case of very serious illness. He did not disapprove of Doctor Jason's methods, which continued as before. Thirteen days after the baby's birth, when she was desperately weak with frequent shivering fits, there was another attempt to bleed her. An incision was made in her arm but no blood appeared, and the doctor tried again after bathing her arm in warm water. Finally he made an incision in her waist and 'drew off two cupfuls of blood.' Two days after this she died. It is, of course, easy to be wise after an event, and especially 130 years after it. But one cannot help wondering if she was killed by the attempted cures at least as much as by the disease itself – whatever that may have been.

The coronation of Queen Victoria in 1838 was celebrated in Dublin by a series of functions in which Henry Rathdowne must have taken part. But Louisa's chronicle deals with nothing but domestic events. Poor William had been left a widower less than a year after his marriage and with a two-week-old baby on his hands. Emily's dying wish had been that her little daughter should be the especial charge of Anne, her own 'second mother', who was now thirty years old. The child Emily was the idol of her maternal grand-parents and aunts and spent several months of each year at Charleville, while a bedroom there was permanently set aside for her father and known as 'William's room'. But Barbavilla was his home and, at least nominally that of his child, and this led to a situation which seems astonishing when one remembers the Monck family's strict views on chaperonage. Whenever the baby was with her father at Barbavilla it was taken for granted that Anne should also be there. It is true that from time to time Anne's parents or one or other of her sisters joined the Barbavilla party. But there certainly were occasions on which Anne was alone with her brother-in-law with no other chaperone than the baby; and when little Emily needed sea air, it was William and Anne who took her to pass several weeks at Newcastle in County Down.

This unconventional arrangement revolutionised Anne's life and was as near as she ever came to being a wife and mother. As the eldest of a large family, she had had plenty of experience, and she showed her understanding of child psychology when she got rid of the nurse and herself took entire charge of Emily. They were at Charleville at the time and the child's bed was moved into Anne's room. 'She had been allowed to get imperious in the nursery,' Anne wrote to William who was at Barbavilla, 'whilst in some respects she was unnecessarily thwarted in little matters, causing small bursts of impatience. I am sure hers is a temper that should, at least while she is young, be *soothed,* without exactly humouring her. She has much improved, even in this one week.:

At Charleville, Elizabeth was now in a position of some importance, as the eldest unmarried daughter at home. Her mother never entirely recovered from the shock of Emily's death and had more than one severe illness during the remaining five years of her own life. Caroline had always been more or less of an invalid, but Louisa and Georgina, aged eighteen and seventeen, would now be able to help look after the two little ones, Harriet and Mary, when they were not with their governess. Fanny and Owen Cole and their children were also at Charleville, so a nursery had to be kept going as well as the school-room.

Georgina, who was always described as being 'very pretty', was herself becoming something of a responsibility. Accustomed as Elizabeth was to being the centre of attraction, it speaks well for her that she was helpful and sympathetic to her younger sisters and never grudged them their 'conquests'. She had, in fact, quite enough going on in her own love life to keep her fully occupied. But for the present we are again dependent on Louisa's narrative which deals at this time with the romantic history of her favourite sister.

An atmosphere of light comedy surrounds the love affairs of that charming lightweight, Georgina. In contrast to the stormy scenes created by Elizabeth's swains and to William's ponderous courtship, the young men attracted to Georgina were a carefree lot. Even Louisa could not be sententious about one who manoeuvred to get a lock of Georgina's hair, and another who 'could not have been very bad' as he afterwards consoled himself with a Juno-esque local lovely nicknamed Mont Blanc. In common with her elder sisters, Georgina was courted by yet another of the seemingly inexhaustible supply of McClintock cousins. He tried to win her approval by giving presents to her sisters, but this had been done too often before to cause much comment. Louisa carelessly noted that she herself 'got a gown and a brooch' out of the affair, before going on to describe Georgina's first meeting with Captain Edward Croker.

This rather dashing young officer was in the 17th Lancers, then stationed in Dublin, and he first saw Georgina and her sisters at Harristown, County Kildare, the home of Robert La Touche who had married their aunt, Lady Emily Trench. On Edward's side it was a case of 'love at first sight', and from that moment he determined to marry Georgina. This he confessed later; on that first evening he was *'very* shy' and merely tried to amuse her by putting his dog through its tricks, 'making it balance bread on its nose'. After this he came more than once to Charleville with a brother officer called Madden. The latter was a friend of Elizabeth's, which may be why the family were slow to realise that Edward came expressly to see Georgina and that her own feelings had become involved. Elizabeth was the first to be aware of what was going on and she 'gave a hint' to Louisa who had been making catty remarks about Edward, saying that she thought him ugly. The two young officers used to drive over to Charleville and accompany the sisters on their country rambles. Mr. Madden entertained them with amusing stories – 'Friend Bess, where are my clothes?' being one which Louisa particularly remembers as setting the party in a roar – and they were all very merry together. Then Edward, no longer shy, spoilt it all by asking Georgina for one of her gloves as he intended to buy her a pair as a present. 'She very properly refused,' Louisa notes approvingly. 'This vexed Edward much, and he complained to his confidant, Mr. Madden, who wisely observed: "Do you think Lady Georgina would let her glove be seen in a barracks?"' It sounds a trivial enough episode but Edward seems to have taken the snub to heart. He went away – 'and it was a long time before we saw him again.'

Georgina pined, her sisters were plunged in gloom on her account, and it may have been in order to distract her that the family moved to Dublin. While they were there, the girls were invited to watch a procession from a friend's house. There was great excitement when they caught sight of Mr. Madden in the military escort; but this upset poor Georgina all over again because Madden was Edward's friend. They returned to Charleville where everything reminded her of Edward. The gardens, the pleasure-grounds, the Glen, walks down the wild and rocky valley of the Dargle river, expeditions up 'Walker's Rock' – the hill which rises abruptly from just beyond the back avenue gate, named after the forge at its foot owned by Walker the blacksmith – all were full of memories. Unlike lovelorn maidens of this century, she was spared the agonising suspense of listening for the telephone. But there were the daily postal deliveries which came by the mail coach from Dublin to Taney (Dundrum) and were conveyed from Taney to Enniskerry. The time of arrival of incoming mail would vary from day to day, which added to the torture of waiting. From the school-room window on the top storey, she could see as far as the first bend in the front avenue and watch the approach of visitors on horseback and in carriages, side-cars, tilburies or phaetons. Hopes would be raised to a feverish pitch by the distant sound of wheels and horses' hooves; then there would be another sickening disappointment when the wrong vehicle rounded the bend.

In describing this period of her sister's life, Louisa writes with spontaneity and real feeling. Otherwise she might have been accused of plagiarism, so nearly does Georgina resemble Jane Austen's 'Marianne Dashwood' both in character and in situation. At this time Louisa herself could have been cast for the part of 'prudent Elinor'. Convinced that they had seen the last of Edward, she blamed Elizabeth for allowing Georgina to confide in her, thus keeping the younger girl's mind in 'a state of excitement'. But Louisa was wrong. One day a beautiful bouquet, tied with white satin ribbon and addressed to Georgina, was sent up from Enniskerry having come out on the mail-coach from Dublin. 'Only one person could be the sender, and only one meaning could it have.' If there were any doubts on that subject they were soon dispelled by the arrival of Edward in person, 'in a Tilbury with a very wicked horse.' Georgina was too well brought up to make him a scene or to ask for an explanation of his long silence. It was enough to be able to see him and to hear his ready acceptance of her father's invitation to join the house-party which was to assemble on the following day. Her long agony of waiting and watching was over.

Edward arrived the next day at dinner-time, bringing a white camellia for Georgina's hair. There was no time to re-arrange her coiffure before dinner; but after they left the dining-room, Georgina went up to her mama's dressing-room accompanied by Louisa and their mother. Louisa remembered every detail of the scene: her younger sister standing on a chair in order to see herself in the glass above the chimney-piece, while she 'settled' the flower in her hair. Frances made no comment while Georgina was in the room. Only when the happy, excited girl had run across the wide gallery and down the stairs did she remark: 'There goes a lamb adorned for the slaughter!'

This is the first time that we hear of her having said anything either for or against Georgina's attachment to Edward Croker. But it is easy to imagine how she must have rejoiced when the affair had seemed to come to an end, while at the same time grieving for the girl's disappointment. The sudden and unexpected return of Edward placed her in a quandary. It would have been hard for an affectionate mother to lock up her daughter and forbid Edward the house when she had seen that daughter's woebegone face suddenly flame into happiness. Then there was the glad relief of the other girls and Henry hospitably urging the young man to get his baggage and return the very next day. As in the case of Owen Cole, Frances knew nothing definite against Edward; she simply seems to have had a 'hunch' that he ought not to marry her child. Meanwhile he was charming and plausible, the rest of the family were delighted with him and Georgina was madly in love. Frances may have decided that her interference might do more harm than good and that matters must now be allowed to take their course.

At first that course looked like being a straight-forward one.

Edward, with his host, climbed to the top of Sugar Loaf mountain, that peak of a little under 2,000 feet which the inhabitants of the surrounding countryside regard as their personal property. Henry may have felt a literal sense of ownership as the grazing rights of the lower slopes were divided between Charleville and Powerscourt and had sometimes been a bone of contention between the two families. During this steep and quite arduous climb Edward came clean about his past life, in particular about his former love affair with a certain Miss O'Grady. Perhaps he was less candid about the fact that he was heavily in debt, because the interview appears to have been satisfactory. At all events, the setting for it was a pleasant change from the orthodox: 'Come into my study, Sir,' and the choice of a mountain-top as an alternative was characteristic of Henry Rathdowne.

However, there were rocks ahead. On Sunday the family and their guests went to Powerscourt Church . . . 'and Mr. Greer preached a sermon which seemed meant for our circumstances,' says Louisa; adding that she herself was reduced to tears by his eloquence. She does not tell us the subject of this moving discourse but it seems probable that the theme was a warning against being 'unequally yoked with unbelievers'. The party divided after the service when Frances and her daughters went to teach in the various Sunday school classes. But when they came home, Frances found Louisa in floods of tears, saying: 'It's so terrible for her to give him up, yet so dreadful to think of her marrying him, after that sermon!' At dinner that day, Georgina did not sit next to Edward but 'sat at the bottom of the table, next Papa. She looked like snow.' Louisa, with red and swollen eyes, sat beside Edward and forced herself to make conversation. 'I talked to E. more than I ever did before; he kept looking at G. and saw something had gone wrong.' Louisa went to Mr. Daly's evening 'lecture' but – 'I cried the whole time, and could not stop. G. and I slept that night and many after in Mama's room, on the couches.' At last Edward managed to corner Georgina in the small drawing-room and 'made his proposals. She confessed her love, but said she could not marry him as she did not think her feelings and his were [at] one about religion. It was a wretched interview.' It was followed by another 'upstairs in "The Refuge", Mama's dressingroom.' We are not told what took place there, only that Louisa had never forgotten the sound of Edward's steps crossing the gallery before descending the stairs and leaving the house. There was a dinner party that night at which the girls had to behave as if nothing had happened, but Louisa admits that she could not understand what her neighbour was saying to her 'and I am sure I answered all wrong.' The following weeks were a time of confusion and indecision on the part of Georgina who 'got herself into a dreadfully nervous state.' Her uncertainty was increased by a correspondence carried on between Edward and Fanny Cole.

During the first seventeen years of their married life, the Coles spent the greater part of their time at Charleville. At one time they were in Brussels and at another in Pau; he appears to have let his house in Knightsbridge, and his frequent letters to Gladstone refer to financial embarrassments in spite of the valuable London property inherited from 'my greatgrandfather, "Old King Cole", the jolly brewer of Twickenham.' His children were born in his wife's home and 'Charleville will always find me,' he told Gladstone. Edward Croker found this young married woman a useful go-between and he wrote to her on the understanding that his letters should be shown to Georgina. Louisa thought this 'a pity' and, in the light of subsequent events, one cannot but agree with her. Fanny was sentimentally romantic and as naïve as Georgina herself. Either Anne or Elizabeth would have made a wiser confidante; but Elizabeth was away from home while Anne, at Barbavilla, had her hands full with William and little Emily, the latter being very delicate.

Georgina's was not a strong character but she remained surprisingly firm in her resolve not to marry a man who did not share her religious faith. At the same time she could not resist reading the letters which Edward continued writing to Fanny. The valley of Glencree is always beautiful but never more so than during the last weeks of summer and during the approach of autumn. While the bracken on the hills was turning to gold and bronze and the heather was fading, there came a brief pause in the correspondence. When Edward wrote again it was to say he had been ill and that during his illness he had been reading the Bible. He had, he said, been particularly struck by a passage in the book of Job: 'If I have done iniquity, I will do so no more.' As a result, 'he had quite new feelings on religion, and begged to know if he would be accepted.' Georgina herself replied, saying that he might come to Charleville when well enough to travel; but, having written the letter, she was again tormented by doubts. In the evenings when the family were assembled in the small drawing-room, they 'looked so happy, she feared she could not love Edward enough to leave home. Then Edward came, and all was right . . . Everything seemed likely to go smoothly,' adds Louisa, until it became necessary for the respective fathers of the young couple to discuss marriage settlements.

Mr. Croker was furious when he discovered that his son was not, after all, marrying an heiress. He wished to contribute as little as possible himself and was dissatisfied with the amount Henry was prepared to settle on the fifth of his nine daughters. Meanwhile Edward had left the army and was living as a gentleman of leisure, entirely dependent on his father. The discussions brought to light the extent of his debts, which discovery did nothing to sweeten the atmosphere. In fact, during the winter months the engagement was continually on the point of being broken off.

It was a humiliating situation for Georgina who exclaimed to Edward: 'If I had been a kitchen-maid with my earnings, your father would have been more pleased!' Finally, Mr. Croker was prevailed on to pay Edward's debts and to give him an annual allowance. This last was so small that, when the young people were married in Powerscourt Old Church, it was on the understanding that they were to live half the year at Charleville and the other half with Edward's parents in County Limerick. Unfortunately there is no record of how this arrangement turned out, nor of how long it lasted. According to Louisa, Mr. Croker did not keep his promises and 'they were not even given anything in their hand to begin with.'

The marriage took place in 1841 and during the next two years Edward and Georgina are often referred to as being at Charleville; but it is not clear whether they were there on a visit, or as permanent residents. There is a letter in the British Museum written four months after the marriage, from Henry Rathdowne to Sir Robert Peel, asking for the post of Stipendiary Magistrate for his son-in-law, Edward Croker. We may be sure that this was only one among many written by Henry in his desperate attempts to put Edward into a position in which he could support himself, his wife and – all too soon – a large family of children. But these efforts were unsuccessful. Edward continued to be idle, extravagant and self-indulgent to the end of his life. His sons and daughters followed his example and the subject of 'Helping the Crokers' occurs again and again in family correspondence.

Pretty, bird-happy Georgina had not the sort of character which is improved by adversity. There is a querulous note in her plaintive letters, so lovingly preserved by her loyal sisters, and though sentiment is laid on with a trowel it fails to conceal an under-lying shrewdness. Throughout the sixty-six years of her life, she remained faithful to the Jane Austen pattern, though cast for a different character in another of that author's works. Her letters written after her marriage recall 'Mrs. Price' in Mansfield Park, who wrote of 'such a superfluity of children, and such a want of almost everything else.' As in the case of that unfortunate lady, Georgina's letters were 'not unproductive'. The burden of supporting the Crokers was born uncomplainingly by one generation after another, though chiefly by Elizabeth and her husband. For that wayward young woman was, at long last, persuaded to join the ranks of the godly matrons. This feat was accomplished, not through any whirlwind courtship by a handsome stranger suddenly entering her life to sweep her off her feet; but by the faithful devotion of a young cousin, five years her junior, whom she had known from childhood.

Notes to Chapter Three

1   O. B. Cole to W. E. Gladstone, October 1834. Gladstone Papers. British Museum.
2   Sir Frederick Burton, a member of the Royal Hibernian Academy, was already famous in Dublin as a portrait painter. After a visit to a Dublin gallery in 1842, W.M. Thackeray noted that 'his [Burton's] pieces were the most admired in the collection.' W. M. Thackeray, *The Irish Sketch-book* (London, 1843). Burton later became a director of both the National Gallery in London and the National Portrait Gallery in London, *DNB.* Burton was only twenty-four when he painted Frances Rathdowne and her daughters.
3   Cole to Gladstone. 1836. Gladstone Papers.
4   Gladstone's Diaries. Vol. II, 1868.
5   Croker Papers.
6   Madden's biography of Robert Daly.

4

'Young' Charles

In the procession of Elizabeth's suitors there is one constant figure; so very much in the background, so immature and unimportant that in the opinion of Louisa he hardly counted as a serious admirer. 'Charles Monck was always dangling after Lizzy.' Louisa's references to her young cousin are always faintly contemptuous. His ideas were too democratic; he was 'hail fellow' with social inferiors; his dress was unconventional. Elizabeth herself told her sisters that she regarded him 'as her son'; and she was, in fact, already twenty-one when he entered Trinity College to read for the Irish bar. Eligible young men came and went, but young Charles was always there; sometimes very much in the way, as when he turned up unexpectedly on the Ballinasloe fair-ground, 'just to see Lizzy'. She and her sisters were staying with their mother's brother, Lord Clancarty, who as usual had an immense party at Garbally Park for the annual October fair. The party from Charleville travelled across Ireland in their own carriage and spent a few days with their aunt, Lady Castlemaine, at Moydrum, a few miles north-east of Ballinasloe, before continuing their journey to Garbally. Louisa's enjoyment of the house-party was completely spoilt by a 'shameless flirtation' between Lizzy and one of their fellow guests. It was certainly a tactless occasion for young Charles to appear, as devoted as ever and showing every intention of attaching himself to their party on the 'Fair Green'. Elizabeth made it quite clear that her cousin was unwelcome and openly showed her displeasure when he accepted Lord Clancarty's kind invitation to return with them and dine at Garbally. This happened on the last evening of the party. The sisters set off very early next morning as they were again to break their journey at Moydrum in time to breakfast with the Castlemaines.

At Charleville, young Charles was such a constant visitor that his presence was hardly noticed. Louisa occasionally mentions the fact that he was there, as a background for more prominent events – such as Georgina's marriage to Edward Croker. 'Charles Monck was continually dangling . . . always after Lizzy . . . writing music for her . . . bringing or sending presents . . . buying comfits for the children.' By Louisa, as by Elizabeth's other sisters, he was looked on as a person of no importance even when, in 1841, he graduated and was admitted to the Irish bar having completed his legal training in London and spent some, at least, of his vacations on the continent. From London he had visited Oxford where he met his cousin by marriage, Owen Cole. When Charles returned to London, Owen entrusted him with a parcel for Mr. W. E. Gladstone, writing from Christ Church a covering note which explained:

> . . . The bearer . . . is a person with whom I should be glad to make you acquainted as he is a *very* amiable and right-minded young man, which is a great comfort to us as he is the representative of the house of Monck after Ld Rathdowne.[1]

One day after returning from a ride, Charles asked Elizabeth to go for a walk with him; not in the Dark Walk, nor in the kindly seclusion of The Glen, but along the carriage-drive known as 'the back avenue' which runs straight across the demesne grass-lands. From here there is an uninterrupted view of the whole range of Wicklow Mountains which Elizabeth would always associate with her childhood. The windows of the nursery at Charleville look out on these mountains – on Djouce, Malin, Tanduff, Warr Hill and Kippure. This was to be no light flirtation, requiring a twisting path sheltered by trees and shrubberies. Charles did right to bring his cousin here when he wanted a straight answer to a serious question. She gave him a straight answer, but not the one he hoped for. She was absolutely firm and unhesitating in her refusal to marry him, thereby proving that she was not influenced by material considerations. As matters then stood, Charles Joseph, the father of young Charles, was Henry Rathdowne's heir. The younger girls do not seem to have been aware of this, but Elizabeth knew that Charles might one day occupy her father's place and that, as his wife, she would be mistress of this home she loved so much. The prospect would have tempted a young woman of less integrity.

Up to now, we have seen Elizabeth only through the somewhat jaundiced eyes of Louisa. It is from her own letters written after her marriage and from the testimony of her many friends, that we learn of her passion for sincerity. Even earlier, in the austerely brief notes she made on her studies in history, in English, French and German literature, and in philosophy, we can trace this search for bare, unadorned truth. Her insistence on reality made her unpopular with those of her sisters who found no difficulty in submitting to the conventions of their creed and class; accepting instruction, religious or secular, in tabloid form, covering up anything that was 'not quite nice' with a wreath of sugary sentiment. Although basically her religious faith never wavered and she was a loyal churchwoman to the end of her days, she could never bring herself to accept that Protestants were always right while Roman Catholics were always wrong. At times this dread of false values and shallow judgments swung her too far in the opposite direction, causing her to stifle her natural impulses; as now, when she told her cousin Charles that 'she had no liking for him.' Young as he was, he may have felt that he knew her better than she knew herself and guessed that she was prejudiced by those very advantages which might be gained by accepting him. This would explain his refusal to accept her decision as final, for he was neither selfish nor insensitive, and would not have persisted had he truly believed that she did not care for him.

For the time being the matter was taken out of his hands. An invitation to go to Scotland with her young married cousin, Gertrude McClintock, gave Elizabeth the opportunity to get away from home and sort out her problems at a distance. She kept her own counsel about her love affairs; so there is no means of knowing whether the separation from Charles made her aware of the true state of her feelings, or whether that came about when she saw him again after her return to Ireland. Reading between the lines in Louisa's note-book, one gets the impression that her parents had begun to discourage Charles' visits and that Elizabeth found it difficult to see him. Why, otherwise, should she have played such a shabby trick on her brother-in-law, Edward Croker, on the occasion of Lord de Grey's first Drawing-room? William Smythe was to go to this Castle function as Louisa's escort and Lizzy 'engaged Edward to look after her'. Louisa is too delicate to say so, but presumably Georgina was kept at home by the approach of a happy event – the first of so many. No sooner had the young people arrived at Dublin Castle than Lizzy 'sent Edward off to fetch her an ice, and never went near him again.' It afterwards transpired that she and young Charles had spent the evening together and Louisa believed that it was then that matters were settled between them.

There was consternation at Charleville when Elizabeth announced that she wished to marry her cousin. Henry and Frances had put no difficulties in the way of Fanny's marriage to Owen; they had, though with more reluctance, allowed Georgina to marry Edward Croker; and they had taken William Smythe to their hearts. But they were horrified by the idea of receiving nephew Charles as a son-in-law. Nobody seems to have objected to the fact that he was five years younger than Elizabeth but: 'There are two objections,' said Henry when Charles formally asked for his daughter. 'One is not to be got over; that is, want of money. The other is being cousins.' Henry's own parents had been first cousins with apparently no ill results, and his brother's daughter Anne had recently married her first cousin, James Napier Webb. Frances' Trench relations were constantly inter-marrying. Perhaps Henry thought it was time to put a stop to this dangerous practice. Frances backed him up, but her unmarried sister, Louisa Trench, took the part of the young lovers, and everyone was at loggerheads.

The want of money was a real difficulty. With Edward Croker, and sometimes Owen Cole on his hands, Henry can hardly be blamed for drawing the line at having to support another son-in-law. As a newcomer to the bar, young Charles would not have been earning anything as yet; and, as one of eight children, could not have counted on financial help from his father; but he had no intention of becoming one of Henry's pensioners. All he asked was permission to be engaged to Elizabeth and he had every confidence of soon being in a position to marry.

At this point a new development arose. His mother, Bridget, died in January 1843, and she left him a little money. There was now nothing to prevent an immediate marriage if the Rathdownes would give their consent and if Elizabeth would agree to live, for the time being, in his father's house. The death of Bridget Monck had placed her eldest son in a difficult position in spite of slightly easing his financial situation. His father was now completely crippled and a very sick man. John and William, the second and third sons, were in the Army, and Anne, the eldest daughter, was married to James Webb; but there were still Henrietta, Isabella, Elizabeth and Richard, all still in their 'teens, and the two last aged respectively fifteen and fourteen. Charles had a strong sense of duty and he knew that he must not abandon his bereaved family. For a while, at least, he must stay at home and look after them; but this would be no hardship if Elizabeth would share the responsibility with him.

At first she made no objection to the arrangement, though privately she may have doubted the wisdom of such a plan. If so, her doubts became certainties after a visit to her cousin Gertrude in County Down. Gertrude had been a LaTouche and she had married her own first cousin and Elizabeth's, Robert McClintock. Gertrude may have had sad tales to tell of disagreements with her own husband's parents, who were also her uncle and aunt. However it may have been, Elizabeth returned from that visit prepared to make difficulties. She still wanted to marry Charles, but he must not ask her to live with his family.

Charles declared that he could not desert his father and sisters just at this time. Though only twenty-five, he was weighed down by family cares. If he were to leave home, what would become of fourteen-year-old Dick? And there was the constant anxiety over brother William and his extravagant ways. None of this was news to Elizabeth; these troublesome people were her own flesh and blood and Charles could not tell her anything about them that she did not already know. She had steeled herself in advance; Charles must choose between his family and herself. Louisa noted that 'Charles went away, very much disappointed'. Perhaps his disappointment was caused more by this new hardness in one who was normally kind and compassionate, rather than because he felt any real doubt about the outcome. Charles seems always to have been quietly confident that he and Lizzy were to marry. Aunt Louisa Trench was highly indignant. She had championed Elizabeth and Charles to the point of quarrelling with her dear sister Frances. And here was that tiresome Lizzy going back on everything and incapable of knowing her own mind from one day to another.

We shall never know how long deadlock would have lasted between these two strong-willed young people; how soon Elizabeth would have given in, for if anyone had to give way, it must be herself. If Charles had had a weak, yielding nature, she would not have wanted to marry him. She would hold out, perhaps, till the end of October or the beginning of November, but in November no-one at Charleville or connected with Charleville had time to think of lovers' tiffs; of who was right or who wrong. Frances Rathdowne was dying.

Until less than a week before her death, Frances had seemed better in health and spirits than she had been for many years. Her daughters had remarked on this with thankful relief for she had been through a terrible time of depression after the death of her grandchild, Emily Smythe, in the previous December. Poor William was heart-broken, as was Anne to whom Emily had been like her own child.

In the loss of her adored grandchild, Frances had seemed to lose her daughter all over again and for a time it was as if she could not get over it. But by the autumn she was again serenely attending to her many duties in her family and on the estate and she was once more entertaining friends and relations. 'Her cheerfulness increased,' wrote Anne, 'and she seemed even to enjoy many things which for a long time had given her no pleasure.' One day she said to Anne: 'What a comfort it is that that depression is gone. I have the light of my Father's countenance shining upon me.' There was now no longer any excuse for Anne to live at Barbavilla though there was still a continual coming and going between the two houses. 'William's room' was always kept ready for him at Charleville; and Anne was often at Barbavilla though usually accompanied by some of her sisters. Frances encouraged her to go there alone, however, to be with William during the sad weeks before and after the anniversaries of his two bereavements. This was a period in which such gloomy occasions were observed with an almost religious fervour; relations and intimate friends were expected to remember the date and to send letters of condolence, and woe betide the careless ones who overlooked it. William's child had died a few weeks after the fifth anniversary of his wife's death so that Barbavilla would be plunged in mourning during most of November and December. Frances thought that William should not be left by himself at such a time and that 'Anne was the best person to be with him.'

Five days before she died, Frances paid her usual visit to the village school, beside the Glebe House. 'Her manner on that day was remarked by all there to be unusually solemn. She spoke very earnestly to the children; talked to them of those who were gone, and of our own dear little child . . . wept and prayed with them. After leaving the school, she went again to the door and took leave once more of the children, saying very solemnly and fervently: "God be with you, my children." They were so much struck as to speak to their parents about it all when they went home.' The next day was Saturday and on that day she always went up to the school-room on the top storey – 'to hear Mary her lesson'. Later in the morning, while sitting in the small drawing-room with a party of relations who were staying in the house, she was seized by a fit of shivering. Her sister-in-law persuaded her to come up to her dressing-room and lie on the couch by the fire – 'with her fur tippet round her shoulders'. By the next day Elizabeth was so anxious about her that she suggested sending to Dublin for Sir Henry Marsh, but Frances would not allow this. 'It would be so fussing,' she said; it was simply an attack of influenza and she would probably be better tomorrow. She also forbade Elizabeth to send for Anne who was – 'better where she was'. William had been unwell and Frances was more concerned about his condition than about her own. However, by Monday evening she had become so weak and feverish that Elizabeth and her father insisted on sending a messenger on horseback to Dublin. Frances dictated the letter to Sir Henry telling him that she had influenza, that she did not want him to come out to Charleville, but to send remedies to alleviate the pain in her bones and in her head. She was still determined that no message should be sent to Barbavilla, with the result that Anne never again saw her mother alive.

Afterwards, Anne made Elizabeth tell her every detail she could remember of the last week of her mother's life, and her written account of that time gives us the most vivid picture that exists of Frances Rathdowne's personality. In the general break-up of the family in 1848, all letters and papers were removed from Charleville. The family were great letter-writers and the daughters would certainly have treasured every note written by Frances; but not one of them survives. Louisa's *History of the Lovers* was written at a later date and is concerned with the characters and doings of her sisters. Written for herself and for them, it contains no pen-portrait of her mother and the immediate impression it gives of Frances is a misleading one: that of a self-effacing and shadowy presence in the background. Yet, although she deferred to Henry in everything and

70

often allowed her daughters to make their own decisions, there is no doubt but that hers was the final court of appeal and that the way of life at Charleville was such as she wished it to be.

In addition to her activities on the estate and in the parish, the smooth running of such a complicated household must have required a high standard of organisation. There was the nursery establishment for Fanny's children, the school-room and governess for Harriet and Mary, the grown-up unmarried daughters, and the young Crokers with their baby. There were dinner parties and house parties, as well as guests arriving unexpectedly, yet we never once get the impression of bustle or confusion. In her gentle, dignified way, Frances was a thoroughly good manager, the more so as she never appeared to be 'managing'. Although order and discipline were maintained by Anne and in her absence by Elizabeth, they were deputising for their mother rather than replacing her. Her children's attitude to her seems to have been one of loving reverence rather than of awe; they ran to her with all their troubles and slept in her room when they were ill or unhappy. Her hand on the reins was light, but she never relaxed her hold on them; and to the last day of her life her mind continued to be occupied by plans for the comfort of her large household. 'Mama was much distressed that the messenger who had been sent to Town should be out on such a wet evening, and desired that he should have hot Negus on his return, and not be allowed to wait at dinner . . . She said to Harriet: "Go and beg of your Papa, now that these disorders are going [about] so much, to be very careful of himself; not to eat crude things, or to get wet in his feet."'

Her manner was a curious mixture of the ceremonious formality of Lady Clancarty's early training and a direct, almost blunt, simplicity of speech. This last was in marked contrast to the elaborate phraseology of that time which was already being adopted by some of her daughters. No doubt there were still traces of the brogue of her girlhood as when, during her illness, she asked for arrowroot laced with wine, remarking: 'I shall go out entirely if I don't have something.' Anne or Louisa would certainly have expressed themselves more elegantly and would have taken longer to explain that they felt faint for want of food. She became so much worse during Tuesday night that, early on Wednesday, she at last allowed Elizabeth to summon Sir Henry Marsh. 'Sir H. arrived

71

about nine o'clock and said at once that there was little or no hope,' and that no time was to be lost in sending for Anne and William. As usual, no diagnosis was recorded; perhaps it was against Sir Henry's principles to give a name to an illness, even if he knew it.

The portrait painted of Frances three years earlier gives her an ethereal, almost transparent, look; and it seems probable that she had been keeping herself going by sheer will-power and that her physical resistance had become too low to combat a sharp attack of influenza. Apart from a feverish cold and cough, with pains in her limbs, her main symptom was intense weakness and faintness, though her daughters noted that, at frequent intervals, she roused herself in order to make 'playful remarks' to cheer them up. In between her bouts of faintness and drowsiness, there were times when she was 'alive to everything', as when she ordered her daughters to go out for a walk and get some fresh air after they had spent the morning in her bedroom. Sir Henry had said he would return late in the evening and she gave directions about preparing a bedroom for him, 'and for whey to be left for him. She gave Marianne particular instructions about having Anne's room and

Frances, Viscountess Monck (1787-1843). Portrait by Sir Frederick Burton *c.* 1840.

William's comfortable when they arrived.' Two days previously, she had had a fancy to be moved into William's room, perhaps because it was warmer than her own; one can easily imagine that William had been given one of the pleasantest rooms in the house. In consequence, he would now have to occupy an inferior room in a distant wing and she 'did not like him to be down there, out of the way'.

Late in the evening, when she was very weak, she heard Louisa say: '"Marianne, go down and see if Sir Henry is come." Mama said: *"Please,* Marianne!" in such a way that Louisa said it made *her* say – "Please!"' In an age when a great deal was made of death-bed scenes with a regular ritual of solemn last words and exhortations, Frances must have been something of a disappointment to the more conventional of her daughters. With no pious homilies or poignant farewells, she approached the end of her life with as little fuss or commotion as if she had been going down to the village and would see them again in an hour or two. She liked her family to pray with her and to read aloud from the Bible but, with her, there was nothing unusual in this. She remained calmly practical and matter-of-fact to the end, which came at mid-night on the Wednesday, four hours before the arrival of Anne and William.

Robert Daly, then Bishop of Cashel, gave the following address at her funeral which took place at Powerscourt Old Church a week after her death:

> Very many loved and valued friends have I seen laid in the adjoining churchyard . . . but among them all I can say that there was not one who for so long a course of years I knew so intimately and valued so highly. I knew her as a child; I knew her in the gaieties of the world, myself there too. I knew her as the first in this parish who openly assumed and acted on principles different from the morality of the world, and far above it. I witnessed her course as a Christian matron acting on these principles and endeavouring to diffuse their light around her. You are witnesses to the truth of what I say. *You* know what manner of life she lived among you. *I* knew, from a long course of most intimate acquaintance and friendship, and the freest expression of thought and feeling on both sides, that the mainspring of the life she lived was Christ. He was the strength

and consolation of her heart through many and deep sorrows, the object which she set before her . . .

The rest of the Bishop's discourse is mainly concerned with the desirability of imitating such an example. Anne wrote it all down conscientiously, perhaps to make up for the lack of any inspiring last words from her mother; and she added a copy of a letter of condolence written to Elizabeth from one of her admirers, also an elegy composed by Owen Cole who had appointed himself poet-laureate to the family.

'She hardly knew she was going, and her last words were – perfect peace,' he wrote to his friend whom he kept informed on every event in the Monck family. 'She died on the day so fatal in her family, the 22. of November, the same on which her daughter, Lady Emily Smythe, died in 1838, and the same on which her grandchild, the daughter of the last mentioned, was attacked with an illness which carried her off in a few days. Lady Rathdowne was an excellent woman, the best I ever knew. In early life she had been very beautiful, but she moved among the crowd of her admirers like a star amid the flitting lights of the North. She soon left the world entirely and devoted herself to God, her children and the poor . . . As you are a poet, I will not apologise for sending you the following tribute to the memory of one you would have loved if you had known her.'[2]

Notes to Chapter Four

1   O. B. Cole to W. E. Gladstone, May 1841. Gladstone Papers. British Museum.
2   O. B. Cole to W. E. Gladstone, 9 December 1843. Gladstone Papers. British Museum.

5

'The Oak King Falls'

Henry Rathdowne was only fifty-eight when his wife died. Though he was 'wretched and ill' during the months following the death of Frances, there must have been many people who expected him to marry again eventually, if only to produce the longed-for heir.

In the meantime, Anne was mistress of his house and, though her position might be a temporary one, she and the other unmarried girls could look forward to many years during which Charleville would still be their home. Deeply as they felt the loss of their mother, it made no fundamental change in their lives, as would have been the case if their father had died. Their home was still there; and with the reins of the household in Anne's capable hands, life at Charleville continued to run, outwardly at least, on much the same lines as before.

Yet, beneath the surface, changes were taking place. Elizabeth had been constantly with Frances during those last days; she had seen her mother die and the experience made a lasting impression on her. We hear of no more flirtations, either then or at any other time in her life. She no longer had the heart to wrangle with Charles as to where they should or should not live, if they married. She would marry him on his own terms, even if these should involve looking after his crippled father and his young brother and sisters instead of having a home of their own. It is significant that all her doubts about marrying him were swept away at the time when, her father having become a widower, there appeared to be little chance that Charles would inherit.

She confided her decision to Anne whose immediate reaction was to carry her off to Barbavilla. It had already been arranged that Anne should go there, taking 'the children', Harriet and Mary. Though William Smythe spent a good deal of time at Charleville, there were occasions on which duty called him back to County

Westmeath, and it was unthinkable that he should be left alone for long. The visit was very well timed from Anne's point of view, if she wanted to get Elizabeth away from home for a while. It is likely that she felt anxious lest this, the most head-strong of her sisters, should be making too hasty a decision as the result of the shock of her mother's death.

The last thing Elizabeth wanted to do was to pay a long visit to William and it is a proof of her chastened frame of mind that she meekly fell in with the plan. They travelled in the family coach with postilions, changing horses at post-houses along the route. Their first stop was in Dublin and here Anne consulted her aunt Louisa Trench about Elizabeth and Charles. By this time Lady Louisa was feeling thoroughly irritated by Lizzy and her shilly-shallying and agreed with Anne that nothing ought to be decided in a hurry. The sisters continued their journey into Westmeath; though well-wooded and with some good pasture-land, it seemed flat and featureless after their home among the Wicklow hills.

Harriet and Mary had always been devoted to William and loved staying at Barbavilla, while Anne found plenty to keep her occupied in a place which had been her home in all but name for six years. But Elizabeth was 'nervous and miserable'. She had many good qualities, but tolerance was not one of them, and in her present frame of mind she can hardly have added to the enjoyment of the party. To be the guest of a disapproving brother-in-law might have tried a more patient nature than hers. She longed to make it up with Charles who had been deeply hurt by her attitude at their last interview, and she had yet to obtain her father's consent to the marriage.

Louisa had been left at Charleville to look after her father, her sister Caroline, and any small nephews and nieces who might happen to be occupying the nursery. That Caroline, now aged twenty, has hitherto played no part in this story is due to the fact that Louisa never mentions her except to refer to her frequent illnesses. There is a general belief, handed down by word of mouth, that Caroline was slightly retarded mentally as well as being physically delicate. There is no documentary evidence to support this belief, but its probability is borne out by subsequent events. While Frances was alive, Caroline had been able to join in the normal family life, at least to a certain extent, and her sisters had noticed no particular change in her condition after her mother's death. But now Louisa

76

sent a messenger to Barbavilla imploring Anne to return as Caroline was 'very unwell'. Anne set off at once, taking Harriet who would stay and keep Louisa company while Caroline was to be brought to Barbavilla.

Elizabeth had been left to look after William, presumably to their mutual dissatisfaction. But Anne had promised her 'to do that wretched office of asking Papa's consent to her marriage'; and she did not leave Charleville until that had been accomplished. Henry gave in, though very reluctantly, saying that they could never be 'comfortable' until after his own death. This proves that he had no thought, as yet, of marrying again, and looked on nephew Charles as his heir. His brother Charles Joseph could be discounted, as his present state of health made it unlikely that he would live very long. Poor Henry could see the day coming when his brother's four younger children would be added to his other commitments; and it would have been a comfort to see Elizabeth married to a man who could support her without help from Charleville. Eventually Anne talked him round, while Louisa attempted to cheer him up by suggesting that young Charles 'might die before him'.

Young Charles still, for the time being, very much alive, was summoned to Charleville. On being told the good news he wished to dash off at once to Barbavilla, but Louisa persuaded him to change his 'frightful clothes' before appearing before his betrothed. She disapproved of his 'bright blue waistcoat'; and she also insisted on providing him with 'a green veil to protect his face from heat and dust'. In her view, Lizzy was acting with her usual lack of consideration in worrying Papa when he was so ill and miserable. She took no further interest in the affair, merely stating that the marriage took place that summer, 1844. We know from other sources that Charles and Elizabeth were married in Powerscourt Old Church on 23 July, two days before the anniversary of her parents' wedding. Presumably they had some kind of wedding tour; after which Charles took Elizabeth to his father's house in Merrion Square.

Elizabeth now had to care for her invalid father-in-law and for his four younger children: Isabella, Henrietta, Dick and Elizabeth. As her own mother had been dead for more than a year, Isabella might have been expected to resent the arrival of her brother's wife as mistress of the house. There are no contemporary personal records to tell us how it all worked out at the time; but that the result was satisfactory is made clear in the correspondence of later years. Isabella was always something of a trial to her relations; she had injured her back as a child and is said to have spent the rest of her life lying on a sofa and playing a harp. This may sound contradictory, but those who have seen the harp state that it was a small one which could be played while in a reclining position. Provided that no one disputed her place on the sofa, she may have been content to leave the running of the house to her sister-in-law, as she and Elizabeth managed to remain on very friendly terms with each other.

Elizabeth was extremely fond of her sixteen-year-old namesake who was soon to become 'Aunt E.' to many nephews and nieces..To avoid confusing her with her sister-in-law, from now on she will be referred to as 'AuntE.' and indeed she seems always to have had the characteristics of a certain type of maiden aunt, angular, rigid and opinionated, but with a kind heart hidden beneath her brusque manner. The elder Elizabeth realised that this sister-in-law was not as tough as she made herself out to be. Her attitude towards her was affectionately protective and in later years she more than once sent her schoolboy son to escort 'Aunt E.' on journeys. A very different type was eighteen-year-old Henrietta; Elizabeth loved her dearly and several years later was to write of her 'sweet, cheerful temper, and her dear pretty face'. In her turn, Henrietta was completely devoted to her brother's wife, while young Dick was Elizabeth's obedient slave to the end of her life. Reading in letters and diaries of the way she and Charles made use of Dick, one cannot help feeling that they sometimes took advantage of his good nature. As Colonel, and later General, Richard Monck, with a wife and children of his own, Elizabeth had only to raise a finger for him to drop whatever he was doing and go to her assistance. 'I have told Dick to meet you.' 'I am sending Dick to London to help you.' These and similar phrases occur again and again in Charles' letters. And Elizabeth would be writing to her son Henry at Eton: 'Dick will come down and take you out.' 'Ask Dick if you need anything.' Dick appeared to be quite happy at being used as a general errand-boy and, when he was in a position to do so, to supply money when it was needed. If Elizabeth was too much inclined to take him for granted, his willingness that she should do so seems to show that he had never forgotten her kindness to him as a boy.

Ann Webb, the married sister, lived at Woodville in County

Tipperary, and John and William were serving with their regiments overseas. John had become Ensign in the 84th Regiment when he was eighteen, and William joined the same regiment at seventeen. At the time of their brother's marriage, the 84th went to India; but in 1844 William transferred to the 7th Fusiliers who were then in Gibraltar. William is said to have been 'wild' but extremely attractive, rather too fond of the opposite sex, and to have had a permanent hole in his pocket. During the process of changing over, he probably managed to get some leave, so may have been at the Merrion Square house when Charles and Elizabeth married. Later in the year, his regiment was ordered to the West Indies, and in 1847 Charles received this letter written from Barbados:

My dear Charles. I was extremely glad to hear from all the letters received from home this packet that you were all going on pretty well. Johnny seems to be enjoying himself very much at Woodville. I am glad to see he is so near the top of the list. I should think he must be the second of purchase for his company, it would be a great thing for him if he could get his company before his leave is up. India will now be the best foreign station, since they have shortened the period of service there.

I have received my account from the Agents by this packet, and on looking it over I find that I have only been paid my allowance altogether since I left England it amounts to £48, whereas by the allowance Papa gives me it would up to this moment amount to £80 since May 1845. I would be much obliged if you would look into it and lodge the balance £32 to my credit at Messrs. Cox & Co. I shall also be extremely obliged to you if you will give me my next year's allowance in advance at the same time, as I shall have to get such a lot of things when I go on to Canada, in the shape of clothes, furs, etc.

I hope My Dear Charles you will not think me extravagant as I assure you this is a most expensive country. Thank God we are soon to leave it, and are going to a cooler and cheaper.

I have no news, so with love to all, including your Lizzy and young ones, Believe me, My Dear Charles,

Yours most affectionate
William Monck

Let me know what you can do for me as soon as you can, as I must raise it by some means or another. Wm.

This letter must have annoyed Charles in more ways than one. By all accounts it was not the only time William had been in a position in which he 'must raise it, by some means or another'. Besides which, it would have been disappointing to receive a letter from a brother stationed in the West Indies, only to be told that he had 'no news'. William had not even the excuse of being always in one place. According to the Regimental Record – 'One of the Companies at Berlico was sent under Lieutenant the Hon. William Monck. to Mahaica for change of air in consequence of the prevalence of fever.'

William's reference to 'Johnny . . . enjoying himself very much at Woodville' (his sister's house), shows that his elder brother was on leave from India at least on this occasion. The hopes for John's promotion were realised, as he became Adjutant of the regiment in the following December.

While adjusting herself to this family of first cousins, Elizabeth did not allow herself to forget that one of them was now her husband. If she had previously imagined that she knew all there was to know about Charles, she would have discovered her mistake soon after her marriage. Here in Dublin he was seen in a very different light from that of the boy cousin who had 'dangled' after her for so many years, and her five years' seniority did not prevent her from looking up to him as her superior. Circumstances had forced him to act as 'father figure' to his brothers and sisters before he was out of his 'teens, and at the time of his marriage he seemed far older than his twenty-five years. Towards his responsibilities he was conscientious and thorough but his cheerful, extrovert temperament prevented him from ever becoming ponderous. His philosophic outlook was very good for Elizabeth who, left to herself, might have become too intense. Charles took life as it came, was more prone to like people than dislike them, and was able to see the humorous side of any situation – even if the joke were against himself. Though tall and heavily-built, he was athletic, passionately fond of horses, and essentially an outdoor man.

He was already interesting himself in public affairs and he introduced his wife to a world which was new to her. His friends and associates were reformers and thoughtful politicians; and it was his strong sense of public responsibility, at least as much as personal ambition, which sent him into politics. As a member of the Anglo-Irish land-owning class he owed allegiance to the English monarchy, while at the same time his personal sympathies were with the Irish people. He realised that their intolerable situation could be relieved only by a complete change in legislation, and, Westminster being the seat of government, he could best help his fellow countrymen by way of a seat in the House of Commons. His letters of that period have been lost; but those he wrote in later years show that he had always strongly opposed the political, agrarian and ecclesiastical injustices perpetrated by the British Government. There is no actual evidence to show that he would have voted against the Union, had he been born fifty years earlier, but he made no secret of the fact that he deplored the results of the Union.

In the eighteen-forties there were over eight million people in Ireland whose only source of livelihood was the land, and who existed almost entirely on potatoes. The other farm produce and the steadily increasing rents were spent by the majority of the landlords in England, while the peasants were continually on the verge of starvation.

The widespread discontent at this time was concentrated mainly in two nationalist movements: the Catholic Association, founded by O'Connell, and the Repeal [of the Union] Association led by Thomas Davis. One of the chief aims of the former was to abolish the tithe system, whereby the Catholic Irish were compelled to support the Protestant Church. Charles Monck's views on the tithe system were expressed in a letter written several years later.

> I have always thought that it is a great injustice that the provision that the State makes in Ireland for the support of religion should be given exclusively to maintain the Church of a small minority of the population, and that minority by far the richest portion of the people of the country.[1]

In 1845 a hitherto unknown potato-disease spread over Europe, ruining the greater part of the crop in Ireland where one-third of the population subsisted on potatoes alone. This was followed by a total failure of the Irish potato crop in 1846. Largely owing to procrastination on the part of the British Government and subsequent inefficient administration of plans for relief, by the summer of 1847 one million people in Ireland had died of starvation and fever, while many thousands had emigrated to America, hundreds of them dying during the voyage. In 1846, Charles Duffy wrote of:

> . . . Deaths of individuals, of husband and wife, of entire families . . . batches of inquests, with the horrible verdict, 'Died of starvation'. In some cases the victims were buried 'wrapped in a coarse coverlet,' a coffin being too costly a luxury. The living awaited death with a listlessness which was at once tragic and revolting. Women with dead children in their arms were seen begging for a coffin to bury them . . . .[2]

By the roadsides were found bodies of people who had died where they fell; an entire family would be found dead in their cabin. Cartloads of dead were taken each morning from the fever-stricken workhouses, to be buried in a great pit in the churchyard. Sixteen thousand pounds-worth of potatoes were destroyed by the blight in that year alone:

> At the same time, the bulk of the remaining supplies, cattle and corn, butter, beef and pork, which would have fed all the inhabitants, continued to be exported to England, to pay the rent of farms which no longer yielded the cultivators their ordinary food . . . .
> The established practice . . . was to despatch Englishmen to a country of which they knew nothing, and entrust them to determine questions requiring minute knowledge and long experience. The English officials determined that work simply, irrespective of its reproductiveness, was the proper system, and that not railways and canals or transforming wastes into corn-fields, but a prodigious extension of highways, was the legitimate application of the national strength. Half a million people were soon employed on this basis, and nearly twelve thousand persons paid for overseeing unproductive labour. Serviceable roads were torn up that they might be made anew, and new lines projected where there was no traffic.[3]

Great bitterness was felt against the numerous absentee landlords;

living in England, they left their estates to the mercy of agents who evicted tenants who could not pay their rents. Among the resident landlords who worked tirelessly to provide relief were John Robert Godley and his friends Charles Monck and William Monsell. 'How I wish you and Monck and I formed a triumvirate to govern Ireland! We are the only people who think alike,' Godley wrote to William Monsell. '. . . I will try to improve Monck's manners, but he is really so excellent and useful that you *must* like him.'[4] Charles Monck was inclined to be too blunt and outspoken to suit an age in which ceremonious speech was the fashion. In spite of this, he and Monsell became firm friends and, with Godley, formed the nucleus of a committee which met every day in Dublin. They called themselves 'The Irish Party', and were joined by the nationalist leader, William Smith O'Brien. They had some difficulty in curbing the latter's wish to turn it into a political group, thereby defeating its object: 'An attempt to combine classes and creeds and interests in Ireland.'[5] In a letter to O'Brien on 20 April 1847, Charles Monck tried to convince him that their common cause was likely to be endangered by the intrusion of party politics. The letter, which combined tactful persuasion mingled with characteristic blunt sincerity, showed that he was on extremely confidential, even affectionate, terms with the nationalist.[6]

The Irish Party drew up a memorandum which was presented to the government at Westminster in January 1847. The memorandum contained a clear and informed summary of the situation and proposed 'a short-term plan to cope with the famine, and a long-term plan to restore the national economy.'[7] Their memorandum was debated in parliament, but few of its provisions were put into effect and in March, Godley admitted to Monsell that 'The Irish Party' had failed in its object.

While pressing for immediate relief, both Charles Monck and John Godley were equally insistent that temporary amelioration of the present distress was only a part of the task which lay before them. They aimed to strike at the root of the evil – 'to bring about a fair day's wage for a fair day's work,' as Godley wrote to Monck in 1847. 'If we can bring that about, we shall be able to bear without fainting any amount of bad government. We shall never be in a satisfactory or wholesome state, but we shall rub on tolerably, till time shall have effected, in some unforeseen way, the social revolution which is necessary for Ireland.'[8]

There was a good harvest in 1847 and, before the end of that year, belated assistance from the government and voluntary contributions from all over the world had done a great deal towards alleviating the suffering. Administration of relief was, tragically, made less difficult by the decrease in the population. The effects of the famine were felt for many years and bitter memories of 'The Hunger' had a lasting influence on the subsequent history of Ireland.

In December 1847, Elizabeth received a letter from her cousin, William Gregory,[9] written from his home, Coole Park in County Galway, saying that he hoped she was 'acting like a truly patriotic Irishwoman, and daily inciting your husband to get a seat in the House of Commons. It is to such Young Irelanders as himself, Godley,[10] Monsell,[11] Herbert[12] and your humble servant that we shall look hereafter when the time comes to influence public opinion in England as regards Irish affairs. I am however rather afraid of your preferring the quiet of home, to the troubled waters of St. Stephens. Hence this hint.'

Charles Monck needed no 'incitement', either from his wife or from her cousin, to try for a seat in parliament, and in April 1848, he stood as Tory candidate for County Wicklow.[13] His defeat by Sir Ralph Howard, Radical member for the county during the past eighteen years, was the cause of an acrimonious correspondence in the *Dublin Evening Mail,* the issue having hung on the contest between the old electoral system and the new. By the old method, influential land-owners would nominate the candidate of their choice, bribing or intimidating their tenants to vote for him; opposed to this was the system of 'free election' laid down by the Constitution since the reform of the franchise and the distribution of seats brought about by the Reform Bill passed in 1832. For many years afterwards the enactments of the Bill were ignored by a number of boroughs and counties, in England as well as in Ireland, and the County Wicklow election was an example of this.

In a speech at the hustings, one of Monck's sponsors described how he, in contrast to his 'absentee' opponent,

> . . . when famine, disease and pestilence stalked over this unhappy land – when the peasantry were stricken on the highways, and their cottages became the temples of death –

was ever found labouring day and night to alleviate their sufferings; one day at the poor law court and the next at the relief committee – in fact, where he best could be of use, there was he to be found.

This and other long speeches were reported in full in the *Dublin Evening Mail* and were followed, six days after the result was declared, by an editorial article:

COUNTY OF WICKLOW ELECTION

The four Lords – two of whom are absentees, one a lunatic, and the fourth the Earl of WICKLOW – have succeeded in returning their nominee for Wicklow, by a majority of ourteen voices over those of the independent constituency of the county. After a contest the closest that has taken place in Ireland for many years, Mr. CHARLES MONCK, a resident gentleman, able, zealous, well-intentioned, and universally popular, has been defeated by the four Lords and their serfs; and in his stead has been returned a creature of the noble quartette who, during the eighteen eventful months that preceded this election, never once set foot in Ireland; who gave £20 to the relief of the starving multitudes upon his estates, and 3,000 guineas for a London opera box. For this man, and in obedience to the four Lords, the Irish SOLICITOR-GENERAL went specially to Wicklow to record his vote.[14]

From her earliest childhood Elizabeth had regarded the helping of her poorer neighbours as a matter of course, though realising that the utmost she and her family could do was a mere drop in the ocean. From Charles and his friends, she learnt that such small-scale philanthopy was not enough. To relieve individual distress might be good in itself; but the main object was to change a system which had created the need. This could only be done by being in a position of authority, even if it meant getting involved in officialdom. The *Dublin Evening Mail* mentioned 'Lady Elizabeth Monck' as being a member of the Ladies Association 'for the encouragement of industry among the female peasantry of Ireland.' Yet she was not committee-minded and, in fact, officialdom and public functions were always to be anathema to her; but she supported Charles in all his schemes and activities as she was to do for the rest of her life.

The atmosphere she now lived in was very different from that of Charleville, where life still moved at the leisurely tempo of a more spacious age. She was living for the first time among those who had not had everything handed to them on a plate. In contrast to her own father, who had stepped into a ready-made position at the age of seventeen, her husband was the son of a younger son, and had had his own way to make in the world. It had at no time been certain that he would succeed to his uncle's title and estates and, with Henry a widower, it was now even less so. It was true that Henry had handed over some of his farms to Charles and Elizabeth, the rents of which were his contribution to their marriage settlement, and this might have been taken as a sign that he regarded young Charles as his heir. But he had done this only a few months after his wife's death when, by all accounts, he was prostrated by grief. Such a situation could not be expected to last for ever, especially in the case of a handsome and vigorous man of fifty-eight. His own mother had made a second marriage, and it could only be a matter of time before Henry followed her example.

Young Charles, moreover, had too much common-sense to rely on an inheritance which was unlikely to take place for at least twenty years, if indeed it took place at all. He continued to work at his profession, though determined to embark on a political career as soon as the opportunity should arise. He had also become keenly interested in farming, not only through having become a landowner by his marriage settlement, but also through his association with The Royal Agricultural Improvement Society of Ireland. He threw himself into the work of establishing a local farming society, one of many which were affiliated to the main organisation. The Society's task was not easy in this nation of small-holders, in which dispossession had all too often been the first step in plans for improved agriculture. 'I am far from expecting any apparent result immediately,' Charles wrote to his neighbour, Sir George Hodson.

> . . . The improvement in the habits of the people must be gradual and brought about by patiently combating their prejudices and proving to them the value of the plans . . . I am quite prepared for present apparent failure and determined not to be disheartened by it.[15]

The family party at Charleville had been gradually decreasing in number. Caroline's condition deteriorated after her mother died, and Anne took her to Wales and placed her in the care of an old friend of the family. The numbers were further reduced by the departure of Edward and Georgina Croker with their children. They had at last set up house on their own, incongruously enough in the Quaker village of Ballitore in County Kildare. This still left Anne, Louisa, Harriet and Mary, while the Coles and William Smythe were there often enough for their occasional absence to require explanation.

Young Charles and Elizabeth had two daughters, Frances and Louise, born during their first three years of married life. Elizabeth never made heavy weather of her pregnancies, carrying on with her normal life as long as possible and resuming it very soon after the birth of each child. In the autumn before Louise was born, Charles' work for the 'Irish Committee' took him to London and Elizabeth accompanied him. While they were there she received a letter from Anne urging them to come to Charleville immediately. Henry Rathdowne had had a paralytic stroke and was dangerously ill.

Until three years before, he had been accustomed to leading a healthy outdoor life, driving four-in-hand, riding, and climbing the Wicklow Mountains. He loved to laugh and joke with his daughters who treated him as if he were their contemporary. But when Frances died it was as if a spring inside him had broken. His daughters thought it natural, as well as right and proper, that he should be heart-broken to the point of illness during the first year and even for two years. But instead of getting better he had grown worse, and his collapse, in October 1846, was the beginning of a death-in-life existence which lasted for two years.

The curious practice of writing a detailed account of the last days of any member of the family may seem distastefully morbid to modern minds; but in the absence of letters these accounts are useful in giving some idea of the background to family life in that period. Louisa recorded that her father 'continued between life and death for some time, his mind quite astray. The Bishop of Cashel came on one of the days of greatest danger, and very beautiful were his prayers with us for our father. One thing he said often came to our minds during this long and trying illness . . . that God would grant him His presence, even if he were quite unable to express himself.'

Louisa and Harriet were sitting in his room one day when he startled them by calling out: 'I cannot find the Saviour.' 'It was a sort of waking dream he had, for he was able to tell us afterwards that he thought he heard someone say: "The Bridegroom cometh", and then, he said, "There was a great fuss, and I could not find the Saviour, and I said – 'But I want to find the Saviour' – and then I thought someone said: 'I will never leave thee nor forsake thee . . . him that cometh unto me I will in no wise cast out'; and I was quite satisfied."' He was often heard repeating those words.

His condition varied; during one period he was able to sit up in a chair, and Louisa wrote that he 'laughed and joked and even sang with us.' 'I never had such clear ideas on religion as since my illness,' he told Louisa; and on another occasion he said with tears that it was 'a terrible thing to slack one's pace in religion.' Perhaps Louisa was too humourless or, more probably, too accustomed to her father's way of expressing himself to note the pathos of such a remark from one who had been a famous whip. When he was able to sit up and his faithful valet, Starr, and Starr's assistant, had helped him into his chair, he liked to sit with his driving-apron over his knees. He was taken in a pony-carriage along the wide paths in the eighteen acres of gardens and 'pleasure-grounds' which were being redesigned by Anne who had expert knowledge of plants and shrubs. He asked William Smythe to look over his will with him to make sure that it was in order. 'My children are so attentive to me. I should wish all about them to be right.' Even after he had a second stroke, his family were still hopeful that he would recover and it was not until after his third and last stroke, in June 1848, that his unmarried daughters realised that their days at Charleville might be numbered.

Louisa, referring in her journal to a rearrangement of their respective bedrooms, remarked: 'How short a time we were to occupy those rooms!' Aunt Louisa, their mother's sister, came to stay and was a great comfort to them; but 'we wished much for William,' mourns Louisa. William Smythe was still very much the son of the house; and although during Henry's worst times Charles sat up with him all night and helped Starr with the nursing, with his sisters-in-law he counted for nothing compared with their dear William. Luckily Charles was never one to stand on his dignity and amused tolerance would have been his only reaction to William's patronising attitude, if indeed he noticed it at all. This unselfconsciousness and entire lack of personal vanity, were to stand him in good stead during his subsequent career, giving him a freedom and poise which some of his colleagues must have envied.

By the time her father had entered on the second year of his illness, Elizabeth had started another baby. Their second daughter, Louise, had been born in the previous year, and it was probably to prevent her from over-exerting herself that Charles took his turn at nursing her father. His own father being a helpless invalid, he had plenty of experience and would certainly be handier in a sickroom than any of the other sons-in-law – William Smythe, Edward Croker or Owen Cole. Louisa does not once mention Owen during the whole time of her father's illness, though he and Fanny were often at Charleville. Owen, however, was to write his usual poetic effusion when the end came, a line from which heads this chapter.

Louisa remembers going out very early in the morning to stand on the front steps and thinking, 'how beautiful the place looked.' On another morning, 'I went out into the Glen to say my prayers, and I heard Harriet crying at our Cottage.' This would be the eighteenth-century 'rustic cottage' mentioned earlier. 'I sat down on a tree that had fallen, I have the look of the tree before me now; and as I looked round the Glen, I thought it might be the last time I would call it ours . . . On one of these sad days, I was busy in my room, and Nanny [Anne] came and said: "I do not want to say he is dying now, but let us now determine that, when all is over, we four will not separate."'

Their father died at two o'clock on the morning of 20 September 1848, and, three days later, he was laid beside his wife in the family vault in Powerscourt Old Churchyard. A descendant of one of those present has been told of the great funeral procession down the back avenue, past 'The Earl's Oak' which still flourishes, and out on to the Enniskerry road where it turned towards the entrance to Powerscourt.

Louisa states that it took place 'very early in the morning', which fact may account for the curious legend circulating among the Moncks' cousins of a later generation that, 'All the Moncks were buried in the middle of the night.'

Notes to Chapter Five

1 Charles Monck to Henry Monck, March 1868. Monck Papers. Canadian Archives.
2 Quoted in Lady Ferguson, *Sir Samuel Ferguson and the Ireland of his day* (London, 1896). Sir Charles Gavan Duffy was a historian, poet and politician. He was a friend of Thomas Davis.
3 Ibid.
4 J. R. Godley to W. Monsell, February 1847.
5 Charles Monck to William Smith O'Brien, 3 March 1847. W. S. O'Brien Papers, National Library of Ireland.
6 Ibid., 20 April 1847.
7 Carrington, C. E., *John Robert Godley of Canterbury* (Wellington, 1950).
8 J. R. Godley to Charles Monck, Unpublished letter, 1847. Monck Papers.
9 Sir William Gregory, 1817-1892. Conservative M.P. for Dublin, 1842-1847; actively supported Poor Relief Act, 1847; Liberal-Conservative M.P. for Co. Galway, 1857-1871, having formally joined the Liberal Party in 1865. Concerned in Irish agrarian legislation. *D. N. B.*
10 J. R. Godley, 1814-1861. Politician. Founded settlement of Canterbury, N.Z. He and Monck were deeply involved in the relief of Irish distress. *D. N. B.*
11 William Monsell (cr. Baron Emly in 1874). Moderate-Liberal M.P. for Co. Limerick, 1847-74. Under-Secretary for Colonies, 1868-1870. *D. N. B.*
12 The Hon. Sidney Herbert, 1810-1861. Statesman. (Cr. Lord Herbert of Lea.) Primarily responsible for Florence Nightingale's going to the Crimea. *D. N. B.*
13 *D. N. B.* states that Monck, on this occasion, stood as a Liberal, while a contemporary newspaper describes him as the Tory candidate standing against a Radical. This apparent contradiction is the result of the confusion, at that time, of party labels. Monck was first and foremost a 'Peel-ite', and supported whichever party represented Peel-ite principals; in this case the principle of 'free election' as opposed to nomination.
14 Report in *Dublin Evening Mail,* 28 April 1848.
15 Monck to Hodson, 18 December 1847. Hodson Papers. National Library of Ireland.

6

The Barbavilla Harem

The old warrior, Charles Joseph, now became the 3rd Viscount Monck; the earldom of Rathdowne, being a new creation, could not pass to a brother. Not that he was old in years; he was only fifty-seven when he succeeded, but for several years previously the state of his health had forced him to lead the life of an elderly man. When his second daughter, Henrietta 'with her sweet, cheerful nature and her dear, pretty face', married Francis Brooke of Summerton, the wedding had to take place in the Merrion Square house, the bride's father being too ill and infirm to get to the church.

Henrietta used to tell her grandchildren of her alarming experience on the day of the wedding. Her father had lent Charleville House to the young couple for their honeymoon and they were to be driven there in the family coach, with the crest and coat-of-arms emblazoned on its panels, which now belonged to Charles Joseph. The postilions having done themselves too well at the wedding, the newly-married pair had a terrifying drive culminating in the horses' bolting down Tinnehinch Hill. At the foot of this very steep hill it is necessary to turn sharply in order to enter the gates of Charleville; but by a miracle the horses were got under control and turned into the avenue without mishap.[1]

The wedding took place on 18 November 1848, barely two months after Henry Rathdowne's death. The fact that Charleville was already available for the honeymoon shows that Anne, Louisa, Harriet and Mary had wasted no time in clearing out. When Anne had said, 'Let us determine that, when all is over, we four will not separate', it is not difficult to guess what was in her mind. According to the convention of those days, it would be taken for granted that their future would be that of scores of young – and not so young – women of their acquaintance. That is, that each of the unmarried daughters should, humbly and gratefully, go to the home

91

of a married sister, to be kept in the background, to be made use of, and to be generally pushed around for the rest of their lives if they did not marry. Unless they acted promptly and firmly they would, after weeks of humiliating discussion, be parcelled out. Anne, however, had other ideas. Was it she or was it William who first made the suggestion that all four sisters should transfer themselves *en bloc* to Barbavilla? William certainly wrote a letter in which he handsomely assured the sisters that 'it is but moving from home to home', proving that he had much true kindness and delicacy in his very complex nature.

Fanny, Elizabeth and Georgina and their respective husbands had, perhaps, already embarked on a seemingly interminable wrangle as to which of them should have which sister. They must have been somewhat taken aback when Anne quietly informed them of the curiously unconventional plan: they were all four going to live with dear William at Barbavilla. Neither she nor anyone within the family appears to have thought there was anything improper in the arrangement; but this was not the case with the rest of the Anglo-Irish world. To this day, there are people in different parts of Ireland who still discuss and conjecture about the Barbavilla ménage, and many legends have been handed down through the succeeding generations. William Smythe, always eccentric where finance was concerned, is said to have ruined himself through having to support the four Ladies Monck. Also, the descendants of William's brother declare that the Ladies refused to go out or to meet anybody and that William was forced to plant trees and shrubberies intersected by concealed paths so that they could take the air without being seen. This last is entirely fictitious as can be proved by existing letters written by, to and about the Ladies, showing that they frequently stayed in Dublin, London and Paris as well as at Charleville while their own relations, besides members of William's family, often stayed at Barbavilla. A pencil-drawing has recently been found at Barbavilla, depicting a pony-carriage containing four females believed to be Anne, Louisa, Harriet and Mary. One of them drives the spirited pony and all are dressed exactly alike in voluminous capes and poke-bonnets with enormous brims. They are seen driving at a spanking pace through a village the inhabitants of which are running out of their houses to wave, while a dog gallops behind the vehicle.

As for their having been a drain on William's resources, each of them received a fat dowry from Charleville, the interest on which was paid regularly, uncomplainingly, but with great difficulty from the heavily-encumbered estate. As William himself received what would have been his wife's portion, and a good deal more, it would be interesting to know exactly what took place between him and his dying father-in-law when the latter consulted William about his will. Barbavilla is not a large house and the *ménage à cinq* must have lived there extremely comfortably as 'charges' on the Monck estate, even without the presents of game which were sent regularly from Charleville. There are letters from Harriet, from Mary and from William himself, thanking for pheasants received and sometimes asking for more.

Yet although his 'harem' was not a financial burden to William, it could have been an embarrassment to him in other ways. Setting aside their lordly disregard of the conventions, the most curious aspect of the affair was its being taken for granted by the sisters that William, aged thirty-nine, would not wish to marry again. Or was there more than a brother-and-sister relationship between William and Anne, who was two years his senior, or between William and Louisa who was nine years his junior? The relations between William and Anne must often have been discussed among their acquaintances during the five years before William's child died. The Church Table of Affinity did not, at that time, allow a man to marry his deceased wife's sister; but because of their long and close relationship, William may have felt as surely bound to Anne as if they had been man and wife, whatever his personal feelings may or may not have been. The fact remains that he did not remarry, and neither did any of his protégées though, in 1848, Harriet and Mary were aged respectively twenty-three and twenty.

One thing is quite certain and that is that they were extremely happy at Barbavilla. The sisters were devoted to each other and adored William; and in his house they had far more importance than would have been the case if the quartet had split up and each gone to live with a married sister. Anne occupied the position she would have held if she had indeed been William's wife; besides acting as chatelaine of Barbavilla, she also made herself responsible for the welfare of the people on the estate and in the village of Collinstown. She was particularly concerned with the young people and had them

Barbavilla, County Westmeath.

taught flax-weaving, the object being to start a local industry. Her first efforts were unsuccessful but later, 'Lady Anne has set on foot a straw-plaiting manufactory,' Owen Cole wrote to Gladstone. 'The flax-weaving was too much for her little workmen and workwomen.'[2]

Louisa was known to be consumptive and her condition deteriorated soon after she went to live at Barbavilla. But even when she became bed-ridden, she was not idle. Two hard-covered notebooks, each containing a year's guide to daily Bible-reading with brief notes on each portion, are still in the possession of the Monck family. This studious and painstaking work was undertaken for the edification of the children of her beloved sister, Georgina, whose marriage to Edward Croker had been a source of grief to her sisters.

There is no record of how Harriet occupied her time, though from what is known of her character, she would neither have been idle nor content with such futile employments as delighted her younger sister; Mary pandered to William's pernickety ways by supplying each bedroom with a card on which was written, in beautiful script, the times of meals, Church services, trains and outgoing posts. William expected his guests to conform to the ways of his house, and by these and other little notices, they knew just what was expected of them and certainly had no excuse for being late for meals.

In addition, Mary had a more robust hobby, and certainly a more profitable one, in the breeding of retriever dogs which, in later years, were much in demand by younger members of the family.

A descendant of William's younger brother can still remember stories told by her grandmother who had spent a great deal of her girlhood at Barbavilla. Other houses might move with the times, but the stately formality of Lady Clancarty's day was still observed by her four granddaughters who kept house for their brother-in-law. Their high principles and ceremonious manners made a deep impression on William's young niece who afterwards tried to bring up her own daughter according to the standards of the 'Ladies Monck'.

While, for the four sisters at Barbavilla, life was tranquil and uneventful, in the case of other members of their family it moved at a quicker tempo. On 8 January 1849, Elizabeth's third child was born, a son whom they named Henry Power Charles Stanley. An ancestor of Elizabeth's mother had married a Power and it was through this marriage that the Trench family owed their descent from the McCarthy clan. The birth of the baby Henry is an important event for the purpose of this book. From his earliest years he was a hoarder of letters, and to him we owe nearly everything that is now known of his family, apart from official documents and references in books.

Undeterred by his defeat in the Wicklow County by-election, young Charles Monck was continually on the lookout for an opportunity to get into the House of Commons as representative of an Irish constituency. This was no easy matter since the old electoral system still persisted in many parts of Ireland. It was against his principles to stand as nominee of one of the influential Anglo-Irish landlords who, in any case, disapproved of his advanced Liberal views. On the other hand, he had many friends and supporters in Liberal circles, some holding government office, who looked on him as a valuable ally and were prepared to use their influence to get him into parliament.

They would almost certainly have succeeded had it not been for the death of Charles Joseph Monck in April 1849 – just seven months after the death of his elder brother. The Viscountcy now devolved on young Charles, thereby dealing a shattering blow to his hopes of a political career, since it put him in a class which he himself later described as 'neither fish, flesh nor fowl' and which was then the only class not represented in the House of Commons.

An Irish peer was not eligible for a seat in the House of Lords except as one of the small groups of representative Irish peers. The other members of this group, who were Tory almost to a man, made it clear that they would gladly elect him as a representative if he would forswear his Liberal sympathies, which he refused to do. An Irish peer could sit in the House of Commons as member for an English constituency but was not allowed to represent an Irish constituency nor to take part in an election in Ireland.

During the summer following Charles Joseph's death, etiquette would not have allowed the Moncks to take part in social functions except by 'royal command'. This came early in August when Queen Victoria with Prince Albert and members of their family, arrived for her first visit to Ireland. In July, Charles proposed the motion of welcome to the Queen, carried unanimously by a meeting – called by the High Sheriff – of 'influential citizens of County Dublin of every shade of opinion.'[3] The Queen went ashore at Cork on 1 August, spent that night on board the *Victoria and Albert,* and arrived in Dublin on 5 August. Charles and Elizabeth attended the dance on 8 August given by the Lord Lieutenant and Lady Clarendon at Viceregal Lodge where the royal party were staying. The 'great and important event' of the Queen's six days' visit to Dublin was the Drawing Room at Dublin Castle on 9 August:

> So early as 7 o'clock the carriages began to set down at the Castle. The scene . . . was one of peculiar brilliancy. Hour after hour the line of equipages succeeded each other . . . and the blaze of light from the Castle, and the Royal Exchange, and other buildings which were illuminated made every object

appear almost as discernible as if it were clear day.

At 12 minutes after 9 o'clock the Queen and Prince Albert, the Lord Lieutenant and Countess of Clarendon, entered the Castle gates, the three state carriages being preceded and followed by a squadron of the 6th or Enniskillen Dragoons. Cheers, fervent and earnest, burst forth on every side . . . Shortly afterwards, Her Majesty, accompanied by His Royal Highness, Prince Albert, and the officers of state, entered the Presence Chamber. Her Majesty was attired in a superb pink poplin dress, elaborately figured with gold shamrocks.[4]

Charles and Elizabeth were among the 1,700 who attended and among the young officers who were present at the Drawing Room was Charles' youngest brother, Richard, now a lieutenant in the 43rd Regiment. On the following day, the Royal party embarked for Belfast.

Elizabeth had been 'presented' both before and after her marriage but now had to go through the ceremony again as 'Viscountess Monck'. On this occasion she was presented by her cousin-by-marriage, Lady Clancarty, as were her younger sisters, Harriet and Mary Monck.

The despised cousin, 'young' Charles, was now the head of the family and Elizabeth became mistress of her old home. She, who so loved outdoor exercise, would now be able to take her walks and rides in familiar places; she would occupy rooms she had known from her childhood and look from their windows at the same glorious views. She would see her children playing on the lawns and running down the wide paths; they would drink spring water from the Glen or new milk from the home farm, and they would have picnics at the top of Walker's Rock. Far from crowing over her sisters, she and Charles almost fell over backwards to avoid any such attitude. Charleville was a family house and 'home' to all members of the family, whether their relationship was near or distant.

Before Elizabeth married, Louisa had criticised her independent attitude, implying that she had sometimes caused offence by her refusal to conform to the family pattern. Whether or not this was true, Elizabeth was deeply devoted to her sisters. After her marriage she kept in close touch with them and was never happier than when they came to stay at Charleville, which she still regarded as their home.

In 1850, Charles and Elizabeth were settled at Charleville with their three children – five-year-old Fan, three-year-old Louise (who was always called Puss), and the baby, Henry. In May of that year another daughter was born and given the Trench family name of Florinda.

Charleville was also the home of Charles' sisters, Isabella and 'Aunt E.', and also of his three brothers when they were on leave from their regiments. In the previous year, Dick had joined his father's regiment, the 43rd Light Infantry, from which he later transferred to the Coldstream Guards. Charles' sister Henrietta was often staying at Charleville with her husband, Francis Brooke, and their baby, George, who was the same age as Henry. To Elizabeth's own nieces and nephews, the young Coles and Crokers, Charleville was like a second home. It has already been said that Charles and Elizabeth followed family tradition in keeping 'open house' for all relations, considering Charleville a home for all the family. At the same time, their methods of entertaining were less haphazard than the Rathdownes' had been. There were now formal house parties and dinner parties; politicians from England came to stay and Irish celebrities were invited to meet them. The Archbishop of Dublin, Richard Whately, would be asked to meet the Roman Catholic Archbishop, Paul Cullen, who later became a cardinal. As an author and professor of political economy, for which he founded a chair in Trinity College, Dublin, Whately was well equipped for his ceaseless efforts to improve the appalling condition of the poor people in Ireland. He and Cullen were both progressive, broad-minded men and, when they were at Charleville, discussions on church and other affairs in Ireland would continue till far into the night.

There was one annual event, however, for which only relations were invited to stay. This was the Harvest Home supper, attended by every man, woman and child on the estate. A great feast was laid out in the laundry, after which there was dancing in the coach-house. The music for the 'long dances', reels and jigs, was provided by a famous local fiddler called John-in-the-Box, or Dargle John. This local character had something wrong with his legs and he and his fiddle travelled the countryside in a box-like vehicle drawn by a small ass. No wake or wedding, feast or fair was complete without Dargle John, though it is believed that, at the Charleville Harvest Home, his fiddle was re--inforced by an accordion or two. On this occasion the house would be overflowing with relations, as the married sisters and their husbands were expected to bring all their children, irrespective of age. From year to year the children, both visiting and local, eagerly looked forward to the Harvest Home supper as is proved by the fact that it is still talked of by descendants of those who attended it.

When it was time for the feast to begin, Charles and Elizabeth conducted their house-party through the long stone passages to the laundry which, with the bake-house and other domestic offices, was in the first quadrangle immediately behind and adjoining the main building. The coach-house formed part of yet another quadrangle adjoining the first. All those staying in the house wore evening dress – the ladies in off-the-shoulder bodices with square or heart-shaped necklines, full ground-length skirts and two or three overskirts looped up with ribbons or flowers. The crinoline over a wire 'cage' did not come in until 1856. The men's cut-away 'swallow-tail' coats would be black, brown, claret or blue, with gilt buttons. After supper healths were drunk, then all trooped across to the coach-house. Charles led the wife of the senior tenant to the top of the set, while that lady's husband partnered Elizabeth. Apart from this bit of traditional ceremony, there was no formality. Members of the house-party danced with tenants and employees, most of whom had known them from childhood.

By the time little George Brooke became old enough to join in the fun, he and his cousin, Henry Monck, were already firm friends and were to remain so for the rest of their lives. George was one of those who in later years was to tell his sons and daughters of the enormous family gatherings at Charleville, with especial emphasis on the Harvest Home supper. In 1850 both he and Henry would have been too young to take part in the festivities, if indeed there were any that year. Before the summer ended, the family were again in mourning for Charles' brother John, who had died in Madras on 12 July. Owing to this brother's service overseas, Charles had seen little of him during recent years. But Johnny had been only one year younger than himself, and Charles could not but be affected by the death of one so closely associated with boyhood memories. In any

case, the family's views on mourning were strict and social engagements would have been cancelled, for a time at least. But even
without entertaining at home, visits to other country houses, trips to
London and attendance at Dublin Castle functions, Charles and
Elizabeth led a full and active life. Charles had his commitments in
counties Dublin, Meath, Wexford, Kilkenny and Westmeath, as
well as in County Wicklow, and he and Elizabeth had undertaken a
strenuous task in giving a 'new look' to the Charleville demesne.

The main approach to the house had been by a drive or 'avenue',
running due east from the front entrance. This drive was now
grassed over and a new approach made. But the most costly and
ambitious undertaking was the new private road from Charleville to
Bray, known as the Dargle Drive. In 1827, a *Guide to the County of
Wicklow* describes this ravine, cut by the river Dargle, as 'a deep,
dark, wooded glen whose opposite sides are so close that there is
only a passage left for the torrent, which appears to struggle through
with difficulty and interruption; both hills are thickly wooded with
oak from bottom to top . . . the channel of the river filled with large,
shapeless blocks of granite . . . The scenery is of the most romantic
description; the grouping of rock, wood and water is peculiarly
beautiful.' The *Guide* adds a footnote: 'This name [Dargle] appears
to be a corruption of Dark Glen, or perhaps the Glen of the Oaks,
which is in Irish, "Darglin".'

The new drive ran from a point immediately opposite the main
gates of Charleville to the outskirts of Bray. The first half of the road
lay through grazing grounds; then it entered the densely wooded
ravine and ran along the side of a steep cliff, high above the rocky
gorge. To prevent cattle from venturing into the dangerous gorge, a
gate with attendant lodge had to be built halfway along the drive, in
addition to a gate and lodge at each end. Today opinions vary as to
why Charles embarked on such an extravagant project. Some say
that his object was to provide employment during the years
following the Great Famine. Others, less kindly, suggest that he
wanted to 'make a splash' in order to help him in his political career.
The latter theory seems an unlikely one considering that one of his
chief characteristics was an intense dislike of any form of ostentation. Whatever his motives may have been, the real mystery is how
he managed to reconcile this and other expensive undertakings with
his perennial financial embarrassments. The too obvious implica-

tion, that the embarrassments were the direct result of spending so lavishly on his home, does not solve the problem. From the day he succeeded his father, he must have known that the estate was heavily encumbered, not only with debts to the amount of £90,000 but also with the many 'charges' on the estate. Annual payments had to be made to Henry Rathdowne's daughters and to William Smythe, also to his own brothers and sisters; and under the will of his grandfather, the first Viscount, to the Webbs and Wilsons and at least two distant cousins. Elizabeth surrendered half of her own portion in order to help meet these charges.

In a letter written in 1874, Charles was able to tell his son that he had reduced the debt on the property to £27,000. To accomplish this and to meet the above family commitments, he sought and obtained a succession of salaried government appointments until a few years before he died. There are many proofs that he was sensible and level-headed about money, and the other members of the family never regretted having taken his advice about their financial affairs. It is therefore hard to account for the lavish spending during his first years at Charleville, unless he was merely continuing with projects which had already been planned, if not actually started, by his father-in-law. There is a certain amount of evidence that this was so. We know that the plan for the pleasure-grounds and gardens was drawn up for Anne in 1847; and that work had already begun on the new approach to the house may have been the reason why the back avenue was used for Henry Rathdowne's funeral procession. Two water-colours painted in 1853 show the front avenue in its present position, with the carriage sweep in front of the main entrance bounded by a sunk wall, and sheep and cattle peacefully grazing where the old avenue had been. In these paintings there is no trace of the old carriage-drive which would not have been grassed over before the new one was ready to be in use. If this work had been planned, put in hand and completed after Charles inherited, the workmen in those days must have been a great deal more expeditious then than they are now.

Charles could not have pleaded the excuse of being married to an extravagant wife. Elizabeth shared his dislike of pretentiousness and ostentation, though with her it was less a matter of principle than of personal taste. She liked the house and the way of life there to be conducted in an orderly and dignified manner; but the idea of

Keeping-Up-With-The-Joneses would never have occurred to her. She and Charles were invited to stay in houses which were far grander and more impressive than their own, but they never attempted to imitate them nor to compete with the ever-increasing splendour of Powerscourt which lay just across the river. Elizabeth and her sisters had always thought their home quite perfect, just as it was; and if it made Charles happy to add to its beauties, she would accept it as a compliment to Charleville rather than as a criticism. She was not, however, in favour of the Dargle Drive scheme. 'I have always thought it would be better to keep it just for a *walk*,' she wrote when for the nth time it was being repaired after heavy rains had caused a landslide.

In her day, and in succeeding generations, the key-note at Charleville has been an easy-going spaciousness combined with dignity, and the leisurely and restful atmosphere of the place has been largely due to this absence of either competitiveness or conscious grandeur.

Charles personally supervised the care of the pinetum planned by Anne in 1847, and himself undertook the pruning of the cedars, Californian pines, deodars, Wellingtonias and Insignia pines. The largest plantations of these were on each side of the Broad Walk which is 7 yards wide and 320 yards long. Today these trees are about 100 feet high and have been so as long as anyone living can remember. It is difficult to imagine them at the stage when Charles was afraid they might be damaged by hares. A stream runs through the plantation and the ground on either side of it was inclined to be swampy. It was partly to absorb the moisture that the trees were underplanted with laurels, though their main function was to provide covert for the pheasants. For Charles was determined to have some good shooting at Charleville by the time his son Henry should be old enough to hold a gun. To supplement the existing stock of wild pheasants, the keepers, William Quin and his son Tom, were kept busy rearing young birds from eggs Charles brought over from England. He also kept a few brood mares and some of the hacks and carriage horses were bred on the estate. During the next few years he built a row of glass-houses for peaches and vines; also an orangery shaped like a Grecian temple, which stood at the end of the Long Walk, a very wide straight path bordered on each side by 'Irish' yews.

The old account books have been destroyed so we can only guess at the number of servants employed by Charles and Elizabeth; but their household appears to have been fairly modest compared with others of the period. Certain names occur again and again in family correspondence; such as Brock who became house-steward at Charleville in 1850. He was still there when he died in 1879 and he was buried next to the family vault. There were several footmen but they were seldom mentioned by name except to say that one or other of them had been complained of by Brock.

Besides Dennis, the farm steward, Hobson the head gardener and Hill the coachman, there were a second coachman and grooms, but after 1849 there were no more references to postilions at Charleville. It does not follow, however, that they were no longer there; there is no mention either of under-gardeners or of house, laundry, bake-house or kitchen staff, and there must have been a considerable number of employees, both indoor and out, in addition to those referred to by name. Dimsdale was Elizabeth's own maid and 'Agga' was the children's nurse. She eventually married Hogan, the ploughman, but continued working for the family until she died. Mathilde was the French nursery-maid and a German governess, Fräulein Denneler, or 'Denny', soon joined the family circle to remain in it, if not as an employee at least as a close friend for the rest of her life.

Elizabeth was determined that her children should speak fluent French and German from their earliest years, as she and her sisters had done; and Stanley, her youngest child, learnt to chatter in French before he could speak English. But in 1850 it is too early, by eight years, to introduce Stanley, that *enfant terrible*. The nurseries on the top floor were occupied by Fan, Puss, Henry and Florinda, though the children were by no means confined to the nursery quarters. Charles and Elizabeth doted on their children and took infinite trouble over planning for them, getting to know them as individuals and gaining their confidence. If they erred as parents it was in not being sufficiently severe. They set a high standard, but when their children fell below it, a gentle reminder and an appeal to the child's better feelings were the usual form of correction. It was already too late when they realised that Henry's happy-go-lucky attitude towards his studies and Puss' headstrong, extravagant ways, should have been dealt with by sterner measures; while nothing short of a good hiding, given thoroughly and often, could have made any impression on Stanley.

In her children Elizabeth found that fulfilment and reason for existence for which she had been seeking all through the years of her spinsterhood and her letters make it clear that they were her main interest and source of happiness. She enjoyed seeing her many friends but, though she was described as a 'gracious hostess', formal entertaining was a duty rather than a pleasure to her. While she found her chief happiness in her children, through them she also knew her greatest sorrows. Early in 1851 Florinda died; Elizabeth was to lose two more babies but it was Florinda for whom she grieved most deeply. It was said by those who knew her best that she never really recovered from the loss of this little girl.

Meanwhile another blow had fallen on the affectionate parents. Gradually they had been forced to face the terrible truth that Fan, their first-born, was a deaf-mute. There is a theory, passed down verbally through two generations, that she became deaf and dumb as the result of a bad attack of scarlet fever; and present-day medical opinions confirm that this could have been possible. However, the descendants of some of Charles' nephews and nieces declare that she had been a deaf-mute from birth and that her case had been held up as an 'awful warning' to them against marriage between first cousins. There is something to be said for the latter theory since Fan's great-grandparents, as well as her parents, had been first cousins.

On the other hand, it is well known that in Britain the diagnosis and training of children born deaf was then in its infancy and that deaf-mutes were regarded as incurable idiots. Now Fan, born in 1845, grew into a charming young woman, lively and intelligent, artistic and very well educated. Full of fun, enterprising and game for anything, with a well-developed sense of humour, her cousins greatly preferred her company to that of her sister 'Puss'.

Fan was a general favourite and it is still remembered at Charleville that 'everyone on the estate learnt to talk on their fingers' so as to be able to converse with her, the manual method being then the only known means of communicating with the deaf. In 1860, when Fan was fifteen, Charles wrote to his son Henry: 'I am putting a thing called Sulphuric Ether into Fan's ears and I think it is making her hear much more than she did before. Perhaps, please God, it may restore her hearing altogether.' This would seem to imply that she was not born deaf and was not, at the time Charles wrote, totally deaf. But even without this piece of evidence it seems hardly credible that she could have reached such a high standard of normality had she been deaf from birth. It is true that Elizabeth made a life's work of the training of her handicapped child. Fan was her mother's constant companion, and when she passed beyond the nursery and school-room stage, never left her mother's side. She joined in all the family activitites, rode and drove, attended dinner parties and went to balls. Elizabeth spared no pains in educating her and in providing her with interests and occupations. Fan's letters are a delight to read; they show that she enjoyed life thoroughly and was a keen observer of all that went on around her. All the same, her condition cannot have been anything less than a tragedy to her parents. And as though this grief and the loss of Florinda were not enough, their second son, born in 1852, died during the same year.

His succession to the Viscountcy had been a great blow to Charles since it placed him, at the age of thirty, in a position in which it seemed improbable, if not actually impossible, that he would ever achieve his aim which was, in the words of William Gregory, 'to influence public opinion as regards Irish affairs.' In the meantime he continued to be active in various charitable organisations and, in 1851, he became a Commissioner for Charitable Donations and Bequests. In this capacity not the least of his tasks was the administration and apportioning of the large sums raised in England and in Ireland to relieve the results of the Famine. This involved him in correspondence with his political friends and chiefly with W. E. Gladstone who, in December 1852, became Chancellor of the Exchequer. Charles Monck's chance came in 1852 when he was elected as Liberal member for Portsmouth, having stated in his election speech that he was 'a Peel-ite and a free-trader'.

The first debate in which he took part was on a proposed change of the procedure of parliamentary elections. The present ruling confined polling to one day only and a spell of bad weather could prevent voters from reaching the polling station in time since many of them had still to travel by road. Monck's speech was in favour of leaving it at one day only in Ireland, thus allowing less opportunity for 'intimidation'. Elections were often stormy affairs in both countries, but were particularly so in Ireland. He conscientiously fulfilled his promise to the Portsmouth electorate that he would not 'doze upon the benches' in Parliament, but support their interests 'as a real working and speaking member', but he also took a vigorous part in debates on Irish affairs, particularly when the subject was land tenure or national education. It was to this end that he had worked hard to get a seat in the House of Commons, but he did not neglect his constituency and spent more time in it than was then considered absolutely necessary.

It was from Portsmouth that he wrote, in 1855, the first of his letters to six-year-old Henry:

There are a great many ships between this & the Isle of Wight. Some of them have seventy four cannons in them, & today they fired off all the cannons & made such a noise. I am very glad to hear from Mama that you are a good boy. I hope you will be able to read a great deal to me when I come home, & that you do not tease dear large sister.

William Monck, Charles' younger brother, arrived at Charleville in 1852 when his regiment returned to England after seven years' service overseas, in Gibraltar, the West Indies and Nova Scotia. William was due for a considerable period of leave, long enough at least to effect plenty of damage to feminine hearts as well as to the family exchequer. The male members of the Monck family followed an unswerving pattern during the nineteenth century. As in each generation there was an eldest son who was conscientious, steady and reliable, so there was almost invariably a wild, younger brother – unstable, extravagant and irresistible to the opposite sex. If it had been hard to refuse William's written requests for 'advances', it must have been infinitely more so when that fascinating individual was there to plead his cause in person, especially after a long absence.

For all his 'wildness', William appears to have been a warm-hearted creature and he must at first have found it difficult to get used to the many changes that had taken place in his family since he had last been at home in 1844. His father and his brother Johnny were both dead. At the age of seventeen, William had joined John's regiment and the two brothers had been together till William transferred to the 7th Fusiliers four years later. He found his little sister, Henrietta, established at Summerton as the wife of Francis Brooke; while his eldest brother had also married and was now head of the family and living at Charleville. Isabella, the elder of his two unmarried sisters, had gone to live in Paris. With a fine show of

106

independence, she had removed herself, her sofa and her harp, to a large apartment in the Champs Elysées where she remained for the rest of her life. The reason given was that the air of Paris agreed with her injured back. However that may have been, her residence there gave all her relations an excuse for frequent visits to Paris on the pretext of going to see 'poor Isabella'.

Elizabeth would have been highly indignant if she had been accused of anything so vulgar as match making. It cannot be denied, however, that she enjoyed seeing her friends paired off and was not above giving them an occasional freindly push in what she considered to be the right direction. Here, now, was her attractive brother-in-law William, badly in need of the steadying influence of matrimony; and here, also, was her favourite niece, Feo, the eldest child of Fanny Cole.

Feo had been christened Frances Elizabeth Owen. In addition to her own mother, there were also Fan Monck and Georgina Croker's Fanny, and it had been at Frances Rathdowne's suggestion that her eldest grandchild was called by a name composed of her three initials. In 1852, Feo was a round-faced, round-bodied, merry little creature of seventeen. Sprightly and kittenish, she was of a type that would nowadays be considered a desperate bore, but which was then already becoming popular with 'the gentlemen'. No family excursion or picnic was complete without Feo, with her peals of coquettish laughter alternating with little shrieks of terror when it thundered, when a horse shied or when a boat seemed in danger of capsizing. She was forever getting herself into the sort of situations that called for the support or protection of a strong, manly arm, which she seldom looked for in vain. The perfect 'house-party girl', she was always ready to join in an unsophisticated round-game of cards, or to delight the company with her singing of simple ballads or comic songs.

There must have been a good deal more to Feo than mere silliness; Elizabeth was extremely fond of her, which would certainly not have been the case if her niece had been no more than an empty-headed flirt. Whether or not she went out of her way to throw the young people together, Elizabeth was delighted at the idea of having Feo as a sister-in-law. It would have been a waste of time to try and pair William off with a demure bread-and-butter Miss. If the family wished him to 'settle down', lively, roguish Feo was the perfect

solution. Though not his first cousin, she was one of the family and
this counted for a great deal with the clannish Moncks. In age, too,
they were sufficiently well-matched; in 1853, William was thirty and
Feo eighteen. There is no record as to why their marriage did not
immediately take place. Perhaps Feo's parents, Owen and Fanny,
had doubts about William as a son-in-law; or the wedding may have
been postponed owing to the death of William's eldest sister, Anne
Webb, which occurred in September of that year. William himself
may not have been in too great a hurry to put an end to his gay
bachelorhood. The fact remains that he and Feo were still only an
engaged couple when, in April 1854, war was declared against
Russia and William's regiment was ordered to the Crimea.

Early in the evening of 20 September, Agga, the children's nurse,
came hurrying in from the garden with the exciting news that
Captain William had come home. No, she could not have been
mistaken; she had just seen him in the front avenue, leaning over the
paling. The joy of the family was mingled with bewilderment. Surely
the war could not be over already? According to Agga, William was
not wounded and had appeared to be in perfect health. Why, then,
had he returned? And why did he not come into the house? After a
thorough search of house and grounds had revealed no trace of him,
they were forced to the sorrowful conclusion that Agga had
imagined the whole thing.

News travelled slowly, but there were rumours of a great victory.
The battle of the Alma had been fought six days after the Allies
landed. The Russians had been totally defeated; but when the
casualty lists came through, William's name was on the list of those
killed on 20 September. Among the Monck Papers there is an
account of the battle of the Alma written by an eye-witness and
published twenty-eight years after the battle took place. It refers to
the outstanding bravery and resourcefulness of "the gallant Monck"
of the Royal Fusiliers and gives a detailed account of the circumstances of his death. Contemporary accounts of this varied but
Kingslake's 'Invasion of the Crimea'[5] bears out the current legend
that 'he was last seen fighting with his bare fists.'

Notes to Chapter Six

1 Brooke, Raymond, *The Brimming River* (Dublin, 1961).
2 O. B. Cole to W. E. Gladstone, 28 November 1851. Gladstone Papers. British Museum.
3 *Freeman's Journal,* 25 July 1849. Quoted in C. Woodham Smith *The Great Hunger* (London, 1962).
4 *The Times,* 9 and 11 August 1849.
5 Kindly supplied by the Army Museum's Ogilby Trust.

7

'Young' Charles in Parliament

Lord Palmerston formed his first Cabinet in February 1855; and on 7 March William Thackeray wrote, in a letter to his mother: 'I see they appointed a new Lord of the Treasury, Lord Monck, last night.' In those days the appointment to such a post necessitated his being re-elected to his seat as Liberal member for Portsmouth. He was opposed, but returned with a handsome majority – 1,478 to 473. From this time there is a marked change in the tone of letters from W. E. Gladstone and others, who wished to enlist his sympathies for causes in which they were interested. A young and comparatively inexperienced member of the House of Commons, he had already made himself known as a man of integrity with no personal axe to grind.

Though himself an Irish landlord, in most cases he championed the tenant farmers in debates on the perennial and vexed question of Irish land tenure. Thus, in a debate on the Tenant Compensation (Ireland) Bill in December 1852, he moved that: 'The only true and just principle . . . was to give a right of property to the tenant for any additional value which, by his industry or his capital, he conferred upon the land.' On the subject of eviction of tenants, except in the case of 'injury or damage wilfully committed [by the tenant] on premises which the landlord was bound to keep in repair,' Monck said that he 'should certainly support any claim that would prevent the landlord from being the immediate enforcer of his own rights.'[1]

Charles Monck's forceful, downright manner was sometimes tempered by a flash of humour, as when he spoke against the 'intolerance and bigotry of excluding Jews from Parliament,' adding: 'The House has been told that Jews feel no annoyance at being excluded from parliament. If so, it must be on the same principle that eels are said to feel no annoyance in being skinned – they are used to it.'[2] His 'liberal' and humanitarian views were far from being universally popular; he could, however, always rely on support and encouragement from John Robert Godley who stayed with the Moncks during the summer of 1855.

During his five years as a member of parliament, though he sometimes stayed with friends or relations in London, he is listed by *Kelly* as 'residing' alternately at the Carlton Club and at 21 Dover Street, the latter being described as 'a private house owned by James Brown.'* This fact could be taken as a refutation of the charge made many years after his death, that Charles impoverished his family by his efforts to cut a great figure in public life. If this had been true, he and Elizabeth would have rented a London house of their own in which to entertain his political friends. Elizabeth was often with him in London; we hear of her at Queen Victoria's Drawing Rooms; at the Queen's Ball and at the Queen's Concert; but Charleville was still their base and it was there that they did their entertaining.

Parliament was only in session for seven months of the year and, even allowing for the time spent in their constituencies, there were long periods during which members could visit each other's homes and discuss their problems at leisure. John Godley was not the only politician who visited Charleville and enjoyed the 'salubrious climate' for which the district was famous. The intimate way in which Charles Adderley, Robert Lowe and Chichester Fortescue among others, referred in their letters to the Monck children, shows them to have been regular visitors. The term 'salubrious' was no mere guide-book hyperbole. There is something peculiarly vitalising in the air, like a light, sparkling wine, the effect of which is both restful and invigorating. From rides and walks in the open, Charles' guests would return with keen appetites for the substantial, unpretentious meals, largely composed of home produce.

In common with similar country houses, the dining room had its own distinctive smell – innocent then of tobacco fumes which were confined to rooms set apart for smoking. The atmosphere, subtly reminiscent of port and other wines, matured cheese and well-hung venison, was overlaid by the more delicate and daily-renewed aroma of home-baked soda bread, ripe peaches and bloomy black grapes lying on a bed of their own green leaves.

The game larder, divided from the vast stone-flagged kitchen by a

---

* Now Brown's Hotel.

Elizabeth after her marriage to
Charles, 4th Viscount Monck.
(Portrait by Mary Severne).

scullery, contained an ingenious device made by Walker, the
blacksmith. This was a tall iron stand, like a six-fingered signpost,
each 'arm' comprising a different day of the week executed in
wrought-iron. Each in their proper season, hare and grouse from
the hills, the occasional wild pheasant, and the inexhaustible supply
of rabbits, hung on massive iron hooks attached to the relevant arm
according to when they were killed.

Dinner was now the last meal of the day and Charles and his
friends sat long over their wine discussing church affairs, the future
of Irish agriculture and the burning question of national education.
Charles had made a speech in the House of Commons where the
system of Irish national schools was being criticised on the grounds
of 'the problem of different sectarian beliefs'. There existed in
Ireland, he said, 'a voracious appetite for education' and he warned
the House against taking any steps that would have the effect of –

> . . . weakening public confidence in a system of education
> which had taken deep root in the affections of the people of
> Ireland, and which was doing more than any other system had
> done to elevate the social condition and provide for the future
> prosperity and happiness of the people of that country.

While ensuring that ample opportunity was given for separate religious teaching outside school hours, he held that 'the basis of combined instruction for children of different denominations . . . tended to cultivate that friendship and charity amongst them which every religious creed ought to inculcate.'

The parties at Charleville were not confined to solemn political gatherings. Friends and relations would arrive and stay for a week or longer, either with or without a special invitation. Each female guest would bring her own maid, while married couples had at least one manservant as well. With the growth of the railway system, it was not always necessary as in the past to accommodate coachmen and horses in addition to personal attendants. This was before the days of select and organised parties composed of a definite number of carefully chosen guests. People would arrive at short notice, or even

Left to right: Louise 'Puss', Fan and Henry Monck. (Portrait by Mary Severne).

without previous warning; room was made for them somehow and they had to adapt themselves to any others who happened to be staying there.

An annual Christmas Tree party was given at Charleville for children on the estate as well as for those staying in the house. In December 1854, Owen Cole wrote to Gladstone that 'at Charleville during the Christmas week . . . there was a large juvenile party assembled round the Tree in the Hall.'

In September 1855, Elizabeth had another son, Frederick, who died soon after his birth; but this did not deter her from entertaining a large house-party during the following month when the Lord Lieutenant, Lord Carlisle, inaugurated a new railway line from Dublin to Ballycurry. The party were at Charleville for several days and included Feo Cole and her brother. Frank Cole had inherited his father's craze for writing atrocious doggerel verse and on this occasion he wrote a very long and facetious ballad describing his fellow guests and how they spent their time. It ends on a regretful note:

> At last they all went off
> In five hack cars and a carriage,
> And in all that large assemblage
> They had not made up *one* marriage.

He had seen no significance in an incident described in an earlier verse, an expedition on foot when his sister Feo had gone on ahead with 'the gallant Captain', Richard Monck. Feo's engagement to Dick's elder brother had been ended tragically the year before, by William's death in battle. Her Monck relations would have expected her to be still inconsolable, and it was not, in fact, until six years later that she became Mrs. Richard Monck.

During that winter Elizabeth established the annual custom of taking her three children to Paris for a few months, renting a house in the rue Nuroc, Versailles, where Charles joined them when his duties permitted. This expensive arrangement was made for the benefit of Fan; at that time Paris led the world in the education of the deaf. In addition to the advantages to Fan of visiting instructors, her parents engaged an English private governess with special qualifications. Like Fräulein Denneler, Miss Frend became a valued friend of the Monck family with whom she remained for several years.

In March 1857, a dissolution of the government followed a motion in the House of Commons by which Lord Palmerston, the Prime Minister, was accused of 'highhanded action' over an incident which occurred in Chinese waters. A trading ship flying the British flag had been boarded by Chinese who seized twelve of the crew, suspecting them of being smugglers. The British demanded an apology and, when this was refused, had bombarded Chinese ports. Charles Monck held that 'it was only fair play' to support agents of the government transacting business in distant parts of the world, when they had carried out their duties honourably and to the best of their ability. He voted in support of Palmerston and consequently lost his seat in the ensuing general election.[3] When he ceased to be a member of parliament, he should have resigned his office of a Lord of the Treasury, and it is not known why he continued in it for another year.

In the Oxford by-election of July 1857, the Liberal party nominated him as their candidate, to stand against William Thackeray. The author of *Vanity Fair* wrote to his young daughters:

My dearest little women, as far as I can see,
The independent Woters is all along with me,
But nevertheless I own it, with not a little funk,
The more respectable classes they go with Wiscount Monck;
But a fight without a tussle it is not worth a pin,
And so St. George for England, and may the best man win.[4]

'The Liberal nominee was Viscount Monck, a wealthy Irish peer of little political strength. Neate persuaded Thackeray to be the Independent candidate, arguing that against such opposition his chances of victory were very good.' Lady Ritchie, Thackeray's daughter, wrote that her father told her of 'a charming little speech made by Lord Monck, which gave him great pleasure at the time . . . A sort of catchword, "May the best man win", was the constant refrain just then. My father meeting Lord Monck in the street, shook hands with him, had a little talk over the situation, and took leave of him with the doggerel, "May the best man win". "I hope *not*," said

Lord Monck very cordially, with a kind little bow . . . It shortly became apparent that Lord Monck could not hope to win. He accordingly withdrew in favor of Cardwell, against whose heavy artillery Thackeray in turn had little chance.'[5]

During the next four years Charles continued to try to get into parliament but was defeated at Dudley in Worcestershire when the Conservative sitting member was re-elected. During the contest he had spoken on the burning question of the day, the further reform of the franchise. He was in favour, he said, of settling first for 'the small end of the wedge' of reform, rather than 'clog the measure' and court defeat by asking for too much at once.

In between election contests he was often in London, sometimes accompanied by Elizabeth. From there she wrote accounts to Henry of 'The Queen's Ball' or 'The Queen's Concert', and of the marriage, on 25 January 1858, in the Chapel Royal, of the Queen's eldest daughter, Princess Victoria.

My pet boy, – I am *so* happy to hear such pleasant accounts of you all – I do not think we can be with you till this day week*(Tuesday)*. Tell Brock to send all the letters that have come to Papa to the Treasury. He need not pay them. *Do not forget.* I hope you will get Denny to read you about *every thing,* in the *Times* when it comes. There cd not have been a more beautiful sight than the Marriage, and we were in the very best places for seeing & hearing *every thing,* in the Gallery, *just* over the Altar, & the gallery is a low one, so that we were quite near. You will read all about it, so I shall only tell you a little. When the Queen came in she knelt down & said a prayer. She had the 4 princes, all with her, all in Scotch dresses – the two little ones were so nice – the three princesses were very nicely dressed in pink & looked very nice. The Queen wd not let one of them *move,* & when the little prince wd move *a little,* she scolded him very much, & at last put him where he cd not be seen. When the princess came up with her bridesmaids, the Queen shook out her dress. She forgot to kneel down & say a prayer till the Queen told her. She & the prince spoke very distinctly – *he* has a very foreign accent. When it was over, the princess kissed the Queen & Prince Consort, & the Prince & Princess of Prussia, his father & Mother, & then the Queen kissed *them* & the

Prince. The Music was very good. We have the paper of the Music & the books with the Marriage Service, for you three. Agga dressed my hair, & put in the plumes, for a naughty Lady made Isadore late; every one said that *she* did it just as well.

In the Evening we went to the Concert, which was beautiful to *see,* but too loud to *hear.* A Lady who had just come from Windsor told me that she had seen all the Eton boys there waiting at the Station to receive the Prince & Princess, & to draw them up to the Castle. There were some beautiful things sung at the Concert. Every one was *so beautifully* dressed. I believe we shall go the Drawing room, & Dot & Pen with us.

Last night there was some of the Wedding Cake cut up on the Refreshment tables, & I took a little *Crumb* for *you three* – give my love to Denny & tell her how happy it makes me to hear of yr being good. Papa was so pleased with yr nice letter. I saw Percy La Touche, & the Parrot & Cat. The Cat is just like Minette.

Kiss Puss for me – yr fond Mama –

Will you send this letter to Aunty I: to read – Agga went out after I had gone to the Marriage, & saw the Princess & all the people *quite well.*

There are great illuminations – Dick was in *such* a good place at the Marriage.

If you *could* have seen the Siamese Ambassadors – I was afraid of them. You know Siam is in Burmah, & I often told you that the Burmese make thr teeth black because Dogs & Monkeys have white teeth, & so their teeth were black. Oh they were so ugly.

When Elizabeth wrote this letter, there was already another baby on the way – and Richard Charles Stanley Mountjoy was born on 2 August.

Earlier in that year old Mr. Croker had died and Edward and Georgina and their ten children went to live in the family house, Ballynagarde in County Limerick. Poor Georgina might be supposed to have entered on a less harassing mode of existence; but two years later, disaster again overtook the accident-prone Crokers. 'My dearest Child,' Elizabeth wrote to Henry who was at school, 'a telegram has brought us some dreadful news. Ballynagarde is burnt down! All are safe, I am thankful to say . . . Your Papa has telegraphed, begging them all to come here . . . I must add, the house is *insured.* Perhaps you don't understand that, but it means that your Uncle will be given money from the Insurance Office to build it again.' The invitation to house twelve Crokers was not accepted. One of the daughters wrote for Georgina saying that they were being accommodated in various houses in the neighbourhood and wished to be near Ballynagarde where 'work of restoration' had already been put in hand. Bitter experience had taught Georgina prudence, and she knew her husband too well to leave him in sole charge of the insurance money.

The most important family event in 1860 was the departure of Henry to Mr. Nind's small preparatory school, Woodcote House, Henley-on-Thames. The first letters exchanged between the homesick boy and his parents started the regular correspondence which was to last for thirty years and which, by itself, forms a family chronicle.

After his defeat at Portsmouth in the general election of 1857, Charles had been offered the governorship of New South Wales.[6] He refused the appointment because at the time he still hoped to get into parliament, and to be offered a salaried government post which could be combined with his duties as an Irish landlord. Lord Palmerston had formed his second government and still Charles' hope had not been realised. At some time during the year 1861 he let it be known that he would accept a colonial appointment if no vacancy nearer home should occur, although this would be to sacrifice his principles which were strongly against absenteeism. But his estate was still heavily encumbered and, owing to agricultural depression, many of his tenants were behind-hand with their rents. With his knowledge of their desperate plight, he would not press them to pay, nor would he follow the example of some of the other landlords who were evicting small-holders in order to farm the land at a profit. Yet money must be found, and if he could earn none at home, he would have to look for a job elsewhere.

Elizabeth sympathised with his disappointment and shared his anxiety about money; yet, in that summer of 1861, she welcomed a period of settled home life. She and the girls had returned from Paris in May, bringing with them Charles' youngest sister who was now living with Isabella in her apartment in the Champs Elysées. 'We

brought Aunt E. home with us,' Elizabeth wrote to Henry at school.
'We are so delighted to have her with us.'

During June, William Smythe spent two days at Charleville and
confided to his diary his impressions of the many changes which had
been made since the place had been his second home. Charles drove
him round by the Bray road to the furthest Dargle gate. From here
they sent the groom home with the 'jaunting-car', and returned on
foot by the new Dargle drive which William had been told was –

> . . . the finest thing in Ireland. It is two miles to the gate of
> Charleville and, with the approach to the house, makes a drive
> of about 3 miles, the first part through oak woods over the
> Ravine of the Dargle, much of it *en corniche* and requiring
> protecting walls; after which it continues through an open,
> undulating Park overlooking Tinnehinch (home of the
> Grattans) whence it emerges on an earthwork bringing it to the
> level of Charleville gate and exactly opposite it . . . The new
> pleasure-ground and garden at Charleville are daily
> improving, and the classical Doric facade of the Conservatory
> (at the end of the Long Walk), if not on too large a scale for
> symmetry, will be handsome and imposing.

Following a visit to Powerscourt:

> . . . We drove down to Enniskerry, passing the New Church,*
> the situation of which is as admirable as the structure is, in my
> mind, deplorable. I cannot like its polygonal stone, its walls
> naked of buttresses, its clumsy slated accompanying spire.
> Then, too, it is said to be far too small for the present con-
> gregation, likely to be annually increased as the very pretty
> village of Enniskerry increases; as it is sure to do, united as it is
> by a flat road to the Bray Station, now frequented by omnibus.
> We walked through the Charleville farm on our return, and

---

* The new church outside the village of Enniskerry had been built to replace 'Old
Powerscourt Church' which stood on the grounds of Powerscourt House, The Moncks
contributed to the new building, but the main expense was borne by the Powerscourt
family. The date of its consecration coincided with the coming of age of Lord Powerscourt, by the wish of his mother, Lady Londonderry.

saw turnips growing and turnips sowing in land in beautiful order.

His visit ended with a stroll 'in some of the old Walks.'

Charles and Elizabeth continued to keep 'open house' for their relations. No day passed without visits to or from their country neighbours; but beyond occasional references to trips to Dublin to the opera, to functions at the Castle, and to a ball at Viceregal Lodge, the letters to Henry were concerned with home news:

> ... The rats are very troublesome in the poultry yard and eat many of my little creatures ... I forgot to tell you that Fleda has such a pretty little foal. *I* say it will be bay; Papa says it will be *white*. It was very delicate at first and had to be fed with *Cow's* milk, for Fleda had none, but now she has. The Pheasants are doing *grandly* – about 140. William Quin gets heaps of ants for them from Sugar Loaf. He said (don't you know his face!) – 'Oh, my Lord, if you'd see the lovely bag of ants I got this morning before 6 o'clock – full of eggs as big as peas.' The idea of ants' eggs as big as *peas* coming from such little bits of wee things as ants! We do see wild ones [pheasants]. Mrs. Karr found 7 little wild ones, and brought them down in her apron.

Mr. Sandys, the agent, had been married, and Fan and Puss went to the wedding –

> ... The new brown horse is lovely, and Papa rides it. Puss rode your pony yesterday. The black pup is a fine fellow. Denny is charmed with your German letter. It will improve you very much, writing German letters, and I think nothing does us so much good as what we do for ourselves ... Your hamper is on its way, and I think you will say it is a good one. The Toffy is so good, I think.

Then, in a double postscript:

> You will remember *Friday* and your verse; try to think some-times thro' the day of what Christ has done for us, and that will make you try to do right.

120

I do not know how many Pheasants they have at Powerscourt.

Those who knew her best agreed that one of Elizabeth's most valuable characteristics was her ability to 'give herself' ungrudgingly to her friends, and this talent formed the basis of the relationship between herself and her children. It was apparent in the tireless endeavour to release Fan from her world of silence, and in her cherishing of Puss' gift for music. Even more striking in a woman of forty-seven who had been educated at home and who had no brothers, was the way in which she identified herself with Henry's school life. She kept a list of his hours, so that she would know what he was doing at any given time in the day; and he wrote to her without reserve, confident of her genuine interest and sympathy. There were occasions, however, on which her advice was contradictory, as when she urged 'self-denial', at the same time promising to reimburse him:

> . . . If I were you, I should subscribe to the library or any other thing that the boys wish to get up. If you will give a good subscription, as good as any other boy, I will give it to you when you come home, or send it by Papa. Even if you do not care particularly about the books, it looks stingy and churlish not to be ready to join in anything that is going on. I will always pay you again. I like you to be ready to join pleasantly with those you are with; do you not think it would be a good way of denying yourself? Think over this on *Friday* – and think of this verse for a Friday verse – 'Christ pleased not himself' – and then perhaps you will think it well to do what they wish about the *Illustrated News,* but I don't quite understand about that. To do what we do not want, to please others, is a very good way of denying ourselves. I will always give you money for that sort of thing, and be glad to do so, so you have no want of money.

Even before the end of June, a holiday spirit infused her letters:

> We are all thinking so much of your coming home; I am going to ask William Maxwell to spend part of his holidays with us; that will be pleasant for you.

And, in July:

> I long to see cricket again. I have asked a new Mr. Trotter
> and a Quin cousin of ours to play here when you come, and
> William La Touche and Henry Sandys [the agent] say they will
> play. I think we shall have an 11 on each side . . . We shall have
> happy and good Sundays, I trust. Sundays would be a great
> blessing to us if used aright. If we gave attention to the services
> at Church, and tried to think then of God, to remember what
> God would wish us to do, and what he had done for us. I trust
> we shall have happy Scripture lessons together.
>   It is such a happiness to think of your being with us so soon. I
> think you will be quite charmed with 'Aunt Sally'.* We like it
> and croquet so much.

Charles always tried to make one of his periodical visits to
London coincide with the end of the school term, so that he and
Henry could go home together, usually travelling by night and
arriving at Charleville in time for breakfast. Before the excited boy
could ride his pony, inspect the livestock, or visit his favourite
haunts, family tradition demanded that he should first go and call on
all the old people 'on the place'. His parents did the same after an
absence from home, as did his aunts and their children. These visits
were no hurried affairs consisting of an exchange of greetings at the
cottage door; an invitation to 'Come in and sit down' must be
accepted, and Henry must show no impatience while his physical
growth was exclaimed over, and devout Catholic blessings were
rained on his head. Since not only the day but the very hour of
arrival was well known in every house and cottage, it would be
unthinkable to postpone this ritual; nor has any child of the Charleville family ever wished to omit what was an integral part of 'coming
home'.
    Only when the tour of visits had been completed was the twelve-
year-old boy free to take part in the cricket matches organised by his
mother, to ride, to fish for trout in the river Dargle, to scramble up

---

* 'Aunt Sally' began as a family or garden-party game and later was relegated to fair-
  grounds. A wooden figure on a pole was stuck in the ground and dressed in a red flannel
  cloak with hood over a goffered, white bonnet, framing the crudely-carved head.
  Wooden rings were then thrown over a clay pipe fixed between 'Sally's' large teeth.

Walker's Rock for a view of the sea or to climb Sugar Loaf mountain. At least once during the holidays he would make the more arduous ascent of Djouce and drink from the spring at the foot of the three immense boulders on its summit. His favourite cousin, George Brooke, came to stay, bringing his own pony so that he and Henry could ride together.

On the evening of 22 August, this idyllic existence was interrupted by a letter from the Secretary of State for the Colonies, offering Charles the governor-generalship of Canada.

Notes to Chapter Seven

1 Hansard's Parliamentary Reports.
2 Hansard's Parliamentary Reports.
3 *The Birmingham Journal,* 9 April 1859.
4 W. M. Thackeray to Anne and Harriet Thackeray, 11 July 1857, My text is taken from *Biographical Introductions,* X, xxxi. *The Letters and Private Papers of William Makepeace Thackeray,* collected and edited by Gordon N. Ray. Vol. IV, p. 49. O.U.P. 1946.
5 *Biographical Introductions,* X, xxxi-xxxii.
6 Letter from the Duke of Newcastle to Sir Edmund Head, 27 August 1861. Newcastle Letters. University of Nottingham.

PART II

CANADA: 1861-1868

8

'An unknown man'

The governorship of British North America was a senior post, second in importance only to the viceroyalty of India. Yet there was not very keen competition for an office which appeared to require an almost super-human degree of tact and wisdom. The extent to which the governor was expected to influence administration was not clearly defined by the Home Government, while any interference was liable to be resented by the Canadian Government.

At the Athenaeum Club Charles heard all the political gossip and knew that there had been difficulty in filling the post. He had already been approached unofficially on the subject, so that the Duke of Newcastle's letter found him sufficiently prepared to be able to write a letter of acceptance by return. '*Your* cock fights, where so many turned tail. Lord Monck accepts Canada,' Newcastle wrote to Delane, the editor of *The Times,* implying that the latter had been one of those who had suggested Monck for the appointment.[1]

Besides the urgent necessity of earning a living, the very difficulties of which Monck had been warned put him on his mettle, the more so as it was generally believed that Lord Palmerston had personally recommended him for the post. Charles had an enormous respect and sincere affection for the seventy-seven-year-old Prime Minister. His letter of acceptance reached the Colonial Office on 24 August, but the appointment had yet to receive the royal assent from the Queen who on that very day was attending a field day at the Curragh in Ireland, where the Prince of Wales was quartered.[2] The royal party visited the lakes of Killarney before re-embarking on 30 August on the *Victoria and Albert* where, among the papers awaiting the Queen's attention, was a letter from the Duke of Newcastle recommending Monck for the governor-generalship of Canada. The Queen replied immediately in a private letter that 'she most readily sanctions this appointment which she thinks an

126

excellent one. We have just seen Lord Monck at the Vice-Regal Lodge.'[3] According to contemporary reports, Queen Victoria was not in the habit of giving such prompt and cordial assent to appointments recommended by her ministers. The few references to Charles Monck in her letters show that she knew him personally and highly approved of him, which may account for the absence of delays and objections when disposing of this very senior post.

Meanwhile the news had leaked out. 'I must tell you a piece of news which has excited me a good deal,' John Godley wrote to Adderley. 'Monck is appointed Governor General of Canada. Very flattering to him in the present critical state of North America.'[4] The publication of the appointment raised an immediate storm of astonished comment and conjecture. In the words of *The Saturday Review,* 'A greater complication of perplexities and dangers never before greeted a young aspirant trying his 'prentice hand at government for the first time.' Several London papers suggested that Monck owed his appointment to his personal friendship with the Prime Minister. These articles were reprinted in Canadian newspapers, the editors of which added their own comments about 'this unknown Irishman', as one called him: 'Though the remark made by most Canadians on first hearing the report of Lord Monck's being chosen . . . – "Who is he? He is an unknown man" – he appears nevertheless to be a man of some mark and thoughtful intelligence.'[5] 'We think that London journals are disturbing themselves a good deal more than the occasion requires respecting the qualities of our new Governor General. What we want is an honest man, who has no whims of his own to serve, and who keeps himself from such personal friendships and antipathies as will influence his conduct.'[6]

Meanwhile the London *Morning Chronicle* defended the appointment. 'Lord Palmerston, knowing well and esteeming highly a person whom the public does not know at all, has thought proper to entrust him with a post of some responsibility and distinction in the colonial hierarchy.' Subsequent events were to prove that Lord Palmerston had known what he was about when he decided that, in this case, character was more important than previous experience. Charles Monck had plenty of common sense, besides the 'thoughtful intelligence' attributed to him by the *Quebec Morning Chronicle.* His outlook was both broad and far-seeing, while his alertness in grasping the essentials of a situation and going straight to the heart of the matter surprised those who had been deceived by his outward calm. He had a warm, friendly manner, and was at ease with all classes of people. His integrity was unshakable, and he was not easily rattled. Perhaps his greatest strength lay in his unself-consciousness and entire absence of personal vanity, so that he did not waste time and nervous energy either in resenting personal slights or in playing to the gallery. All these qualities would be valuable in the governor of a colony consisting of self-governing provinces, split by regional, political and cultural squabbles.

Immediately after seeing the Queen, Charles had to go over to London to be briefed by the Duke of Newcastle, Secretary of State for the Colonies. He first drew Charles' attention to the most vital problem of the day, Canada's urgent need of military defence. Relations between Britain and the United States of America were strained to breaking point owing to Britain's determined neutrality in the American civil war. The situation resembled a barrel of gunpowder in which the smallest spark was liable to cause an explosion and if this should happen, Canada, with 3,000 miles of undefended frontier, would be the obvious point of attack from the United States. Over the greater part of this frontier the only means of communication was by water and by overland treks. Only one third of the whole colony was 'settled'; this third comprised the three Maritime Provinces and Newfoundland on the eastern seaboard, and Upper and Lower Canada. The ancient fortified city of Quebec, built on the heights overlooking the St. Lawrence river, was the capital of British North America and, at present, the seat of government for Upper and Lower Canada, these two provinces having recently united to form one legislation. Newfoundland had a separate government, as had each of the three Maritime Provinces. Rupert's Land and the wild north-west, with their untapped mineral and agricultural potential, were governed by the Hudson's Bay Company which held the monopoly of the fur, timber and fishing trades. Thus 'Canada' was a loose term applied to six independent governments linked to the British Crown by the governor-in-chief or governor general.

Although the Imperial Government had usually supported former governors in their efforts to deal with the teething troubles of a self-governing colony, Newcastle was shrewd enough to be aware that some mistakes had been made. He had agreed with the Prime

Minister that Monck could be the right man for the job, though some of his reasons for doing so differed from Palmerston's. The Duke saw, or thought he saw, how the various problems should be tackled, and seems to have decided to do so by means of back-seat government from the Colonial Office. It suited him, therefore, to send out as governor one whom he imagined to be a useful piece of raw material, inexperienced and willing to be guided, rather than an experienced administrator who would have ideas of his own.

If Charles left the Colonial Office feeling that he had bitten off more then he could chew, he did not allow himself to betray any anxiety even to so intimate a friend as John Godley, who saw him in London and described him as having been 'very cheery'.

While Charles was being briefed for his difficult assignment, it fell to his wife to prepare for the removal of her family and household to the other side of the Atlantic. A governor was expected to bring his own domestic staff, horses and carriages, furniture, silver, linen and china. It was fortunate for Elizabeth that the complicated preparations left her little time for brooding anxiously over the future, although accounts of the harsh Canadian climate made her extremely doubtful of its suiting the children's health, and three-year-old Stanley was rather delicate; also, in those days of frequent wrecks, the thought of the voyage was in itself enough to daunt an anxious mother. Iron-clad ships were gradually replacing wooden vessels, and all were equipped with engines, the earlier paddle-engines having given place to the 'screw' or propeller-driven type. But all ships still had their full complement of sails, to which the engines were a supplement rather than the chief means of locomotion. The perils of the voyage to Quebec were not confined to the actual crossing of the ocean, to the icebergs off Newfoundland or to the fogs in the Gulf of St. Lawrence. To reach Quebec it was necessary to sail up the river St. Lawrence and ships were often wrecked in the river itself.

The education of the three elder children presented a serious problem. Henry had only four more terms at Mr. Nind's preparatory school before he was due to go to Eton. Fan would be debarred from the annual visit to Paris and the expert teaching of professors from the School for the Deaf. She and Puss, now aged sixteen and fourteen respectively, must soon be learning to take their place among the daughters of their parents' friends, and Elizabeth doubted whether 'the wilds' of Canada would provide an adequate preparation for social life.

Her misgivings were not confined to her concern for the children. While conscious that a great honour had been conferred on her husband, she was also aware that his predecessors had not always found the position a happy one. However, it was not her province to decide whether or not the appointment was in itself a suitable one, nor at that date would she be required to play a prominent part as governor general's wife. No publicity had been given to the wives of former governors; when these had accompanied their husbands, they usually did so for short periods at a time, and then remained very much in the background.[7]

The problem of Henry's education was solved by extricating a certain Mr. Wilkinson from the staff of Mr. Nind's school, and engaging him as private tutor. Henry could therefore accompany his parents to Canada and stay there till he went to Eton. Miss Frend and Fräulein Denneler would take care of the girls' education and Mathilde would look after Stanley. The domestic staff would include, among others, Elizabeth's maid Dimsdale, Brock the steward, several footmen, a coachman and grooms.

The decision of what to take with them was made doubly difficult by the impossibility of finding out where they were going to live. There was some excuse for the Colonial Office's evasiveness on this point, for the very good reason that there was no governor's residence in Quebec. Until recently the seat of government had been Toronto and it was there that the retiring governor, Sir Edmund Head, had had his headquarters. Charles could obtain no precise information beyond the assurance that he would be told where to go when he arrived in Quebec.

At last the preparations were complete. Elizabeth sadly took leave of her sisters and sisters-in-law, and of her favourite niece Feo, whose marriage to Charles' young brother Dick had taken place in August. Farewell visits were paid to all the people on the place. Henry Sandys, the agent, and Flood, the solicitor, were put in charge of the estates; and the children's nurse Agga, who had married Hogan the ploughman, was to take care of the house.

Charles had booked their passage for 11 October in the *North Briton,* a three-masted, iron-framed ship of the Allan Line. Sailing from Liverpool, the *North Briton* would put in at Derry for Irish passengers, including the usual large intake of emigrants. The Moncks and their party travelled to this northern port by train; from the railway station horse-drawn vehicles conveyed them to the wharf on Lough Foyle, where they boarded a tender by the simple method of stepping on to the paddles and from there to the deck. It took the tug more than two hours to reach the mouth of Lough Foyle where the *North Briton* lay. Somebody lent Elizabeth a 'spy-glass' through which to look at the ship which was to carry them away from Ireland. She could see nothing but still held the glass to her eyes to hide the tears which blinded her.[8]

There was a fresh wind blowing and it had been choppy enough in the Lough. Out here, with the tug 'dancing' and the ship swaying, there was some delay before the constantly slipping gangway could be fixed between them. At last they were all hustled on board where Charles and Elizabeth were received by the Captain in person. While they were being shown to their cabins, above the shouting and commotion and the noise of wind and waves, there rose the voices of the sailors singing 'a wild song' as they hauled on the ropes, hoisting the sails.

They had a rough crossing and Charles and Fan were the only two of their party who did not succumb to the violent pitching and rolling of the *North Briton*. Fan's handicapped state had sharpened her other perceptions and made her keenly observant of all that went on around her. She would be up early, walking on deck, and never missed the meals at the Captain's table. She loved watching the other passengers and was thrilled by the sight of a whale spouting and, towards the latter part of the voyage, of icebergs.

After the first week Elizabeth was able to join her in 'long walks on deck' and to take an interest in her fellow-passengers – 'such pleasant people'. She also revelled in the unaccustomed leisure. 'It is so nice to read so much in quiet, and not to have to do anything else,' she wrote. 'I love the sea air too.' After eleven days at sea, the welcome words: 'Land in sight!' were passed from one to the other. As they entered the Belle Isle Straits, Elizabeth brought little Stanley up on deck and showed him the wild, rocky coasts of Labrador and Newfoundland. Their ship crossed the Gulf of St. Lawrence and steamed up the river, threading her way between islands and the mainland. On their right towered the high, steep cliffs of the Laurentians, but on the more gradual slopes of the opposite shore the travellers had their first sight of Canadian woods in the blazing colours of the fall.

At nine-thirty on the morning of 23 October, the *North Briton* docked at the Grand Trunk Railway Wharf where, though it was raining, the new governor was greeted by a cheering crowd and a guard of honour from the 17th Regiment. A band played as he and his party disembarked and a salute of guns was fired. The newspapers reported that Charles 'gracefully acknowledged the cheers by bowing repeatedly'; after which Colonel Irvine, representing the retiring governor, conducted the party to a convoy of carriages. In these they were driven up the steep, narrow streets of Quebec between wooden, tin-roofed houses and shops which bore French names. All along their route, more crowds waited in the rain to cheer them on their way.

At the grim, barrack-like Parliament House, Sir Edmund Head was waiting to receive them and to explain that temporary accommodation had been made for them in this building until a more permanent residence could be prepared. A former governor's house, three miles from Quebec, had been burnt down two years earlier and was in the process of being restored. It was characteristic of Charles that, on the day of his arrival, he walked out to inspect this house, Spencer Wood, which was subsequently to become his family's much-loved home in Canada.

Notes to Chapter Eight

1   Newcastle to Delane, 6 September 1862. Quoted in Arthur Irwin Dasent, *John Thadeus Delane, editor of "The Times"* (London, 1908).
2   'Bertie marched past with his company, and did not look at all so very small.' Queen Victoria to the King of the Belgians, 26 August 1861, from Vice-Regal Lodge, Phoenix Park. *Letters of Queen Victoria.* British Museum.
3   Queen Victoria to the Duke of Newcastle, 30 August 1861. Newcastle Papers.
4   J. R. Godley to C. Adderley, 28 August 1861. British Museum.
5   *Quebec Morning Chronicle,* 26 September 1861.
6   *The Globe* (Ontario). 17 October 1861.
7   Princess Louise was the first governor general's wife to be given prominence during her husband's term of office (1878-1883).
8   Elizabeth Monck to Henry, 11 October 1863.

9

'I was sworn into office'

On his arrival, the new Governor was immediately plunged into official business. He had to be sworn in as administrator of the province, receive and reply to addresses of welcome and meet the executive council which was headed by M. Cartier as Prime Minister and by Mr. John Alexander Macdonald as Leader of Upper Canada, the premiership at that time being a dual role.

He also embarked on a series of conferences with General Sir Fenwick Williams, a Crimean veteran, now General-in-Command of the Imperial Forces in British North America, that is, of regular troops sent out from England. Williams confirmed that the precarious position of Canada in relation to the United States had not been exaggerated in England, but rather the reverse. American suspicion of Britain was matched in Canada by strong feeling against the 'Yankees' (of the Northern States) and the most trivial 'incident' was liable to result in an immediate declaration of war.

Since the American civil war began, the Northern States had built up an army described as having become 'almost overnight, the greatest military power on earth.'[1] In terrifying contrast, the Canadian forces consisted of a so-called 'active' militia numbering 5,000 cavalry, artillery and riflemen and also a 'sedentary' militia. The latter could hardly be said to exist since of late years they had received no training and had neither arms nor uniform. A supply of arms had been promised from England but would not be sent out until the spring. They were now at the beginning of November, spring seemed a long way off, and before the end of the month the St. Lawrence would be ice-bound and closed to shipping. If war should break out during the winter, Canada would be cut off from reinforcements from England, while all too accessible along her virtually undefended frontier.

Before leaving England Charles had been warned against any

Charles, 4th Viscount Monck, Governor General of Canada (1819-1894).

sudden and ostentatious preparation for war. To demand an additional battalion from home, or to call for a special session of Parliament, would come under that heading and might provide the very 'incident' all were anxious to avoid. With this need for caution on the one hand, and his own awareness of their dangerous position on the other, Charles felt desperately anxious and could only hope that events would justify the *mañana* attitude of his ministers. The

Elizabeth, Viscountess Monck.

expense of training and arming a defence force would fall on the tax-
payers. The ministers were extremely frightened of the Yankees, but
a great deal more frightened of losing votes.

Meanwhile, Elizabeth was doing her best to make her family and
household comfortable in their makeshift quarters. They must be
equipped with suitable clothing for the Canadian winter, which they
were told would come early this year, the Indians having reported

that the beavers were already at work on their winter 'houses'. Fur coats must be bought for men as well as women, and fur caps – to be worn pulled down over the forehead. They must also order fur robes as coverings in the sleighs or 'carioles' which were being built for them by Gringras, the sleighmaker. The carioles were to be painted red and hung with bells, and Elizabeth had three robes, of bear, buffalo and wolverine skins.

Her country-bred children were enjoying the novelty of living in a garrison town. Fan could not hear the military bands and the bugle-calls, but there was always something new and interesting to be seen from the windows: the sunlight turning the spire and tin roofs to 'burnished gold', the sunsets more brilliant than any they saw at home and the ships plying up and down the river far below. There were drives into the surrounding country, to the Heights of Abraham above the city, or down to the shores of the river to visit the great timber cones from which the lumber was shipped; and for Henry and his sisters there was skating on the covered rink beside which the band played.

Elizabeth could be happy so long as her children were well and enjoying themselves, but she was not finding it altogether easy to adapt herself to her new life. Entertaining presented a problem in these temporary quarters; they were expected to start giving official dinners immediately, and anyone who came from a distance to confer with Charles had to be put up for a night or longer. Brock, the house-steward, was being troublesome, and complained ceaselessly of his assistants. Having spent most of her life on her family's country estate, Elizabeth had had no experience of domestic problems, and had wondered why they were the chief topic of conversation among the ladies of Quebec. She was careful to keep this and all other difficulties from Charles who already had more than enough to contend with.

His preoccupation with momentous affairs did not exempt him from trivial annoyances. While despatches and letters passed between Quebec and London, a complaint with regard to Government House social etiquette was made by a certain Lord Aylmer who had come to live in Canada, in a private capacity. He had been a guest at one of the Governor's official dinner parties which was also attended by members of the Canadian executive council. The table of precedence in Colonial Regulations laid down that Ministers of State should take precedence of all others; and when Lord Aylmer found that he was being 'sent out' (sent in to dinner) after a mere 'Mister', he was deeply offended and lodged a complaint. At about the same time, Charles and Elizabeth were also criticised by two Canadian newspapers for accepting an invitation to visit the Ursuline Convent and Laval University, in doing which they were said to be laying themselves open to 'undue Papal and French influence'.

These pin-pricks did not help Elizabeth to feel happier at having brought her young family to a country which was liable, at any moment, to become a theatre of war. She could not share her children's eagerness in looking forward to the freezing of the St. Lawrence when, with the United States hostile, they would be cut off from the outside world. By those officers on their father's staff who were already familiar with Canada, Henry and his sisters had been told of the landmarks in the Quebec calendar; of the date when the last steam-boat should pass down the river, soon after which the 'ice bridge' would form and they would be able to walk or drive across the St. Lawrence to the opposite shore. They could hardly wait for the day when they would no longer go about on wheels, and the city would be gay with the sound of sleigh-bells.

Charles and Elizabeth treated their staff officers, whether married or single, as part of their own family. Colonels Irvine and Duchesnay, Captain and Mrs. Retallack and Captain Pemberton were soon on nearly as intimate a footing as the Denis Godleys and Henry Brand[2] who had come out to Canada with the Moncks.

Denis Godley, the younger brother of Charles' great friend John Robert Godley, was the Governor's private secretary. He has been described as 'a hardworking official, adept at making the most of his opportunities', who earned the ungracious nickname of 'Almighty' from those who had to deal with him.[3] To increase the consequence of his own post, he tried to insist that his permission be asked before anyone could approach his chief. Charles detested ostentation and, in Canada, earned a reputation for being 'easy and accessible.' It would be a puzzle to know why he put up with Godley's bumptious behaviour, but for the fact that he never saw it. In the relaxed and informal atmosphere of the Moncks' family circle, Godley showed none of the pompous bustle which offended those who knew him in his official capacity. Of the other aides-de-camp, Colonel Irvine was very deaf, and Elizabeth used to worry about his health. He looked, she said, as if he might be going to have a stroke, and a few years later her gloomy prophecy came true. Captain Pemberton was an enthusiastic cricketer and a keen horseman, consequently he was young Henry's favourite.

Informal entertaining became easier when the Moncks moved to their new home in the Rue St. Louis where two houses had been made into one. Even so, it was rather on the small side considering that it was to be, temporarily, the official Government House, and that some of the rooms had to be made into offices for Monck and his staff. In the remainder of the house, besides ordinary reception rooms, there was the girls' school-room presided over by Fräulein Denneler, or 'Denny', and Miss Frend. The latter specialised in the teaching of deaf-mutes, so Fan's education was her particular charge. In the nursery, French Mathilde tried, not always successfully, to cope with Stanley's mischievous ways; while a separate study was provided in which Henry was ostensibly being prepared for Eton by his indulgent tutor, Mr. Wilkinson, though both found it hard to concentrate when surrounded by so much that was new and interesting.

From the Moncks' letters it is possible to deduce some idea of the normal day's routine which formed the background to their social life and official receptions. At the nine-thirty breakfast, extra places would be laid which might be occupied by personal friends dropping in or by a Minister who had come to talk to the Governor. A good deal of the business of the day, either work or outdoor recreation, had already taken place before the family met at the breakfast-table, including the assembling of everyone in the house for family prayers. Monck and his family had been in the habit of walking several miles each day, and in the mild Irish climate there had been few days when they could not ride. During the Canadian winter, with the land snow-bound, the skating rink was therefore a great blessing to them, as was the squash racquets court on which Monck and members of his staff played during their rare periods of freedom. During those first weeks, however, most days were fully occupied, either with official duties or with social engagements, both formal and informal.

The officers from the garrison were constant visitors and in their turn the Governor and his family were invited to the frequent regimental balls, concerts and amateur theatricals. Besides these contacts, Elizabeth had begun to make friends in Quebec. She greatly admired old Bishop Mountain whose father had been the first Anglican bishop there. The present bishop died early in 1863, but she continued to be on intimate terms with his wife and family during the whole of her stay in Canada and afterwards. Lasting friendships were also made between her and the Prime Minister, George-Etienne Cartier; with the family of John Rose, M.P.P., until recently Minister for Public Works; and with Thomas d'Arcy McGee, the statesman and poet. He had been an Irish patriot, and escaped to America after the defeat of the Young Irelanders' rising in 1848, but was now a staunch supporter of the British Crown. In addition to these public figures, she and her daughters were on informal visiting terms with several less prominent families; also, in defiance of the more extreme Protestant press, with the French sisters at the Ursuline Convent and at the Hôtel de Dieu. Yet, though Elizabeth gradually found many congenial companions, especially among the older French residents, there were some aspects of Canadian society which dismayed and repelled her. The years had taught her to be tolerant, but she had little patience with what seemed to her 'bad manners', irrespective of the social rank in which it was displayed. Under this heading she classed the 'Yankee' customs and slang which had seeped across the border and been unconsciously assimilated by some of the British North Americans. Many of these 'Yankeeisms' were the same as those which so startled old-fashioned people in England during the first quarter of the present century, so that it is small wonder that Elizabeth, in 1861, found it hard to adjust herself to them.

But these social embarrassments were as nothing compared with the indignation she felt on Charles' account when she saw him harried and badgered by the intricacies of Union politics on the one hand, and on the other by the Colonial Office which blamed him for the vacillations and inefficiency of those over whom, officially, he had no control.

She heard these matters discussed in her own drawing room, since Charles was in the habit of inviting one or another of his Ministers to spend an evening at his house where they would talk over their problems informally. She approved of this practice and gladly made them welcome – so long as they conformed to her standard of behaviour.

139

Their most frequent visitor was John Alexander Macdonald, the Attorney-General for West Canada and Leader of Upper Canada. In his letters to England, Charles was extremely guarded, particularly since he received a warning from one of his friends there to be cautious when replying to that prolific letter-writer, Sir William Hayter – 'Everything you write to him is repeated in the London clubs.' It is therefore difficult to learn his personal opinion of individual members of the Canadian Government. It is clear that he liked and admired John A. Macdonald, constantly consulted him and had a great respect for his sound judgment and statesmanlike qualities. Judging by Macdonald's letters, the liking and respect were mutual, but there is a barely perceptible impression that it was tempered on each side with certain reservations, because of their very different personalities.

Owing to his breeding and training, and to an innate dislike of ostentation, Monck's instincts were all for under-dramatising a situation. The more other people bustled and panicked, the calmer he became. He did not mean to be irritating; it was an unconscious, reflex action. In times of crisis, a display of histrionic temperament affected him in the form of that *'sangfroid habituel'* described by Macdonald, who later interpreted him as being 'constitutionally incapable of rising to an occasion'.[4] Macdonald's vivid personality and witty conversation made him a welcome addition to any gathering, while his clear and well-balanced assessment of the political situation was of enormous value to Monck. Macdonald had all the gifts which constitute a great statesman. Wise, subtle and well-informed, he had the intricacies of Canadian politics at his finger-ends, and a gift for oratory which could sway a mob. But like many another brilliant leader, he was flamboyant and emotional and not entirely reliable. Under the strain of a political crisis, he was apt to take refuge in a drinking bout, the results of which were all the more disastrous owing to the extent to which his colleagues had relied on him. Sir Joseph Pope, Macdonald's private secretary, wrote: 'It would be futile to ignore the fact that there was a period in the life of Sir John Macdonald when excess in the direction I have indicated interrupted his usefulness, gave pain to his friends, and furnished his enemies with a weapon of which they never hesitated to avail themselves'.[5] Charles Monck was accustomed to men who drank heavily; but he could not believe that so intelligent and influential a man would allow such lapses to interfere with his public duties, and overlooked the occasions on which Macdonald visited him when not entirely sober.

Elizabeth, too, was a product of the Georgian rather than of the Victorian era and was far from being prudish in such matters, but she showed her displeasure when the Attorney-General for West Canada visited her drawing room at times when he would have done better to remain quietly at home. There is no record that she or her husband ever told anyone of these incidents, but there is reason to believe that their children were not so discreet – not at any rate when they returned to Ireland and regaled their cousins with anecdotes of the lighter side of their life in Canada. According to the descendants of those same cousins, John A. Macdonald got himself into Elizabeth's black books by being sick over the new chair covers in her drawing room. This anecdote is apocryphal; the Irish were ever loth to spoil a good story for lack of a ha'porth of exaggeration. And even if poor Mr. Macdonald really had this embarrassing experience, it was just as likely owing to the Moncks' dinners having disagreed with him.

During these informal evenings, the subject of internal politics would give way to the engrossing one of the American civil war. In general, Canadian sympathy was with the South; and each southern victory made it less likely that the Yankees would be able to turn their attention to Canada. If this uneasy peace could only be maintained till the spring, then the volunteers, though untrained, would at least have guns in their hands and, if need arose, reinforcements could be sent from England. Charles was maddened by the refusal of the Ministers to supply arms to the volunteers, thereby wasting valuable time which could have been spent in training them. It was like sitting on a rumbling volcano, when a jolt or an unwary movement might cause an eruption.

Notes to Chapter Nine

1. Stacey, C. P., 'Lord Monck and the Canadian Nation' *Dalhousie Review*.
2. Henry Brand: son of Rt. Hon. Henry Brand, Liberal Member for Lewes. cr. Visc. Hampden 1890.
3. Morton, W. L., *The Critical Years* (Toronto).
4. Pope, Sir Joseph, *Memoirs of Sir John A. Macdonald* (London, 1894).
5. Ibid.

10

'The Trent Affair'

The dreaded blow fell on 8 November and the news of it reached
Charles Monck in a telegram in cypher from Lord Lyons, the British
Ambassador at Washington. The *San Jacinto,* of the United States
Navy, had stopped the British mail packet *Trent* in the Bahamas
Channel, boarded her and arrested two Confederate agents, Mason
and Slidell, with their secretaries. The forcible removal of civilian
passengers from a neutral vessel was in itself a violation of
international law; but to make matters worse, the two Southern
envoys had been sent on a diplomatic mission to England, to lay the
Confederate case before the British Government. It was also
rumoured that Captain Wilkes of the *San Jacinto* had not acted on
his own initiative, but with the consent and approval of the
Washington cabinet, and that news of the arrest was even now
causing 'exultation' in Washington. Lord Lyons, the British
Ambassador, telegraphed that he was awaiting 'orders from home',
which implied that he was packing his bags. Charles Monck and his
Ministers had little doubt as to the outcome. This was it. War
seemed inevitable, and Canada would be involved in it immediately,
if not before, news of its declaration reached them.

Monck had been in office for three weeks and during that time he
had summed up the military situation and decided what he would do
if given a free hand. Now, at the risk of offending his Ministers and
the tax-payers, he proceeded to put these ideas into action. In the
crisis which became known as the *'Trent* Affair', he acted with
promptness and efficiency, shouldering the responsibility for
decisions which might be criticised as unorthodox.

Having learnt that lack of equipment was the only obstacle to the
immediate increase of the volunteer force to double its present
strength, he applied to General Sir Fenwick Williams for the issue of
the necessary arms, 'on tick', from the garrison ordnance stores. At

the same time he demanded that the Canadian Ministers pass an order in council, guaranteeing that the arms should be paid for as soon as the money should be voted at the next session of Parliament. To all this Sir Fenwick gave his full approval and support, and placed the arms under his control at the Governor's disposal. It was an unorthodox proceeding, but Monck was certain that the present emergency justified it. 'I take entirely upon myself any risk involved in the suggesting and carrying out this arrangement,' he assured the General. To the Colonial Office he wrote of the patriotic enthusiasm which was sweeping the country. No longer hampered by his Ministers' fears of sticking their necks out – 'I have *carte blanche* to do what I think right.'

Each of his letters home ended with an urgent request for information as to how the news of the *'Trent* Affair' had been received in England. The United States Minister in London reported to Washington that 'English feeling is almost out of control. The people are frantic with rage, and were the country polled, I fear 999 men out of every thousand would declare for immediate war. Lord Palmerston cannot resist the impulse if he would.'[1] Lord Palmerston told Queen Victoria that an American general had arrived in Paris to propose that France join the Northern States in war against England, offering in return 'the restoration of the French Province of Canada'. The same general had stated that the seizure of the Southern envoys had been planned and ordered by the Washington cabinet.[2] On 29 November, the Foreign Secretary submitted to the Queen the draft of a despatch to Lord Lyons in Washington. The British Ambassador was to demand the release of Messrs. Mason and Slidell – with an apology – within seven days. 'In case these requirements should be refused, Lord Lyons should ask for his passports.'[3] Russell's despatch, which amounted to an ultimatum, intercepted and revised by the Prince Consort – the last official action of his life. He modified the defiant wording to an assumption that Captain Wilkes had not acted under instructions, that a mistake had been made and that the United States Government would doubtless wish to offer 'such redress as alone could satisfy this country, viz. the restoration of the unfortunate passengers and a suitable apology.'[4] This gave the Washington cabinet time to cool off, as well as an opportunity to climb down without losing face.

On the other side of the Atlantic, Charles Monck shared the

Prince Consort's conviction that the fact of being 'in the right' did not in itself justify sending thousands of men to their deaths. While urging forward the preparations for war, he wrote to the Duke of Newcastle that he sincerely hoped and thought that they would prove unnecessary: 'I see a great deal of the American press, and it strikes me that their tone generally is not so swaggering as I expected it would have been. They seem inclined to rest on the fact that Captain Wilkes acted on his own responsibility.' He reported that his Finance Minister, Alexander Galt, had been to Washington and, while there, had had an interview with President Lincoln':

> . . . The latter expressed his wish and intention to maintàin friendly relations with England. Someone who was by said rather sharply' "What about Mason and Slidell?" on which Mr. Lincoln turned to him very abruptly and said: "There will be no quarrel about that; I guess we'll fix it." I am afraid, however this cause of dispute may end, we shall have to fight them sooner or later.[5]

Monck was not the only one to hold this view, and his next instructions from the Colonial Office were to prepare barrack accommodation, and make provision for a safe passage up the river for eleven battalions of regular troops who were already on their way from England to Quebec. Welcome though this news was, it raised an immediate problem owing to the setting in of an unusually early winter.

Canada, as distinct from the Maritime Province, had no winter port. When the St. Lawrence became ice-bound, passengers disembarking at Halifax, Nova Scotia, could only reach Quebec by way of Portland in the United States. The passage of the *Persia* bearing troops across the Atlantic became, therefore, a race against climatic conditions as much as against a possible outbreak of war. It was easy enough for the Colonial Office to issue orders regarding safety precautions for the passage of the ship up the St. Lawrence where navigation was made dangerous by the numerous islands and submerged rocks. By the time it was known in Quebec that the troops were on the way, the upper reaches of the river were already ice-bound, and it was impossible to send craft down the river to relight the lighthouses which had already been extinguished 'for the season'. Monck and Sir Fenwick Williams made minute enquiries as to the safety of passage of shipping to Rivière du Loup, lower down the river, and elaborate arrangements were then made for disembarking the troops and their stores there. These plans were thrown into confusion when the officer sent from Quebec to assist in the disembarkation, reported that the commander of the *Persia,* in defiance of orders, had anchored at Bic, further down the river. It was largely due to the prompt co-operation of the civilian population that the British troops were not left stranded indefinitely there. In the storms and extreme cold of January 1862, seven thousand men were transported in sleighs from northern New Brunswick, through the snow-choked Madawaska Road to Rivière du Loup, and thence to Montreal. 'The troops are now arriving in considerable numbers from Halifax to New Brunswick,' Charles wrote to Lord Lyons. 'The only casualties I have as yet heard of have been a few deserters to whom every inducement is held out by the Yankee borderers. Is it possible Mr. Seward may have expected to add a regular body of troops to the U.S. army by this process?'[6] The troops had barely settled into the accommodation prepared for them, when the original cause of their coming was removed. The United States Government released the Confederate agents and 'disavowed' Captain Wilkes, which was the nearest they could bring themselves to making an apology. In writing home, Monck expressed his fear that the fact of having been made to 'climb down' had intensified the Americans' grudge against the British. He was glad to be able to report that the majority of British North Americans shared his view, and that there was no slackening in the efforts to improve defences.

He also took special pains to assure the Duke that the apparent lack of response in Lower Canada to the call for volunteers for the militia did not arise from any reluctance to serve. The reverse was the case and, although the French population refused to adopt the volunteering system, they were quite ready to serve if selected by ballot. In confirmation he enclosed a copy of a *Mandement* (Mandate) issued by the Roman Catholic Bishop who evidently regarded a possible conflict with the United States as a Holy War:

'. . . Nous avons la confiance, nos Très-Chers Frères, que partout l'on empressera de répondre à l'appel du Représentant

145

de notre graciéuse Souveraine . . . Tous nos jeunes gens doivent
donc avoir à coeur, en ce moment, de servir une si noble cause .
. . Quant même le danger que nous appréhendons viendrait à se
dissiper, nous ne pouvons toutefois nous dissimuler que de
nouvelles difficultés peuvent surgir, à la première occasion, et
nous obliger à prendre les armes.'

The surviving letters written by Charles during the crisis known as
the *'Trent* Affair' are all official ones dealing with military matters
and with the political and international situation. None from
Elizabeth have survived but she confided later to one of the family
her wish that they had never left Ireland. She had brought her four
children, the youngest three years old and the eldest a deaf-mute, to
a country which was inadequately defended, and likely to be invaded
at any moment. Even when the immediate international crisis
subsided, there would still be danger as long as the civil war across
the border continued. The situation, however, had got to be lived
with. This was made easier by the novelty to her, as to her children,
of life in old Quebec where every day brought fresh interests. Having
settled into the house in the Rue St. Louis, they were looking
forward to their first Christmas there which promised to be gayer
and more festive than any they had been accustomed to. But a few
days before Christmas, their preparations were halted by a telegram
from England announcing the death of the Prince Consort.

Unknown to anyone but himself, Prince Albert had been a sick
man when, a fortnight before he died, he had redrafted Russell's
dispatch to Washington which, but for his intervention, would
almost certainly have led to war between England and the United
States. After completing the writing of the revised dispatch, he had
collapsed; and as the Queen's doctor either did not realise or refused
to admit the seriousness of his condition, his death came as a great
shock to the royal family as well as to the general public. Since the
Governor General was the Queen's representative, it was necessary
for his household to observe court mourning. Consequently, the
Moncks' first Christmas in Canada was a quiet one. The children
were debarred from attending the annual festivities which included a
rink ball, when the rink was —

. . . lit with gas, and decorated with flags and ornaments; there were tables with refreshments on the ice, and the regimental band playing. It looked like a fair in a Dutch picture; most of the girls wore *very short* red petticoats, and grey or black dresses; some wore scarlet and some white feathers in their fur caps, and most of the officers were in their mess uniforms, dancing quadrilles, lancers, or valses.[7]

Carioles (sleighs) were now the only means of transport. The roads were first ploughed, then rolled, and their boundaries marked by small fir-trees stuck in the snow. Even so, there were occasional upsets caused by the frequent holes, called *cahots,* in the roads. There was constant traffic on the ice-bridge, which was merely a term used to describe the frozen surface of the St. Lawrence. The best routes on this, either up or down the river or across to the opposite shore, were indicated by little fir-trees, as in the roads on land. Charles Monck wrote home enthusiastic descriptions of the country, its climate and its winter sports. 'Henry has become a first-rate skater,' he wrote to his Wicklow neighbour, Sir George Hodson:

. . . It has been a great amusement to him all this winter. It is carried on here in a large wooden building like a riding house, called a rink, as from the quantity of snow the ice out of doors is unpracticable. Sleighing also is a great amusement here in winter, indeed it is more than an amusement as it is the only way we have of going about, as you cannot use wheeled carriages. As long as the snow is deep and the frost hard, it is a very pleasant mode of travelling and you can go along very quickly . . . The scenery about here is most beautiful, and I think your artist's eye would be well rewarded for a trip across the Atlantic by a sight of one of our sunsets. It is scarcely possible to exaggerate the intensity of the colouring on the sky in the west, and the whole country is covered with a pink tinge like the halo one sees in representations of scenes in tropical climates . . . We are suffering the effects of reaction now after the state of intense excitement in which we were kept all the winter. It was not a pleasant inauguration of my official career here.'[8]

Notes to Chapter Ten

1. *Oxford History of England,* 'The Age of Reform'.
2. Palmerston to Queen Victoria, 29 November 1861.
3. Russell to Queen Victoria, 29 November 1861.
4. Queen Victoria to Russell, i December 1861.
5. Monck to Newcastle, December 20, 1861. Nottingham University Library.
6. Monck to Lyons, 22 January, 1862. Lyons Papers. West Sussex University Library.
7. Monck, Frances, *My Canadian Leaves* (Original edition in facsimile, Canadian Library Service).
8. Monck to Hodson, 11 April 1862. Hodson Papers, National Library of Ireland.

11

Spencer Wood

On 21 March 1862, Charles and Elizabeth Monck were driven to the Parliament House in a 'shut sleigh' drawn by four horses. Troops lined the streets and a guard of honour awaited them at the Parliament building. Wearing the Governor General's blue and gold uniform, Charles read his speech clearly and distinctly, first in English and then in French. To satisfy both Upper and Lower Canada, both languages had to be used during parliamentary sessions, the rule sometimes resulting in a mixture of the two. The Governor's young son Henry was always particularly amused by the phrase, *Sanctionne ce bill.*

The story of Charles Monck's seven years in Canada has been told elsewhere.[1] No attempt is made here to give details of the intricacies of nineteenth-century Canadian politics or of Monck's successes and failures in his efforts to strike the balance between an autocratic Colonial Secretary and a self-governing colony, jealous of its independence. However, some mention must be made of the more outstanding events which took place during his term of office, in order to explain why that term lasted for seven years with a minimum of home leave, and why those seven years were referred to as 'an era in colonial history'.[2]

The most important of these events was the union under one central government, of all the provinces comprising British North America. The confederation scheme, as it was called, became Monck's chief objective, and he was asked to remain in office until it was achieved. This took longer than he or anyone else had foreseen. The general scheme met with a certain amount of opposition, besides which there was immense difficulty in evolving a system of government which would satisfy the different provinces. The Colonial Secretary insisted that union be postponed until after the construction of an inter-colonial railway, linking the port of Halifax with Quebec. From day to day the British Government expected a declaration of war by the United States, and they dreaded a repetition of the events of the previous winter when troops sent from England had been conveyed from New Brunswick to Montreal in privately-owned sleighs.

Charles invited the lieutenant-governors of Nova Scotia and New Brunswick to visit him in order to discuss the railway project and the confederation scheme. Photography was becoming very popular, and a souvenir of the occasion in September 1862 has survived in a photograph of the three bearded Governors: Charles Monck, Lord Mulgrave and the Honourable Arthur Hamilton Gordon, posed with their aides-de-camp on the citadel at Quebec.

Of more immediate importance than either union or railway was the need to increase military strength. The Governor was able to see some of the results of his efforts in this direction during an official tour of what, in those days, was known as 'The West'. He took Elizabeth and the children with him and the party included the Assistant Adjutant-General, the Prime Minister and various members of the government. They travelled by river-steamer and railway. Long train journeys were no hardship to the Governor-General and his family; their carriage consisted of a large sitting room, bedrooms and a smoking room furnished with chairs, sofas and lamps. In each town Charles received and replied to addresses, visited centres of industry, schools and universities, and attended military parades mounted on horseback. A great part of the tour was spent in inspecting the newly-formed Canadian regiments, to one of which Elizabeth presented colours. In most of his addresses he referred to the need for defence, praising what had been done and urging them to still greater efforts.

The Canadian press commented on the 'fine, frank and manly bearing' of 'the goodlooking Governor . . . He walks with a fine step and is very upright, muscular and active . . . Our new Governor possesses the happy knack of placing those who meet him quite at their ease . . . He does not notice mistakes.' He 'even made Buchanan laugh . . .', that member of the Canadian parliament being noted for his forbidding manner.

Throughout the tour Charles had shown that he was particularly interested in agricultural development, describing himself as 'a practical farmer', which surprised those who had only heard of him in

connection with politics. There was an even greater surprise when, at
Trinity College, Toronto, he was admitted to the bar honorary
degree. During the ceremony he was asked: 'What is the highest
estate known to the law of the land?' and promptly replied: 'A fee
simple'. Few of those present knew that he had been a barrister.

At the end of September he left Elizabeth and the children at
Niagara Falls where they stayed in an hotel run by Americans
though in Canadian territory. Two years later, her niece described
the hotel as being 'enormous and very comfortable, though over-
heated by large stoves. In all Yankee and Canadian hotels there is a
ladies' parlour, with chairs all round the room – no table – a stove, a
bad piano, a large jug full of iced water, and some tumblers . . . The
men are supposed to "liquor up" in the bar. We were waited on at
dinner by niggers, in white jackets and aprons.'[3]

Meanwhile, Charles 'took French leave', as he expressed it, across
the border for a few days' shooting in Illinois. He left no record of
the success or otherwise of the expedition, nor of what game he had
pursued. He did, however, report his impressions of the effect of the
civil war on the American people; of the strain on them caused by
'the drain on the population' and by the depreciated currency. He
returned to Canada in time to make a speech at Kingston and review
troops in Montreal, arriving back in Quebec before the end of
October.

The Moncks had their own private reasons for regretting the
absence of winter communications between Quebec and the port of
Halifax. Henry was to go to Eton in the January of 1863 and would
have to sail from a port in the United States. At this critical juncture
in Canadian affairs, Charles could not ask for leave of absence, and
it was arranged that Mr. Wilkinson, the tutor, should take the boy to
New York and sail with him in the *Scotia* at the end of December.
An aide-de-camp, Captain Pemberton, travelled with them as far as
Montreal, and Sergeant Lambkin, the orderly, escorted them to
New York. Henry's dog 'Nora' completed the party. Henry's parents
waited anxiously for news of his journey through a hostile country in
which the civil war was at its height. The party was stopped at the
frontier by the American 'look-out man', but fortunately Sergeant
Lambkin had procured a pass in Montreal, and the rest of the
journey passed off without incident.

In Henry's first letter to his parents, he wrote of the great kindness he had received in Montreal from Sir Fenwick Williams. Monck had already received a letter from the General, which had contained some tactful remarks about Henry. In writing to thank him, Monck said: 'I have given your messages to Lady M. You always held a high place in her favour but what you have said about our boy has *crowned* you . . .', using an idiom which was, and still is, common in Ireland.

They sailed on 31 December and landed in time to allow Henry to spend a few blissful days at Charleville where he was looked after by his old nurse, Mrs. Hogan ('Agga') and the keeper, Tom Quin.

Henry found his cousin, George Brooke, at Eton as well as several boys from Woodcote, his preparatory school. During his first week he wrote of the 'great deal of work' that he was expected to do at Eton, and declared that the place was colder than Canada. In March he described the 'great doings' celebrating the marriage of the Prince of Wales and Princess Alexandra, of whom he had a 'capital view' when they drove through the town. Mr. Wilkinson again took charge of him during the Easter holidays, which began with a visit to Paris ostensibly to see 'Aunts' – his father's sisters. The rest of the holidays were spent at Charleville of which Charles demanded a detailed account, especially of the mares and foals.

> . . . I think the pheasant eggs answered so badly last year I got them, that it is useless to bring them over again; but if Dick* could get a few live pheasants in London (about 2 cocks and 6 or 8 hens) and send them over soon to T. Quin, I think it would be a good plan. You ought to write to Sandys and tell him to have a place prepared for them.

Meanwhile Charles was preparing to move his family out to Spencer Wood, the rebuilding of which had now been completed. The house in the Rue St. Louis had not proved an ideal situation for the children, unaccustomed as they were to the intense heat of a Canadian summer, while Spencer Wood, three miles from the city, standing high above the river and enclosed in large private grounds, was the perfect answer for a couple with a young family.

Charles would still have his offices in the Rue St. Louis, and the

* 'Dick' was Charles' younger brother, Richard Monck.

Spencer Wood.

state apartments in the Parliament Buildings could be used for Vice-Regal Drawing Rooms and strictly official functions; but the rooms in Spencer Wood could accommodate quite large receptions, dinner parties and balls, which could there have the intimate and informal character which the Moncks preferred. It had been necessary to redecorate the rooms before a move could be made; and, more important from Charles' point of view, alterations and repairs had to be made to the stables.

Elizabeth was delighted with Spencer Wood and impatient to get there, though it would entail moving house for the second time since their arrival in Quebec. And now they no longer had Brock to supervise the packing and removal of their household goods; after becoming increasingly 'difficult', he had left them and taken a post in Montreal. As so often happens on such occasions, the Moncks now remembered his good qualities rather than his tiresome ways, and Elizabeth neither liked nor trusted Esden, the new butler. When Henry had broken his journey to New York at Montreal, Brock came to see him on purpose to say how 'very sorry' he was to have left the family and asking to be taken back. 'I wish you would,' Henry wrote to his father, and his letter was followed by a contrite one from Brock himself. 'Papa heard from Brock and he hopes soon to come,' Elizabeth wrote to Henry in January; and in March a letter from Charles reported that 'Brock has come back, and is reinstated just as before, with a most tremendous beard.'

They did not wait for his arrival before getting rid of the unsatisfactory Esden. 'Captain Retallack has taken up all the plate, etc., from Esden, and he is gone, I am happy to say, and Sergeant Lambkin is taking care of everything, and now all seems quiet,' wrote Elizabeth to Henry. 'It is a blessing to get rid of such a man as Esden, and I am sure he was always a thief, only not discovered. God always brings sin to light . . . ' She added inconsequently: 'If you ever get into any difficulty of any sort, *write at once to Dick.* He will always give you good and kind advice and help you in every way. If you find your money not enough for *reasonable* and rational demands, tell Papa, but *do not borrow.*'

Elizabeth's letters to Henry are, in the main, disappointing, being mere covering notes to her 'journal' – a circular letter containing a diary of events such as the formal receptions she held every Saturday evening and descriptions of the people she had met. Henry had to forward it promptly to his aunt, Fanny Cole, after which it was circulated among all Elizabeth's sisters and sisters-in-law. After being read by Georgina Croker at Ballynagarde, the four sisters at Barbavilla and Henrietta Brooke at Summerton, it was forwarded to 'Aunt I.' and 'Aunt E.' in Paris. The only parts of the journal that survive are two or three fragments which Henry managed to recover.

Her personal notes to Henry contained, therefore, little in the way of news – 'You will read it all in my journal.' They were usually dashed off in a hurry in time to catch the out-going mail, but they made up in spontaneity what they sometimes lacked in coherence. As in the foregoing letter, her infrequent comments on people or events were interspersed by loving and anxious little homilies, which made it puzzling for Henry to decide whether or not the subjects were connected. Brief references to Quebec balls and to sleigh expeditions with her neighbours and officers from the garrison, would be followed by a lecture on punctuality –

. . . Never keep people waiting. Do break that bad habit . . . it is not right . . . I like so much writing to you on Sunday. I well remember that lovely Chapel, and it was most interesting to see the statue of old Dr. Heath of whom I had so often heard my dear Father speak – headmaster in his time . . . I was much pleased at yr *accounts.* Sardines are very good things to buy but, as you say, to sit and *munch* at a Confectioners (Laytons I suppose?) is neither good for mind or body. Papa and I shd like you to have a bath, so you can ask for it from us.

She was relieved when 'Papa' bought Captain Retallack's pony carriage, which Puss and Fan took turns to drive. 'It made me sick to see Puss driving a great waggon.' Sixteen-year-old Louise was fearless and energetic, but a temporary stop was put to her driving of either waggon or pony carriage by a 'sad accident' while skating. 'Your letter reached us while I was holding her poor *broken* arm to be set.' 'I hope you think of *Lent,* my dearest Child,' Elizabeth added in a postscript. She liked writing to Henry on a Sunday, and told him she felt that the fact that he and his family were both taking part in the same form of service made them 'together though separated'. On one occasion she wrote that she was thinking of him in church – 'though I know not which church'. Although their new parish church at home was now in regular use, services were still sometimes held in the old church in the grounds of Powerscourt House. On returning to Ireland, Elizabeth would soon have found out 'which church' her son had attended on a certain Sunday in April 1863, when he had occupied his time there by cutting his name and the date on the family pew. He made a thorough job of it and the lettering can still be seen* – a memorial to Henry's inattentiveness and to his tutor's lack of supervision.

Charles, too, wrote to his son every week. 'All the world' had called on him on New Year's Day, as was the custom in Canada and in America. In February, their friend Bishop Mountain died and the synod elected Dr. Williams of Lennoxville to succeed him, to the disappointment of those who, like Elizabeth, had hoped that the late Bishop's son would be chosen. He wrote of the smart appearance of the volunteers – 'especially the cavalry' – at the opening of

---

* In Powerscourt New Church.

Parliament of 14 February; and described a tremendous snow-storm, 'drifts 12 feet high . . . opposite my office', and a narrow escape of some people crossing the ice-bridge on the river:

> . . . A couple of days since, Mama and I were looking at the bridge from the Governor's Garden; there were a number of people on foot and three or four sleighs on it, when suddenly the ice parted right across the river and began moving up with the tide. Fortunately there were canoes near, and they took off the people at once, and the sleighs and horses after some little trouble.

The family letters during March were full of the approaching move to Spencer Wood and this finally took place at the end of that month. Charles Monck wrote enthusiastically of the comfortable rooms, of the conservatory – a 'must' at that date – which had been built on to the end of the house, and of the 'very fair' cricket ground. Built during the latter part of the eighteenth century, Spencer Wood was described as 'a very long house, only two stories high . . . in a lovely spot just over the river. There are thirty windows in each side of the house, and the rooms are, some of them, large. The servants' rooms, kitchen, etc., form a sort of wing.'[4] One of the pleasantest features was the long and deep verandah running the whole length of the house on the side overlooking the river. The family had breakfast and tea there in fine weather; they could watch the ships plying up and down the river below and look across at Point Levis on the opposite shore, with the magnificent view beyond.

It is not surprising that the Moncks preferred a home in the country, since they were surrounded by a menagerie of animals wherever they went. The 'improved' stables contained horses for each member of the family to ride, also the carriage horses and a pony for Stanley; in addition to which there were fifteen dogs and seven cats in the house. At least one of the dogs was the property of Captain Pemberton, aide-de-camp, who also kept his tame birds in the new conservatory. These were soon joined by a tame owl which he had bought in the Quebec market. Another of the dogs belonged to Sergeant Lambkin, the orderly. It was so taken for granted that each member of the household should be allowed to indulge his own particular taste in pets, that Brock's performing fleas were never commented on in family correspondence. It was left to George Augustus Sala to describe them after he had visited Quebec in 1864 and been 'hospitably entertained at viceregal dinners' at Spencer Wood. 'Lord Monck's butler,' he wrote, 'was the proprietor of the original Industrial Fleas; and his talented troupe included the flea that drew the cannon, the flea that rode in the sedan-chair, and the flea that impersonated Napoleon Bonaparte's charger, "Marengo".'[5]

Lord Frederick Paulet was one of the first to stay at Spencer Wood when he came from Montreal to inspect the troops at Quebec. During his visit, the Moncks made up large parties for excursions, on horseback and in carriages, to the Montmorency Falls where they showed him the 'natural steps' – a rock formation like a staircase beside the falls; – and to the ruins of Charlebourg, a country house which had belonged to the French governors of Canada.

Charles wrote to Henry of 'a day of alarms' on the occasion of one of their dinner parties:

> . . . When they arrived they found the fire engine out and the soldiers all ready to put out the fire . . . which turned out to be a large log of wood smouldering in a stove the pipe of which ran into my chimney, and this produced the smoke! We went to dinner and all went well until the party were just breaking up when Retallack [Military Secretary] came into the room and told me that Mr. [John A.] Macdonald and an American gentleman, who had been dining with me, had been upset in a calèche and were very much hurt. I ran out and found the Yankee lying on the ground and very much stunned. We got him into the house and put him to bed and sent for the doctor, who said he would be all right next morning. He was able to depart after breakfast.

Captain Retallack had reported the casualties as being in the plural, yet there is nothing in Monck's letter about the treatment of Mr. Macdonald's injuries, if indeed he had any. The silence on the subject might be thought to imply that Monck blamed him for the accident as being the result of Macdonald's well-known failing; but it is more likely that special attention was given to the concussed

American for diplomatic reasons. Charles had received emphatic instructions from the Colonial Office to lose no opportunity for keeping on friendly terms with 'the Northern Federation'.

A succession of Federal (United States) victories had increased the feeling of tension in Canada, since a final defeat of the Southerners would free the Northern army to turn its attention to British North America. John A. Macdonald and the Governor promptly took advantage of the alarming situation to exert pressure on Canadian Government, with the result that their volunteer force was considerably strengthened, and an effective Militia Bill passed in August 1863. This marked a definite step forward in the progress of Canadian defence, which continued to develop, slowly but surely, in the ensuing years.

Congratulations on the passing of the bill arrived from members of the British Government, many of whom wrote personal letters to Charles. Some of them commented on the Governor's growing tendency to 'think Canadian' on occasions when Canadians differed from the Colonial Office. Charles shared Elizabeth's hatred of 'humbug' in any form, and it seemed to him the height of hypocrisy to support a theory of self-government in a province, while reserving the right to dictate its policy. The Duke of Newcastle was inclined to be suspicious and disapproving of this attitude; but Adderley, writing from the Colonial Office, complimented Charles on his skill in holding the balance in the difficult position of being responsible to the independent Canadian government while being answerable to the home government. 'I really quite agree with you in your last remarks on Canadian leading-strings having so lately been broken.. If Ministers at home will only stand out of their way when learning to walk, I shall be satisfied.'[6]

'Of your personal success I hear on all sides, and with the greatest pleasure,' wrote Robert Lowe. You seem to enjoy the very highest popularity, and that in a land where it is not easy to be popular much or long.'[7] Charles was always grateful for news from Westminster, either serious or frivolous. Lowe was one of those who kept him posted, and concluded this letter with the latest gossip about Lord Palmerston, now nearing his eightieth birthday:

> . . . Our politics here are very simple. As long as Lord Palmerston [Prime Minister] lives and abstains from any con-

spicuous folly the Government is likely to last. As Palmerston himself says – we lose seats but not votes. The Tory party are so disorganised that two thirds of them like him better than their own leaders.

You will have heard of a little scandal, which has occasioned hopes in some quarters. I believe the plaintiff, late Editor of the *Derry Sentinel,* the respondent, and the attorney, to be all persons of the basest character. Unfortunately that does not altogether prove that the charge is not true, however no one would be so unjust as to condemn Palmerston till the case has been tried and that will not be for a year and a half. What may be decided at that time may be a curious question of biography, but can hardly, considering that Palmerston is in his 80th year, be regarded as a matter of much political importance.

'In town and country, nothing was talked of for days than the Palmerston case,' Lord Clarendon wrote to Lord Cowley, the British Ambassador in Paris.[8] The known facts were that a journalist called O'Kane sent his attractive young wife to see Lord Palmerston 'on some political matter' and subsequently sued him for £20,000 worth of damages for having committed adultery with the said wife, both then and on other occasions. Palmerston denied this and refused to pay, upon which O'Kane petitioned for divorce citing Palmerston as co-respondent. 'Mrs. O'Kane not only denied committing adultery, but claimed that she had never been legally married to O'Kane.' Since O'Kane was unable to prove either the fact of his marriage or of the adultery, the case was dismissed.

The affair served as a diverting talking-point for several months. Contrasting attitudes were adopted, varying according to temperament and to political views. 'The lady has been a governess and an actress,' wrote Clarendon, 'and is good-looking and said not to make unnecessary difficulties . . . Party spirit hoped to arouse British hypocrisy "to protect its widowed sovereign from the approach of her licentious minister." Lady Palmerston talked gaily of the case and . . . treated the allegations as ridiculous, and as a bare-faced attempt at extortion.' Gladstone and his friends were greatly distressed and feared the effect on the non-conformist M.P.'s and voters in their party. Disraeli, on the other hand, was afraid '. . . that it would make Palmerston more popular than ever,' and 'playfully suggested that Palmerston had deliberately spread the story abroad because he was intending to hold a general election.'[9] Whether or not Disraeli was right, 'Pam' certainly 'gained both ways': while he stood vindicated and innocent in the eyes of the non-conformist Liberal voter, the naughtier elements of the population '. . . believed the worst about Lord Palmerston and loved him all the more for it.'[10] And the wits went round saying: 'The lady is certainly Kane, but is Pam Abel?'

It was a spicy titbit with which to enliven correspondence with friends serving overseas, and Monck received other letters referring to the same 'little scandal', including one from Chichester Fortescue who was one of the many who were convinced that it was merely 'an attempt to extort money' from *"le vieux Pam, dont la seule infirmité paraît être la surdité"*, as the *Revue des deux Mondes* says.'[11]

Notes to Chapter Eleven

1   Elizabeth Batt, *Monck: Governor General* (Toronto, 1976).
2   Cardwell to Monck, 1864. Monck Papers.
3   *My Canadian Leaves* by Frances Monck.
4   *My Canadian Leaves* by Frances Monck.
5   George Augustus Sala (1828-1895). *Things I have seen and people I have known.* (London, 1894).
6   Adderley to Monck, 1863. Unpublished letter. Monck Papers.
7   Lowe to Monck. Unpublished letter, November 11, 1863. Monck Papers.
8   Lord Clarendon to Lord Cowley. Quoted in Jasper Ridley, *Lord Palmerston* (London, 1970).
9   Ibid.
10   Ibid.
11   Chichester Fortescue to Monck, 5 November, 1863.

12

Letters to Henry

Neither Charles nor Elizabeth could be easy while the Atlantic separated them from Henry. Their letters during that summer show that he was never out of their thoughts and that they lived for the day when he would rejoin them for the long summer holidays. Their joyful anticipation was mixed with dread, which increased each time they heard of another wreck. There had already been two that year and in one of them, off Cape Race, 200 lives had been lost. Monck's confidence in the Canadian line had been shaken. To avoid the dangers of the Gulf of St. Lawrence he arranged for Henry to come by way of Boston in the United States. This would be merely the lesser of two evils, owing to the present strained relations between England and America. He arrived safely, however, in the last week of July, attended by Mr. Wilkinson.

One of the horses was Henry's special property and there were riding expeditions, Charles having already explored the surrounding countryside. Both father and son were keen fishermen and, in Canada, this sport could be enjoyed on a scale they had never known in Ireland. A steam-ship, the property of the Canadian Government, was at the disposal of the Governor, and in this they cruised down the St. Lawrence to its tributary, the Saguenay. From the deck of the steamer they admired the mountain scenery and the Montmorency Falls, but the object of the expedition was the excellent trout-fishing in the wild and beautiful Saguenay river. At some points they would leave the steamer and take to rowing-boats and canoes to reach the best places for fishing. Henry would have preferred to fish all the time but, for the benefit of any guests who had lately arrived in Canada, the steamer would continue down river, and the party would go ashore to see places of historical interest or an Indian settlement. The cruise lasted for several days during which they slept on board, the party including the whole

Monck family with some of their servants, a dog or two, and any friends who cared to join them.

Soon after they returned to Quebec, it was time for Henry to leave Canada. His parents then went through three weeks of agonised suspense before they received the welcome news that he and Mr. Wilkinson had landed in Ireland.

At Spencer Wood entertaining was continuous and varied. Charles gave a large, parliamentary dinner for men only each Saturday; besides these dinners, Canadian ministers and other dignitaries were invited, with their wives, to smaller dinner parties at which the presence of a few senior officers from the garrison ensured the unofficial nature of the gathering. Clergy and judges with their families, the Quebec librarian and his wife, as well as a miscellaneous collection of neighbours within visiting distance, were regularly invited to luncheon, tea or dinner at Government House. A dinner party was often followed by an impromptu dance, to the delight of M. Cartier who was an energetic performer and who would, furthermore, be disappointed if he were not asked to sing *Il y a longtemps que je t'aimais*. On a smaller and even more informal scale breakfast was a sociable meal. If Charles wanted to have a confidential talk with a minister before the day's political business began, he would invite him to come out to Spencer Wood at 9.30 a.m. and breakfast with the family, aides-de-camp and any officers or other friends who happened to drop in.

One dinner party included several officers who were full of the latest gossip about a certain Captain Herbert of the Grenadiers. As a consequence of having married a Canadian, he was to sell out, Elizabeth wrote to Henry, 'and his Father will not let him come home.' She made no comment on this shattering statement; but less than four months later, the lady in question was already being referred to as 'the runaway wife of Captain Herbert'. At a ball in Quebec she 'danced the fast dance with a rose in her mouth,' wrote Elizabeth, 'and then leaped a kind of *hurdle race* over the seats, with an officer.'

Another diversion was provided by the arrival in Quebec of Barnum's troupe of midgets – '"General Tom Thumb", with his diminutive wife, sister-in-law, and "Commodore Nutt".' Elizabeth took her two daughters and Stanley to see the show, the famous midgets were presented to her and she invited all four to lunch at

Spencer Wood. 'They drove out in their miniature carriage-and-four and, after lunch, Stanley got into their carriage and drove about in it.' Tom Thumb gave the Moncks a photograph of the troupe bearing all their signatures, and more photographs were taken during their visit to Spencer Wood.

Regimental cricket matches continued throughout October, as did the garrison races on the Plains' of Abraham. As with those described in Thackeray's novels, only two horses were entered for each race, officers from the different regiments racing against each other. Elizabeth took a keen interest in the races, writing out all the results for Henry, while explaining that she had said nothing about them in her journal, which was sent round the whole family, because 'Aunts do not think it right to go to races.' Stanley was charmed, and said it was *'si amusant'*. At five years old he still spoke French more readily than English, a sure passport to popularity with the French-Canadians, though in fact it was merely the result of having had a French nurse.

The Moncks had invited some of the officers to spend Christmas at Spencer Wood. As that season approached, they received the usual spate of letters from friends and relations offering to have their elder son to stay in the holidays. Young Henry was in a predicament familiar to any orphaned, or temporarily orphaned, boy with many kind relatives. He grudged any time spent away from Charleville, but Charles insisted that he accept, for the first time, the invitation which kind Mr. Adderley gave before each holiday. His mother's four sisters at Barbavilla had to be fitted in somehow, also his father's two sisters in Paris, while plaintive letters from his aunt Georgina Croker urged Henry to spend at least part of his holidays with her and her ten children at Ballynagarde.

In the meantime, his parents wrote him letters of advice and warning, designed to cover any or all of his plans. 'If you go to Bally-nagarde, I hope you will be very careful about fire-arms,' wrote Charles. Among the Moncks' relations and friends, the Croker family was the only one to conform to the pattern beloved by old-fashioned Irish novelists. The slapdash, easy-going way of life at Ballynagarde, the four harum-scarum daughters, the six spend-thrift and almost illiterate sons whose companions were stable-boys and poachers and whose favourite amusements were local boxing-matches and race-meetings – all might have posed as models for a

163

romantic story of Ireland in the nineteenth century. Charles knew that the young Crokers would certainly take his precious son out rough-shooting without any supervision; and in any case, they had long been beyond parental control.

While Charles feared for the boy's physical safety, Elizabeth was chiefly concerned with his spiritual welfare: 'I trust my dearest Child you think sometimes of Advent *and its work: self-examination –* self-denial – earnest prayer. During holidays I hope you will do, each morning, as you did with me; read the Psalms and lesson for the day – learn the collect, one verse of Xtian year, one verse of a Psalm.' While at Charleville, he was to go twice a week to Mr. McDonough, the curate, to be prepared for his confirmation which would take place in Quebec the following summer; and in Paris he was to resist his aunts' efforts to entice him into a new form of churchmanship they had recently adopted. 'If Aunty E. wants you not to go to Mr. Gurney's Church, say to her that I wish you to go there. It is very wrong of anyone to try to prevent your going to the Church your parents went to.'

By mid-January, Henry's letters from Ireland had arrived. Charles wrote to thank him for telling him 'all the sort of things I wanted to know about Charleville,' and in return gave him news of the various horses, two of which he had been driving tandem 'in a sleigh'; and of two regimental balls which Fan had very much enjoyed. Henry, he said, might have Bass's beer next half, and should start learning German, while being careful not to neglect his French. The most important bit of news was left to the end: 'Please God, it will seem a very short time until you will be coming back to us again, and then I think Mama will go home with you.'

For nearly three years Fan had been without the specialised tuition supplied by the Institute for the Deaf in Paris. The plan under discussion was that Elizabeth should return to Ireland with Henry at the end of his summer holidays, taking the two girls and Stanley. She would rent a house in Paris for the winter, where the girls were to attend classes and, in the case of Puss, music lessons, and go back to Charleville in May, when Charles expected to go home on leave, for which he was long overdue.

Fan's education was of the first importance, but another con-sideration was the need to keep personal contact with the Irish estates. Charles could not reconcile himself to being an absentee landlord, and if unable to go home himself, Elizabeth must deputise for him. She was the more willing to go home on account of Stanley, who had had two severe illnesses since being in Canada. By the first week of February, the proposed plan had become definite.

A fragment from Elizabeth's 'journal' describes sleigh-accidents, visits to sick neighbours, dinner parties, a snow-shoe race and then a charity concert in Quebec at which she had to 'say a few words'. She and Charles had invited some of their Canadian neighbours and several of the officers to go with them to see the frozen Montmorency Falls. Captain Retallack took Fan in his sleigh, and arranged for his servant to drive so that he could 'speak' to her on his fingers. It says a great deal for the kindness and tact with which Fan was treated in Canada, that this is almost the only reference made to her handicap during the whole of her stay there.

> . . . I was so afraid of the *frightful* place going to the falls (you remember it, Henry), that I walked all the way to the falls from the high road, *up* and *down,* a very long walk. We lunched at a funny little inn some little way from the falls, and then went on to see the marvellous sliding. The cones are small this year. There is a nice little house made of ice, with tables, sofas, etc. Some of our party tobogined; how I wonder any Lady can do it as it is done there . . . It frightens me to watch it . . .

Elizabeth's nervousness was caused by the bad condition of the roads which were full of *cahots* (deep holes), and three of the sleighs upset on their way home. None of the party was hurt, and they all assembled for dinner at Spencer Wood.

'The roads are passable again, and so Papa can have his great sleigh to open Parliament. I *believe* I am to receive tomorrow after Papa's Parliamentary dinner,' Elizabeth told Henry on 19 February. As always, Charles had to read his Speech from the Throne twice, first in English and then in French. In his letters he showed that he sympathised with the French-Canadians' anxiety to conserve their traditions, language and culture; but on this occasion, he wrote to Henry: 'they gave me a tremendously long speech to read, and did I not wish *"notre langue"* at the bottom the sea!'

After telling Henry that eleven men had been killed by an explosion in the laboratory at the Artillery Barracks, that there had

165

been another wreck of a ship of the Canadian Line in which thirty lives were lost, and that one of the officers had been ill and was convalescing at Spencer Wood, Charles added: 'I want you, the next time you see Uncle Dick, to give him a piece of your hair, to have it put in the locket of a bracelet which I am going to give to Mrs. Retallack. It is to have in it Mama's hair, mine, yours, Fan's, Puss's and Stanley's.'

Richard Monck, who had married his cousin, 'Feo' Cole, in 1861, was now stationed in London and had recently been made brigade major. Charles and Elizabeth still expected him to be at their beck and call, to keep an avuncular eye on Henry and to execute their many and varied commissions – such as despatching sittings of pheasants' eggs to Ireland, in default of the 'two cocks and six or eight hens' – which could not have been easy to find in the environment of Chelsea Barracks. The comparatively simple task of designing a bracelet containing six locks of hair was occasioned by the imminent departure from Quebec of Captain Retallack, who was to join his regiment in April. The loss of his military secretary gave Charles the opportunity of providing yet another job for Dick, who was offered the post and accepted it.

This delightful plan for a family re-union was somewhat marred by the flat refusal of his wife Feo to cross the Atlantic. She hated and dreaded the sea, not only on her own account, but also on that of her baby son, Cecil, from whom she could not bear to be separated. However neither she nor her husband considered this sufficient reason for disobeying his elder brother's summons and thus, 'Colonel Monck tells me he is going out alone,' Mr. Cardwell wrote to Charles. Feo was not alone in shirking the voyage. When in that same year the delegates from Canada were presented to Queen Victoria, the Queen told them that, much as she longed to visit their country, she would never have the courage to cross the Atlantic.

After Parliament reassembled, there was little in the way of social chit-chat for Elizabeth to write either in her journal or in the covering notes to Henry:

> . . . There is no gaiety going on now, on account of its being Lent. I never was in any place where Lent was so well observed as here. It is very bad of members of the Church of England to leave the observance of Lent to the Romish Church, as if *they*

166

were the only people who should observe it. 'Protestants' have a way of excusing their own avoidance of what bores them by saying that it is *Romish* to do so and so. They ought to remember that they were originally *one Church,* and have the same creed, but it was the introduction of *some few errors* which separated the two Churches. There is nothing we are more apt to do, as to cheat our consciences by making false excuses when we do not wish to do something that is unpleasant to us. I should like you always to remember this – but do not think I mean to preach a Sermon.

God bless you my dearest Child,
Yr. fondest Mother, E.L.M.M.

I delight in the thought of the Pheasantry.

In another letter she congratulated him on having won a race, the first of many triumphs in that line during his school and university career. He had now 'settled down' at Eton only too well and was no longer the earnest, industrious, respectful little boy of a year earlier. Mr. Walford, his tutor, wrote that he was inclined to be 'a *leetle* unruly in class' and Henry himself informed his parents that:

> . . . Old Snow's wife is just dead and I am now up to the fellow I was up to my first half, Austen Leigh. I hope old Snow will not come in for some time as he is such an old brute and so dreadfully strict. I am still up to old Frewer in Mathematics and it is the finest fun in the world bullying him. I like being up to him very much as he affords great amusement to us, for we humbug him awfully . . . I had a fight the other day with a boy in this house. I think we had about 4 or 5 rounds. I came off *victorious*!! having succeeded in giving him an awful black eye!! This has been my first fight since I have been at Eton, and I hope if ever I have any more I shall be as successful as I was in this.'

His parents' replies to this letter were characteristic of them both:

> . . . I *suppose* it is quite right for boys to learn to box and fight, but to me it is horrid. Like the Roman Gladiators! However I am very glad you were victorious!

I need not say that I am ever thinking of you and praying for you; it is a solemn time, having Confirmation in view, and preparing for it. May God bless it to you.
Ever my dearest Child your fondest Mother.

Charles merely remarked that he was 'glad you had the best of your fight, but I advise you to have as few "rattles" as you can.' He may have been struck by the similarity between the behaviour of his schoolboy son and that of the members of his present government, a more than usually stormy session in Parliament having culminated in the fourth dissolution in two years. Charles had previously tried and failed to bring about 'a junction of the best men on both sides.'[1]

Now, in a memorandum to his Ministers, he stated his conviction that 'the time had come when an appeal might with propriety be made to the patriotism of gentlemen on both sides of the House to throw aside personal differences and unite in forming a Government strong enough to advance the general interests of the country.'[2] It was no mean feat to persuade life-long enemies to work together; the article quoted above gives Charles a large share of the credit in the forming of what came to be known as 'The Great Coalition'. His persistent refusal to 'govern by a party' had prevented him from becoming conspicuously popular with any one faction. But it had the result that, in a crisis like the present one, men of all parties knew that they could trust him, while many of them had come to know him well owing to his habit of encouraging them to visit him in his own home.

The forming of the Great Coalition was, in reality, a step towards the greatest project of all: a federation of all the provinces of British North America. A new incentive was given to this when, during the summer of 1864, Edward Cardwell succeeded the Duke of Newcastle as Secretary of State for the Colonies. Besides being a personal friend with whom Charles could correspond informally, he was already strongly in favour of the project. Accordingly in October representatives from all the British North American provinces attended a conference in Quebec and worked out a detailed scheme to be laid before the Imperial Government.

Notes to Chapter Twelve

1   Monck to Chichester Fortescue, 21 April 1864. P.R.O.
2   R. G. Trotter, 'Lord Monck and the Great Coalition' in *Canadian Historical Review*.

13

Feo's journal

During this summer in which Charles had been more than usually preoccupied in his public life, a change had taken place in his household. The family had been roused before breakfast by the arrival, accompanied by peals of merry laughter interspersed by little shrieks, of the Governor's cousin, sister-in-law, niece-by-marriage, all combined in one short, plump person encased in an outsize crinoline over a wire 'cage' – by the arrival, in short, of Feo.

'Feo and Dick arrived a little after 7 this morning,' Elizabeth wrote joyfully to her 'dearest Child', Henry. 'I think her looking so nice and well and *how pleasant* it is to have them both . . . Was it not *most extraordinary* Feo taking leave of Dick at Ryde, and Dick embarking at Liverpool, and Feo getting *immediately* so unhappy she made Blayney [Feo's schoolboy brother] take her to Queenstown* and sailed with him. Another passenger got out at Queenstown and forfeited his passage, he was so wretched. She says she would have got out at Queenstown if she had sailed from Liverpool. She told it all out at breakfast, *and there was such a shout* . . .

Feo's first act had been to set the breakfast-table in a roar with a highly-dramatised version of her welcome but unlooked-for presence. As usual several people had come to breakfast at Spencer Wood and were entertained by Feo's spirited account of her wild race from the Isle of Wight to Holyhead, accompanied by her young brother and a maid; the fog in the Irish Sea – 'We stopped in the middle of the sea and nearly ran down a brig'– and her husband's delight when she suddenly appeared among the crowd of emigrants who boarded the ship *Asia* at Queenstown. Then there was the terror

---

* Queenstown, now Cobh, the harbour at Cork, was so named when Queen Victoria landed there in 1849.

Colonel (later General) the Hon. Richard Monck.

and sea-sickness on the voyage; her first sight of the Northern lights; and the excitement when a Canadian passenger was arrested by a detective on landing at Boston, suspected of being a Confederate sympathiser and a blockade-runner. She and Dick had spent two nights and a day travelling by railway and river steamer since they landed at Boston, but Feo was quite ready to go for 'a lovely walk' in the grounds after breakfast. 'Oh! The beauty of this place! I can't

The Hon. Mrs. Richard 'Feo' Monck.

describe it,' she wrote in her next letter home; while Elizabeth was soon writing again to Henry: 'Feo is in the greatest force – *so charming,* and it does make *such a difference* to have them.'

Feo was a shocking snob. 'I can't tell you the bliss of seeing a Guardsman in this land', and 'It all seems so weird and odd – the Monck liveries, and everything like home, and to think we are across the Atlantic, at the other side of the world.' She was incurably frivolous, making no secret of her indifference both to politics and to world events. She was not, however, a complete bird-brain. She had been given a good education, and her diary shows that she could write good English. Before her marriage she had travelled with her parents in Germany, France, Spain and Belgium; her mother gave musical parties in their Knightsbridge house, and her father 'collected' writers, artists and actors. Nobody could have guessed, listening to her frivolous and sometimes futile conversation, that she had all her life been accustomed to intellectual society – nor that she had psychic powers. Her dislike of thunder-storms was not simply girlish panic; she was peculiarly sensitive to natural phenomena and could 'feel' an earthquake or earth tremor in a distant part of the world.

Her snobbishness was too naïve to be offensive and there is no doubt that her infectious gaiety acted like a tonic on her aunt's spirits. Elizabeth herself was not deficient in humour, but she needed someone to laugh *with*. Above all, accustomed to the companionship of many sisters, she had been feeling the lack of congenial feminine society. Feo had been reared in the same traditions as her own; and though there were twenty years between them, and though Feo called her 'Aunt Lizzy', their relationship was always to be that of sisters rather than of aunt and niece. It was such a help, too, to have Dick for instance when there were dinner parties every night as well as military displays and inspections, in honour of General and Lady Sarah Lindsay who had arrived with family and staff for a ten days' visit.

The Lindsays' visit was followed by the even longer one of Mr. and Mrs. Dundas.* The Moncks had promised to show them some of the famous views, and many excursions had been planned, as well as official dinner parties and a great reception and ball at Spencer Wood.

All this time, poor Elizabeth was having to deal with a domestic crisis, beginning with the death of one of the footmen. 'There has been such bother among the Servants,' she wrote to Henry –

> ... Just before poor James' death, Edward went away because he was told to go to Church. He said he would not go and be

---

* Governor of Prince Edward Island.

stuck up like a monkey at Church. It was the first time I ever heard of a monkey being at Church! Then Brock *could* not get a man who would do for footman in his place and had to make a footman of the pantry boy – *that* was instead of Edward, he has not *yet* replaced poor James. King then got drunk and abused Brock, and then said: "You know you can't do without me, you'll just have to go *skedaddling* thro' Quebec to look for a Servant"! To hear Brock stating the case to me! . . . It is rather a bother having all these people, only Feo is such a help. I am so hunted.

'Hunted' was the word Elizabeth used to describe having more to do than she could easily cope with, and at this time her niece was being a help to her psychologically as well as practically. Elizabeth had been taught self-discipline at an early age, and it was now an ingrained habit with her to conceal her personal troubles from those around her. Feo took the opposite line, emitting squeals of dismay at the heat – '92 degrees in the shade!' – ; at the mosquitoes and flies – 'like the plagues of Egypt' – ; at the frequent thunder-storms; at the bad roads and the alarmingly fresh horses; at the easy familiarity of some of the Canadians – '. . . The people out here are all hearty and kind, but their manners are quaint – I mean they are "hail-fellow-well-met" with you in one moment . . .' – and at her own social blunders. It was impossible to take the trials of daily life too seriously or too heavily while in her company, since she laughed at them and at herself even while she comically complained.

She followed her aunt's example in writing her letters home in the form of a 'journal', faithfully entering in it her sprightly comments and descriptions every day for a whole year. She described a fourteen-mile drive to Lake Beauport with the Dundases, and an excursion to Cap-Rouge: '. . . Oh! I never could tell you the beauty of the drive through the bush . . . then glimpses of the deep blue St. Lawrence, and the blue hills and green woods; it was all too beautiful.'

On the day of the reception and ball at Spencer Wood, she and Mrs. Dundas helped Fan, Puss and the maids to make wreaths and garlands of greenery 'mixed with bright flowers' to decorate the ballroom –

. . . The heat had been stifling all day, but the nights are cool here. The verandah was veiled in about 180 yards of fine white muslin, nailed down to keep out the mosquitos and insects, or ' bugs ' as the Yankees call them. The 17th band was outside the curtain. The verandah was lit up, and all the soldiers and their lights looked so very pretty. We assembled in Aunt L.'s [Aunt Lizzy's] sitting room, and then all walked in procession. Then the presentations began, and lasted a few minutes. The dresses were very good, and a few of the girls nice-looking; all were quiet. They all bowed *very* low to Aunt L, and two people backed out of the room. The couples all enter the room arm-in-arm, and some come up three abreast! . . . I danced all night, and enjoyed myself much . . . It was nice walking in the verandah between the dances. Fan went in to supper with old Sir E. Taché, and Louise [Puss] with old Cartier, two little old men, and they looked so funny. Mr. J. A. Macdonald took me in. When everyone was gone but our own party, Cartier and Colonel Gordon sang *The Cure* and most of the gentlemen danced it. Cartier jumped higher than anyone.

Several ministers came to another dinner party two evenings later: '.
'. . . We sang choruses; first a Canadian song, and then the Christy Minstrels; I also sang two solos. Mr. Cartier was enchanted; he sang the solo of the Canadian song . . . He is the funniest of little men, like a terrier.'

At the end of June the Governor and his party embarked on a tour which included Lennoxville College, the Eastern townships, Montreal and Ottawa. They were accompanied by two ministers, Alexander Galt and d'Arcy McGee. They made the first part of the journey by train, then continued their tour in a fleet of open wagons, and were met by a band of musicians as they entered each village. They crossed Lake Memphragog by steamer and spent the night at a hotel called the Mountain House, re-embarking at 7.30 a.m. next morning.

Feo noted that the Governor was received very well at Newport – 'though a Yankee town, gay with flags in honour of the 4th of July' – rather a tactless date to have chosen for a visit from Queen Victoria's representative. A large coach with six white horses carried them to Stanstead, a border town between Canada and the United States.

They lunched at the house of Mr. Knight, Member of Parliament for Stanstead – '. . . so thoroughly Yankee, stiff and unlived in, chairs all round the room, no books, no comfort, only show and stiffness and state . . . There were some speeches at lunch, and then we had to clear out, as all our servants had to feed in the dining room on what we had left.'

Snobbish Feo was more in her element when they arrived at Montreal, where their train was met by General Lindsay and his staff, with a guard of honour of Grenadiers. There were four days of ceremonial functions, including a trooping of the colour on the Champ de Mars and a concert at the Convent school where Elizabeth 'presented prizes most gracefully, and the G.G. made a very good speech.' The Governor and his party were invited to stay by Sir Fenwick Williams on his 'heavenly island', the Île d'Orval.

> . . . We all got into carriages and drove a long way to La Chine, the embarking place. We were rowed across, in the General's barge, by the Grenadier soldiers.
>
> The island is almost covered with primeval forest and green grass, only one road in it. The house is a red brick cottage with four bedrooms in it. Most of the gentlemen were in tents, and the four maids slept in one out-house room together.
>
> . . . The General had a *horn* blown every morning to call us to breakfast . . . He gave each of the ladies a rose-bud every morning.

While Charles and Elizabeth went on to Ottawa, Feo and Dick remained in Montreal where parties were given for them. They all arrived back at Spencer Wood in the middle of a heat wave – '96 degrees in the shade' – with thunder-storms which sent Feo scuttling to the cellar.

> . . . Mr. Stanley* arrived to stay with a letter [of introduction] from his father. He has 'strong Northern proclivities', has been travelling all over the North [of the United States], and gave a frightful account of the way the South treat their slaves, and showed a photo of a slave's back frightfully lacerated. He

* Unidentified. Possibly the son of Lord Stanley of Alderley.

says he saw some emancipated slaves, some of them *brutish* still, but some happy.

On a later occasion Feo was told –

> . . . how very kind the Southerners are to their slaves; they are just as we are with our servants, and till lately a Northerner would not *speak* to a black . . . *Uncle Tom's Cabin* has done much mischief. One can't believe what Mrs. B. Stowe says, as she was only a short time in the South.

Feo was favourably impressed by the behaviour of the Roman Catholic children who came, with the Vicaire-Général, to a school feast at Spencer Wood: 'I never saw so nice and orderly a set. The children were half Irish and half French-Canadians, some of the latter looking like Indians, almost quite black, with round Indian eyes.' They were a pleasant contrast to the children from the English-speaking school, who had attended a separate school-treat and shocked Feo by their bad manners.

Her 'journal' did not meet the same fate as Elizabeth's, but was treasured by her doting father, Owen Cole, who had ten copies privately printed under the title, *My Canadian Leaves*.[1] It is a purely personal narrative and she entirely ignored the momentous affairs which were taking place around her, except in so far as they interfered with her social engagements or her physical comfort. 'A ministerial crisis, so the G.G. [Governor General] can't come,' she wrote on 15 June before setting out on a seven-hour expedition, thus lightly dismissing the collapse of the Ministry. The series of political crises in June 1864, had taken place at the same time as the receptions and dinners at Spencer Wood so much enjoyed by Feo. The conferences which led to the 'Great Coalition' had coincided with the Dundas visit; and an eve-of-Waterloo atmosphere had pervaded the reception and ball on 16 June.

The social activity at Government House had its uses. Ministers and members of the Assembly would meet each other at dinner there and discuss their problems informally. Oblivious that Canadian history was being made, Feo described these evenings with her usual twittering inconsequence. She saw no significance in Charles' having craftily introduced George Brown to her on 18 June as 'one of the new Ministers', showing that he took it for granted that Brown would consent to enter the Coalition cabinet. However, she was a great asset at the Moncks' parties, since it was impossible to be stiff or shy in her presence. Men of all ages enjoyed cracking a joke with Feo, who did not mind being laughed at, and was never so happy as when she was being teased by 'the gentlemen'. 'Flies are very impertinent; they love handsome women's blood,' old Sir Etienne Taché told her gallantly when she complained of the insect life.

Henry and Mr. Wilkinson arrived in July in time to join his family and their friends in a trip down river in the government steam-ship, *Queen Victoria*. Their first stop was Rivière du Loup where Stanley had been sent with Fräulein Denneler during the hottest part of the summer. From there the ship cruised in and out of the bays and tributary rivers, the party sleeping each night on board and making daily expeditions in canoes and rowing-boats, the boatmen singing traditional Canadian songs. After visiting an Indian settlement, they went on to Tadoussac where Elizabeth was given a bouquet by the priest-in-charge of a Catholic chapel, on the site of the first Christian church ever built in Canada.

Fishing was the main object of the expedition and on one day they caught 162 trout in the Marguerite river. Sitting on the bank, they lunched off the fresh trout cooked over an open fire, with wild raspberries and blueberries for dessert. Feo's inevitable adventures and mishaps had provided comic relief for the rest of the party; any boat she was in was sure to stick on a sandbank or nearly capsize. There were plenty of men to come to her rescue or to soothe her when she shrieked, though none took such care of her as her schoolboy cousin – 'dear, kind Henry'.

Back at Spencer Wood, she wrote of 'very large dinner-parties' nearly every night, and a non-stop succession of house parties. Sometimes people turned up without any warning and had to be put up for the night. Henry was confirmed in Quebec, soon after which came the sad day when Elizabeth with her four children embarked in the *Peruvian*. 'This dreadful day I shan't forget in a hurry,' wrote Feo –

> . . . We got up at 7.15 with terrible wind and rain beating against the windows, and everything looking the picture of desolation and despair. We went on board the *Peruvian* with

the travellers and, having inspected the cabin, we all sat together in the saloon before the ship started. At last the bell rang, and we took leave. We then stayed in the wind and rain to see the ship move off into the river. How terrible it is to see a ship move off for so long a voyage! I thought so of 'Gone' when I saw the ropes undone, and she moved slowly off. Then we drove home; the house is so sad and deserted; it is bitterly cold to add to everything else.

In the evening –

> . . . Fires blazed in every room, and everyone cold! The small table at dinner was by no means a cheering sight, and the misery of the animals was sad to see.

Charles, who always hated being separated from his family, tried to speak cheerfully of his impending leave, and of how quickly the time would pass until the spring when he was to join them. But – 'I am to be alone all the winter,' he had written sorrowfully to Lord Lyons when confirming the dates for the Ambassador's second private visit to Spencer Wood.

Lord Lyons, with his attachés, arrived at Spencer Wood on 21 September. A peace-loving, cultured man, he was also a shrewd diplomat. Charles Monck liked and admired him, respecting the alert intelligence and sound judgment by which he steered Anglo-American relations through the stormy years of the American civil war. While relaxing on holiday, the Ambassador showed a different side of his character, and it is hard to recognise the level-headed diplomat in the portrait of him which emerges from the pages of Feo's journal.

On Lord Lyons' first visit to the Moncks, he and Elizabeth had been greatly taken with each other; but his disappointment at having missed her by a fortnight was made up for by the presence of her niece. Feo was the perfect antidote to the strains and stresses imposed on him by his post. In many ways her artless prattle was more soothing to the harassed Ambassador than Elizabeth's informed sympathy would have been. He excelled at the sort of sprightly badinage in which Feo revelled, and after dinner preferred her card-table, at which 'Old Maid' was succeeded by 'Grab', rather than join the whist players. From the first day of his visit, she firmly took him under her wing, and was by his side during the many excursions arranged to amuse him. They saw the waterfalls at Chaudière and at Shawinigan; visited sawmills at work and watched the timber being shot down slides into the water; and the *Queen Victoria* took them down the St. Lawrence river to St. Anne's: 'Lord L. hates ships and water as much as I do . . . He was in bliss at getting out of the ship.' Feo was equally terrified when they travelled by road – 'on dirt roads, which are no roads,' she complained. She squealed and clutched at the reins when the waggons jumped and skidded, and Lord Lyons recited poetry to calm her, and talked to her about books, confessing that he never travelled without a copy of *Cranford*. 'He told me a funny story about Mr. Lincoln.* He is always running off with the umbrellas of other people, and one day he wanted one, and said to his boy aged about seven, "Go and get my umbrella from the hall." The boy returned without one saying, "Father, I guess the owner's been round."'

Lord Airlie was also staying at Spencer Wood, and Feo reported 'a large dinner party' every night. She neither knew nor cared anything about Canadian politics, and was equally indifferent to either the reason for or progress of the American civil war. Her references to 'a grand ball' and 'a drawing room' in honour of delegates from the Maritime Provinces are typical examples of her inconsequent attitude to anything which did not concern her personally. In fact the assembly of delegates was nothing less than the Quebec Conference, one of the most momentous events in Canadian history, since the foundation was then laid for the present Constitution of the Dominion of Canada.

On 20 October 1864, when the Quebec Conference was in full swing, the Governor received a telegram informing him of the most serious threat to British neutrality that had yet taken place. A band of southern Americans had crossed the border and used Canadian territory to make a raid on the United States town of St. Albans, where they held up and robbed the banks of 200,000 dollars before retreating across the frontier. Monck immediately ordered out the militia, who captured thirteen of the raiders and 19,000 dollars of the stolen money. The American papers praised the Governor's prompt action, and Seward, the United States Secretary of State, wrote to

* President of the United States.

thank him for it. 'It is so clearly to the interest of the United States to appreciate the fairness of your dealings with them,' wrote Cardwell, in his reply to Monck's report on the incident.

In spite of this, Seward gave the necessary six months' notice for the abrogation of the 1817 Convention limiting armaments on the Great Lakes. At the same time, the United States Commander, General Dix, issued a proclamation ordering his troops to cross the Canadian frontier in pursuit of marauders, in the event of further 'outrages'. Dix himself told Lord Lyons of the order, and the Ambassador protested privately to Seward. 'Mr. Seward's answer to Lyons appears to me very uncandid and evasive,' Monck wrote to Cardwell –

> . . . I do not believe the order was acted on, nor have I heard that any infringement of our territorial rights (by the United States army) occurred, but I must say it is too bad of Mr. Seward, after having *volunteered* a Despatch thanking me for my conduct in this very affair, – to speak in the present note as if no precautionary measures had been adopted by the Canadian Govt. . .
>
> The examination before the magistrate (in Montreal) respecting the St. Albans people has not yet ended, and no warrant for their extradition can issue until they are committed.[2]

Anglo-American relations were gradually simmering down to their former uneasy but unbroken state, when the judge at Montreal, without consulting the Attorney General, dismissed the case against the Southern raiders, and released them.

M. Cartier brought the news to Spencer Wood. Feo described the scene when Charles Monck, urgently summoned, left the dinner table remarking facetiously: 'I suppose this is an invasion of the Yankees!' But he soon learnt that it was no joking matter. He and Cartier were joined by John A. Macdonald, Langevin and Macdougall . . . 'John A.'s appearance was grotesque,' Feo commented, 'with his hair flying in all directions, like a Spanish caricature. The fuss was great fun.' She was the only person to be amused by the incident which inflamed anti-British feeling in America even more than the original raid had done. Monck called out 2,000 volunteers and reinforced the policing of the frontier; five of the raiders were re-arrested; and once again the United States Government was persuaded that its opposite number in Canada had not been responsible for what had appeared to be a deliberate act of defiance.

Far from hindering the discussions on confederation, the raid which so nearly resulted in war gave fresh impetus to those delegates who believed the future strength of their country to lie in legislative union. The Canadian Premier, Sir Etienne Taché, presented to the Governor General the seventy-two resolutions which became known as 'The Quebec Scheme', and which, with certain modifications, formed the basis of the British North American Act. The scheme would be submitted to the five Provincial Parliaments on the opening of their next sessions early in 1865; after which it would have to be approved and passed by the Imperial Government.

Notes to Chapter Thirteen

1   Frances Monck, *My Canadian Leaves* (ed. W. L. Morton, Toronto). Feo would be surprised to find one of the original copies of her 'journal' in the British Museum today, and *'My Canadian Leaves* by Frances Monck' included in the bibliographies of twentieth-century works by Canadian historians, as well as in the enry on Monck in the *Dictionary of National Biography*.

2   Monck to Cardwell. Private letter, 14 November 1864. Windsor Castle Archives.

14

'The Botheration Scheme'

On 20 January 1865, Charles wrote to Henry: 'I opened Parliament yesterday, and I hope most sincerely it is the last *Canadian* Parliament that will ever assemble. I trust next year we shall have the Parliament of the Union.' Expecting the session to be a short one, he foresaw nothing to prevent him from going home in May, as arranged, for several months' leave. Cardwell had written to warn him that, owing to the continued strained relations with the United States, his leave might have to be postponed; to which Charles replied: 'I think you overestimate the chance of misunderstanding with the United States, and also of the benefit of my presence here should any arise.' He continued to hope for his release; and when, on 11 March, the Quebec Resolutions were passed by the Canadian Parliament by a majority of ninety-one to thirty-three, and Cardwell's invitation to send a deputation to England was accepted, it seemed certain that he would be in London during the discussions. On 1 April, Cardwell was still writing of his hope of having Monck with him at that time, referring to the fact that the Governor had been at his post uninterruptedly for three-and-a-half years; yet, a fortnight later, he withdrew the permission he had so nearly given. 'I cannot venture to say "Come", in answer to your expression of your wish to be here. Looking at all that is going on around you, I think your presence at this moment in Canada could not be spared.'[1]

Cardwell had more than one reason for cancelling Monck's leave. On Saturday 15 April, Feo noted in her journal: 'The news has just come in of Lincoln's death by stabbing; it took place in the theatre last night. Is it not too horrible? What will happen next? He kept off war with England always . . . What will become of America?'

Early in the same month the main army of the American southern States capitulated. The British had believed President Lincoln to be

182

the chief advocate of peace between his country and their own; and now, with the southern army defeated, the northern army was free to invade Canada if provocation should arise. Meanwhile Lord Lyons had resigned his post at Washington, having become so seriously ill that he was unable to carry on until his successor, Sir Frederick Bruce, arrived. Feo had heard rumours that 'the people here are terrified at the idea of the G.G. going home when everything is unsettled, and Lord Lyons gone.'

Charles had told Cardwell that he thought the Colonial Office exaggerated the value of his presence in Canada when relations with the United States were unsettled. He himself, Charles declared, had perfect confidence in General Sir John Michel, who would act as administrator in his absence. This may have been modesty, perhaps coupled with a very natural desire to take part in the discussions in London on confederation, as well as to join his wife and family. Or was he really unaware of the confidence and sense of security he inspired by the fact that he had been *persona grata* with the late President Lincoln and also, which was far more difficult, with the American Secretary of State, William Seward? His sister-in-law bewailed the 'G.G.'s' lack of sympathy with herself, her husband Dick and the young aides-de-camp in their fervent wish that the southern army might win; because, declared Feo, only in the South can 'gentlemen' be found. 'We get so angry with the G.G.,' she complained. But whatever his private feelings may have been, the Governor General never forgot that he represented Her Majesty's government, and that as such he could not have diplomatic exchange with any American power except the existing government in Washington.

During those years there was a very real danger of war between Britain and the United States, whose army was then the strongest in the world, and whose first objective would be a mass invasion of Canada. Owing to the rash actions of hot-headed southern sympathisers, there were times when war seemed unavoidable. That this disaster was averted was largely due to Lord Lyons, the physically frail but indomitable British Ambassador in Washington. But at the time credit for it was also given to Monck, as is proved by letters of the period and allusions to his tactful dealings with American heads of state.

Later in 1865, Cardwell wrote that present relations with the

United States might make it 'objectionable' that Monck should be absent from Quebec. 'It will certainly render it, I think, impossible that you should be absent long.' In retrospect, C. P. Stacey[2] wrote of Monck: 'It is not too much to say that he deserves to be remembered, along with Lord Lyons and Charles Francis Adams [United States Ambassador in London] . . . as having made a great contribution towards preventing what would have been from every point of view a most shocking catastrophe.'

Everyone else seemed to be going on leave – Arthur Gordon in June, and the Richard Moncks on 20 May. When the latter date was fixed, Feo was thrown into a state of agitation, uncertain whether to be glad or sorry. 'Of course I am *enchanted* to see you all again,' she wrote to her parents,

> . . . but at present I am thinking too much of the horrors of the passage to realize anything else. I said last night at dinner that I hoped it would not be supposed at home that I knew anything about the American war, because I know *nothing*. The G.G. advised me to say – 'The *Times* is wrong,' then people would be shocked for a few minutes at my presumption. Then I am to say – 'I have been in America, and saw it with my own eyes!'

A guest at dinner tried to calm her fears of the vogage by quoting Sir Samuel Cunard who had said that the reason the ships of his line were so safe was that they were 'well prayed over'.

When Elizabeth and her children had left Canada in September, it was on the understanding that Charles would follow them in the spring. It was the first time in twenty years that he and his wife had been separated for more than a few days and, knowing how disappointed she would be over the postponement of his leave, he was glad to hear that Henry was spending his Easter holidays with her in Paris. Elizabeth had rented a house at Versailles where the girls' education was continued by visiting masters, and Stanley's by Fräulein Denneler. 'Aunt E.', Charles Monck's sister, accompanied them on sight-seeing expeditions, including the one on which the French coachman had been so drunk that he had 'fallen off the box', and their own footman, John, had driven them home. Unaware of the bad news on the way, Elizabeth had written cheerfully to Henry in March:

. . . I hope the time will pass quickly until we are all together again. Papa may soon be able to name a time for coming. I trust the federation will be carried, as there seems every prospect of. I have been reading the debate on the defences of Canada.

We are all going on the same way – masters, Church, etc. Stanley is so much a better child, I am happy to say, & his education is making progress.

I am longing to know when I may have the happiness of seeing you. Take care to know *exactly* to what *day* the Easter holidays last, that there may be no mistake . . .

I suppose being in the 5th form gives you more things to do with money. Anything you tell Papa about *that,* he will be sure to enter into, only my dearest Child, let *nothing* induce you to go beyond your allowance, or to go into debt. If you have not money to pay for anything, *exercise self-control & do without it.* I think F. Burrowes* is a good example of that. Surrounded by expensive young men, & he with *so* little money, only what he earns, & he never goes beyond. Always remember the misery your Uncle Croker** has brought on *every one* belonging to him, for want of self-control to do without what he could not pay for.

God bless you my dearest Child.'

Meanwhile the confederation scheme, which had been passed by the Canadian Parliament, was meeting a certain amount of opposition in New Brunswick and Nova Scotia. One of the Nova Scotian newspapers referred to it as 'The Botheration Scheme'.

Elizabeth's next letter to Henry broke the sad news that 'Papa sees no hope of coming over before July.' She dwelt particularly on the fact that he would not be able to 'come to London'. She was not, as might be supposed, referring to his absence from the Canadian Ministers' negotiations with Cardwell, but to a more personal matter. Having never doubted that Charles would be with them in May, at the latest, it had long been settled that Fan should be presented at the Queen's Drawing Room held during that month. She was in her twentieth year and the ceremony could no longer be

* Her cousin, Francis Burrowes, was employed in a civil service post in Canada.
** Edward Croker had married Elizabeth's younger sister, Lady Georgina Monck.

delayed, though it would now have to take place without the support of her father. This was the reason for Elizabeth's especial distress on Fan's account. In spite of the girl's courageous disregard for her handicap, and her determination to lead and thoroughly enjoy a normal life, her presentation at Court and her *début* in London society were bound to be something of an ordeal even if, like the other débutantes, she were to be accompanied by both her parents. In the meantime, Henry's arrival in Paris did a good deal towards cheering them, and it was arranged that he was to act as escort to his mother and sisters when they travelled to London. 'I know you will be a great comfort to Mama at Paris, and will take good care of her coming over,' Charles wrote to him.

> . . . I want you, next time you write, to tell me particularly how you thought Mama was looking. She rather frightened me in her last letter by complaining of the heat, and I want to know what you thought about her . . .
>
> I suppose you will sometimes get leave to run up to London while Mama stays there. I daresay you will see little Cartier cutting about London, as he arrived there I think this week . . .
>
> Don't forget what I asked you about Mama.

In his letter of 17 April, he had written:

> . . . I think the South is what they call here - 'pretty nearly played out!'. The surrender of Gen. Lee's army is very nearly a coup de grâce to their chances of success. I am very glad of it. I think the rebellion was unjustified in the first instance, and the object of the South certainly was the maintenance of slavery with which I could have no sympathy . . .

'I dare say you will see Dick almost as soon as you get this,' he wrote on 19 May. 'He will go on to London to be with Mama, but I think Feo will stay in Dublin.'

The Richard Moncks landed at Greencastle, in Ireland, early on the morning of 30 May, and were in Dublin by six o'clock that evening. Their little son, Cecil, was with Feo's mother, Fanny Cole, at her house in Leeson Street. Fanny had also temporarily taken charge of Stanley, while Elizabeth and her daughters were living it up in London. Feo had remained in Dublin with her mother and her child while the obliging Dick hurried on to London to look after Elizabeth who, soon afterwards, moved into a house in Eaton Square belonging to a distant connection. Short of being present himself, Charles had done his best to smooth the way for his wife in the matter of presenting their deaf-mute daughter, with the result that, on 8 May, the Lord Chamberlain had written a private letter to Elizabeth:

> Dear Lady Monck – I had the pleasure of receiving a few days since a letter from Lord Monck, and I have the honour to inform you that I have received the Queen's Commands to invite your Ladyship and Miss Monck to a Ball at Buckingham Palace on the 16th Instant, and I would venture to observe that it would of course be consistent[?] that Miss Monck should be presented at the evening Drawingroom of the 18th Inst.
>
> I have also been commanded to send an invitation for Her Majesty's Reception at Buckingham Palace on the 15th Inst.[3]

Fan wrote to her father an account of these functions in which Puss was not included, her own presentation being deferred to the following year, though she joined in many of the gaieties. Henry wrote to Charles that 'Mama and Sisters' had been down to Eton for the Fourth of June, the celebrations for which had actually taken place on the Sixth, the Fourth having fallen on a Sunday that year. It was the first time since he went to Eton that he had had his family with him on the 'Fourth', and he may have been over-excited and showing off a little to his older sisters, which would account for the letter Elizabeth wrote him next day:

> My dearest Child. – You are such a good child to me, and such a comfort to me, I want you to do one thing for me – to do it now for my sake. You *will* see the benefit of it, and see, I trust, the *necessity* for *rules* and the duty involved in keeping them.
>
> Will you, to please me, not go to the tap . . . drinking beer between meals comes to be a *real* bad habit. I remember the present Lord Clonmell, as nice a looking youth as any I saw yesterday – he began by taking glasses of beer between meals – we used to laugh at him – he went from one thing to another,

and is now *insane* from drink, taken care of by your grand-father's old servant, *Starr*.

Another thing I ask from you, is not to get into the habit of betting. No words could express the misery that I have known result from that habit.

Knowing that there is nothing I would not *do* or *give up* for *you,* will you do those two things for me.

How I enjoyed yesterday.

How I shall enjoy Saturday and Sunday, please God.

The awful example of this warning against drinking between meals, was the 3rd Earl of Clonmell who died a few months later. Naturally Elizabeth did not then know that his youngest daughter, Edith Scott, was to become her dearly-loved daughter-in-law. The next Saturday and Sunday were to be one of the occasions on which Henry 'managed to run up to London and see Mama' as his father had hoped he would.

In all his letters to Henry, Charles showed that he was continually thinking of his wife and children, following their movements with affectionate interest and with a certain degree of anxiety –

. . . When you see Mama, give her a scolding from me for getting up so early in the morning after having been up late at night . . .

I hope you do not smoke much because you are really too young, and many fellows hurt their health by smoking at an early age. Indeed I should much rather, while you are at Eton, that you did not smoke or do anything against the regulations of the place . . .

I hear great accounts from London where Mama and the girls seem to be amusing themselves very well.

The time spent in London was ostensibly for the sake of 'amusing' the girls, but there is no doubt that Elizabeth, too, was thoroughly enjoying herself. During that summer there was a good deal of excitement over the general election in which the Liberal govern-ment was returned; added to which, in political circles at least, Canada was 'in the news', partly owing to the continuing threat of war with the United States, and partly as a result of the interest aroused by the proposed scheme of union. Political hostesses vied with each other in entertaining the visiting Canadian ministers, and Elizabeth received a certain amount of reflected glory as the wife of the Governor General. She did not, however, confine either her friendships or her acquaintances to the social-political circles. She was the reverse of what is now called a 'name-dropper', and was not in the habit of keeping the letters she received. The fact that some of them have survived is due to her encouragement of one of Fan's hobbies, which was the collection and careful arrangement in albums of autographs, crests and photographs – the latter being still something of a novelty. A packet of miscellaneous letters, forgotten or perhaps rejected by Fan, somehow escaped destruction, and these show that Elizabeth knew and corresponded with contemporary writers, artists and musicians. She was also very faithful in seeking out and keeping in touch with people who had been friends of her childhood but who were now in 'reduced' circumstances. 'I think Mama intended to leave London about the 22nd [June], but perhaps she may stay a little longer,' Charles wrote to Henry, and his forecast was correct. On 24 June, Sir Julius Benedict wrote: 'Dear Lady Monck, – I shall be very happy to give Miss Monck a lesson on Tuesday next at eleven o'clock if perfectly convenient.'[4] Puss could not be allowed to miss the opportunity of being given a singing lesson from a man who was then considered a celebrated musician, and this entailed their remaining in London until after 27 June.

By this time poor Dick had been allowed to return to his wife and to the child whom he had scarcely seen. Charles' next commission to him was to buy a horse for Henry whose old pony was now too small for him. Charles had arranged for him to have one of the home-bred colts, but the agent, Henry Sandys, reported that it would not be sufficiently schooled for him to ride during the holidays. Early in July, Elizabeth tore herself and her daughters away from London and crossed to Ireland.

'I am greatly afraid that I shall not be able to get home before your holidays begin,' Charles had written to Henry in June; then, a month later: 'I am afraid you will have returned to Eton before I get home.' Again and again, permission to go on leave had been given, then retracted owing to hostile threats from America. It was not till 16 September that he was able to name a definite date. He was to sail on the 26th in the *Himalaya,* he told Henry, expecting to land at Portsmouth on 9 or 10 October. 'I shall telegraph to you on landing, and I suppose you will have no difficulty in getting leave to come up and meet me in London. I shall be in too great a hurry to get home to allow of my going down to Eton, as I shall be busy with Cardwell, etc., all the time I stay in London. I shall go to Thomas' Hotel in Berkeley Square.' His hurry to get home was the greater since Cardwell had written again to say that the leave must be very short, instead of the several months for which Charles had hoped. It was more than a year since he had seen his wife and children, and he had been away from home for exactly four years.

Notes to Chapter Fourteen

1   Cardwell to Monck, April 1865. Monck Papers.
2   C. P. Stacey, *The Dalhousie Review* (London, 1934).
3   From Monck Papers, in possession of Mr. J. J. McCann.
4   Sir Julius Benedict to Elizabeth Monck. From Monck Papers in possession of Mr. J. J. McCann.
    Sir Julius Benedict, 1804-1885. Conductor and composer. Conducted in Vienna, Naples, Lyceam; and Drury Lane, London. Accompanied Jenny Lind on American tour, 1850. For many years conducted the Norwich Festival. *D.N.B.*

15

'We'll go and conquer Canada'*

Lord Palmerston, the Prime Minister, died on 18 October 1865.
Charles had arrived in London in time to attend the funeral, after
which he got through his business with the Colonial Office as
quickly as possible, and at last returned to Charleville. He had
settled with Cardwell for three months' leave, which was not long for
all he wanted to do in Ireland; for catching up on four years' arrears
of estate business, and seeing his numerous friends and relations. In
November he and his family drove to County Westmeath and spent
a few days at Barbavilla, the home of Elizabeth's widowed brother-
in-law, William Smythe, and of her four unmarried sisters, Anne,
Louisa, Harriet and Mary. Charles had a day's rather indifferent
shooting with one of William's neighbours before he and his party
journeyed on, by road, to spend a week at Garbally in County
Galway. While they were there, Elizabeth wrote to Henry: 'This was
my mother's old home where she and her brothers and sisters spent
their childhood . . . I went to see one of her cousins [at Woodlawn],
and we talked much of her and of her holy life.' The present Lord
Clancarty was Elizabeth's first cousin, though belonging more to her
mother's generation than to her own. His eldest son took Charles
snipe-shooting, and to visit the model farm of the county – ' . . .
which is quite wonderful. He showed us 496 beasts tied up to fatten
in one yard, the house all lighted with gas and everything about them
as clean and nice as possible. This is only *one* farm. He told me that
he has altogether 2,400 beasts in the stalls fattening. He has also a
large horse-breeding establishment and showed us a great number of
very promising young horses . . . I do not intend to shoot at all in
Charleville until you come home.' They went back to Charleville in
time for Henry's holidays and for the 'Christmas together at home'
to which they had so long looked forward.

* Marching song of the American Fenians.

191

Cardwell had arranged with Charles that the three months were to be considered as a little on account towards the far longer period of leave owing to him; and when he left Ireland in January 1866, it was understood that he would be back again before the summer. He therefore decided against his wife and daughters making the expensive double journey for such a short time, and only his brother Dick was with him when he embarked in the *Australasia*. Before going on board at Queenstown, Charles wrote a farewell letter to his 'dearest Fan and Puss': 'God bless and keep you both, my own precious children, and make you a comfort to Mama while I am away from her.' They landed at New York on 9 February and Charles wrote to Henry from Brevoort House, New York:

> . . . We had a very good passage, though rather slow in consequence of head winds. The *Australasia* is a very fine ship and is the most comfortable passenger ship I have ever been in. I never missed a meal the whole voyage, and had my tub every morning as regularly as if I were on shore. We had only one very cold day, but that day all the rigging was covered with ice and the sea *smoking* from the cold. Dick was a very bad sailor on the voyage, but is quite well now. Judging from its present appearance, New York is not a very inviting place. The streets are full of snow half-melted so that it is bad both for wheels and runners. I mean to remain at Montreal till the time for the meeting of Parliament.

The session was to take place, for the first time, in the new Houses of Parliament in Ottawa, which Trollope had described in 1861 as 'a town still to be built on a river of that name.'[1] The choice of Ottawa as the seat of government was very unpopular with the majority of the parliamentarians. The decision had been made as a compromise between the claims of Upper and Lower Canada. George Brown wrote scathing criticisms of the site in general, and of Rideau Hall, the future Government House, in particular: 'The Governor General's residence is a miserable little house . . . To patch up that building will cost more than a new one.'[2]

Nevertheless the Government decided to patch up, or rather make an extensive addition to, the existing 'miserable little house', and the work on it was in full swing when Charles and his staff moved into the original Rideau Hall on 2 May 1866. 'We were all agreeably surprised by this house,' he wrote from Ottawa on the day after they arrived there. 'It is small as far as the *number* of rooms is concerned, but the rooms are all good and they have been papered and painted and furnished, so that everything is clean and comfortable.' Every week he wrote of the good progress the workmen were making with

Left to right: The Hon. Richard Monck, Captain Pemberton and Charles, 4th Viscount Monck.

the new building, and what an 'excellent house' it was going to be. He also thought there were great possibilities in 'the place', which to anyone from County Wicklow meant the grounds in which the house stood. 'It requires a good deal done to it, and I mean to set them to work at once so as to have it *decent* before I bring Mama here.' He was pathetically anxious that 'Mama' should form a favourable impression, knowing that his family had heard continual grumbles from their political friends in Quebec, about the move to Ottawa. 'I think you will like Ottawa pretty well,' he told Henry, 'as there is very good boating on the river.' He wrote frequently of the splendid rides which could be had in the surrounding country which was 'very well cleared and settled', and far from complaining of the dirt roads, mentioned them as a particular advantage for horsemen, since 'none of them have been macadamized and you can go as fast as you like.'

Extra land had been added to the grounds of Government House, so as to give access to the river. Dick and Captain Pemberton had both acquired boats, while Charles solved the difficulty of the bad road into Ottawa by going there each morning 'in a six-oar policeboat . . . the crew all dressed man-of-war fashion . . . in regular sailors' shirts and white hats, and they look very smart. We have an awning to the boat which makes it very comfortable in the sun. It is a great luxury, as we can land close to the public buildings and it saves us the dusty road in hot weather.' He admitted that the flies and mosquitoes seemed more numerous there than at Spencer Wood, but was confident that mosquito-netting over the blinds would defeat them. His philosophic outlook set the tone for his staff, and Captain Pemberton obligingly gave up his bedroom and slept in a tent when Admiral Sir James Hope spent a night at Rideau Hall 'and there was not a single spare room in which to put him.'

'All the members are dead tired of this place already, it certainly is not lively,' he wrote to Henry in June and, after Parliament recessed, he confessed that he was glad to be back at Spencer Wood after the cramped conditions in which he and his staff had lived at Rideau Hall. 'However,' he reiterated, 'the new house, when it is finished, will be very comfortable.'

It had been understood that Charles would return to Ireland for the rest of his leave as soon as the Canadian Parliament rose. In fact, he did not get home until the following December. Confederation had been carried in Nova Scotia and, at long last, in New Brunswick. But it was the threat of invasion which had finally convinced the anti-confederationists of the necessity for union.

Throughout the spring Sir Frederick Bruce, Lord Lyons' successor at Washington, had been writing to warn Charles of the possibility of attack by members of the Fenian Brotherhood in America. The Brotherhood was an underground movement in Ireland which looked to America to help them fight on Irish soil for political independence. It was only certain of their leaders who were in favour of attacking Britain through Canada. These were Irish-Americans whose parents had emigrated during and after the Great Famine, and who had been brought up on their parents' bitter memories of the ill-treatment of Ireland by the English. In the American civil war they had formed a considerable part of the northern army, now disbanded, and were experienced and well-trained soldiers. The situation was summed up in one of their marching songs:

> Many a battle has been fought
> Along with the boys in blue,
> So we'll go and conquer Canada
> For we've nothing else to do.[3]

Charles had proved in past years, and was to prove in the future, that he sympathised strongly with Irish resentment of the mis-government which had caused so much suffering in Ireland. But for the present his duty was to Canada, now again threatened by invasion, and he would not leave the country until the danger was past. He was in close and constant communication with all preparations for defence, including those on the Upper Lakes and in the St. Lawrence river. 'Pray take care of your own personal safety,' warned Sir Frederick Bruce.* 'Assassination to produce confusion is a means to which these people would resort. It would be a serious publick calamity were anything to happen to you during this crisis, for I think Seward would do more for you than for most men in your position.'[4]

Fears for his personal safety were also expressed in letters to

---

* British Ambassador in Washington.

Charles from his son, who had been 'very much frightened' by rumours published in English newspapers. Charles replied reassuringly, emphasising the thoroughness of preparations being made against an attack which he did not believe would come. 'There are to be three ships of war in the St. Lawrence to protect us from the Fenians!' Charles told Henry, treating the matter lightly, and passing straight on the good news from Charleville that '"Fleda" is in foal this year. I hope she will continue to breed, as her foals turn out so well.'

In April Bruce wrote that, according to reports he had received, the Fenians were on the wane.[5] In consequence, when 'a force of between 800 and 900 Fenians crossed the Frontier from Buffalo to Fort Erie on the morning of June 1st,'[6] they out-numbered the body of volunteers who attacked them at Limestone Ridge, and who were forced to fall back 'under heavy fire'.[7] Reinforcements of regular troops were rushed to the spot, but the Fenians had retreated across the border before they arrived, leaving sixty-five prisoners in the hands of the volunteers. This enterprise had been intended to be the spear-head of an invasion on a larger scale, and there were reports that forces amounting to 10,000 Fenians – veterans of the civil war – with arms and ammunition, were assembling at different points on the American side of the frontier. Charles told Cardwell that he believed this to be an exaggeration, that 5,000 would be nearer the mark, although there was no doubt that a large-scale attack had been planned.

'The American Government behaved very well about the Fenians,' he told Henry, to whom he had been writing regularly since the invasion,

> . . . They stopped the men coming, seized their arms and arrested their bodies. At the same time we had a large force waiting for them . . . I think we should have beaten them easily enough even if the U.S. people had not interfered, but then it would have cost much money and probably bloodshed too.

In the 'Battle of Limestone Ridge', six volunteers had been killed and thirty-one wounded. The spirit and discipline displayed by the volunteer force was highly praised by Charles in the final account he wrote to Cardwell. He also paid tribute to the prompt action of the

196

officers and men of the Canadian Militia and of the regular troops, and to the officers of the Royal Navy 'for the rapidity with which they extemporized gunboats for the defence of the St. Lawrence and the Lakes.'[8]

At the end of a telegram despatched on 7 June to Cardwell, announcing that the 'invasion crisis' was over, Charles added: 'Please send a copy of this to Lady Monck, Charleville.'[9] 'I don't think Mama had heard of the Fenians when she wrote,' Charles told Henry in his letter of 22 June. 'I am very glad of it, as she would probably hear at the same time of the attack and its failure.' Others besides himself were concerned for Elizabeth's feelings. At the end of a very long letter to her, written on 4 June, d'Arcy McGee wrote from Montreal:

> . . . You must not be too anxious if this present mail does not tell you that the crisis is past, and the invader crushed or repelled. Another week, or at the outside another fortnight, *must* finish the Fenians. Our population are up and united as one man . . . we shall have this week 12 to 15,000 regulars. We have improvised *six* gunboats, with fighting crews supplied by Admiral Hope . . . I am here for one day, returning to Ottawa in the morning. Lord Monck whom I saw on Sunday is in excellent health and spirits. He is worked very hard, gets little or no sleep, but keeps up his hearty look, and has the same zest for a joke, as if the seventh part of a continent was not entrusted to his charge. Ottawa, you may depend on it, the fillibusters will never see. The railroad can in an hour be rendered impracticable and the highroad, nearly 60 miles or three days' march, leads through woods and marshes and over so many 'creeks' – that a single Company of Artillery could defend, that there is no possible danger of the new Capital.[10]

The Atlantic Cable was not completed until two months after these events took place, and all Charles' considerate precautions could not prevent his wife and children from reading the first newspaper reports of the invasion before they received his own messages. The account in the *Evening Standard* of 13 June had greatly alarmed Henry. 'I really hope you are in no danger,' he wrote to his father. *Do* write as soon as you get this and tell me all about it.' 'Thank

God everything went so well,' Elizabeth wrote to Henry after the excitement had died down; and she admitted that she, too, had been in 'a great fuss'.

She remained at Charleville after Charles returned to Canada, leaving it only for visits to her sisters and to other friends in Ireland. Her letters to Charles consisted mainly of news from home; the bay colt had been backed and promised to be a grand horse; the 'little horse' was expected to do well after he had been turned out to grass; Puss had started riding 'the grey' and was greatly delighted with it. Stanley, too, was riding every day. There was also plenty of local news, since the fact of having no carriage, and of keeping house with a 'skeleton' staff, did not prevent Elizabeth from continually visiting and being visited by the neighbours. She described luncheon and dinner parties; her sisters and others came to stay with her. In the second week of July, she and the girls went over to England and joined Henry in London, in time for the Eton and Harrow match at Lords. Before leaving Charleville, she had received a private letter from Edward Cardwell:

> My dear Lady Monck, – I have Lord Russell's authority for saying to Monck that the Queen has signified her pleasure that he shall be made an English Peer. Lord R. says 'I have said "Baron Monck".' Do you know whether he would prefer any other Title? If you have anything to say on the subject, pray let me know *forthwith*. Of course we are right in believing that he wishes to be an English Peer? Pray accept my sincere congratulations and Believe me, always truly yours, Edward Cardwell.[11]

There is no means of knowing how Elizabeth replied to the embarrassing question as to whether her husband would prefer 'any other Title', but it may be presumed that she intimated that an English barony would do very nicely for the present, since this honour was duly conferred on him. The announcement was not altogether a surprise, as two months earlier there had been premature rumours in the English press. 'I saw that paragraph you speak of about my getting an English peerage,' Charles had written to Henry on 3 May, 'but I have heard nothing about it myself.'

If Henry had any doubts about the genuineness of the announcement in *The Times* of 4 July, they were dispelled by the arrival on the same day of Cardwell's letter, forwarded to him by Elizabeth. *'The Times* of this morning praises you very much,' he wrote to his father in his letter of congratulation. The Prime Minister had recommended other people for peerages, but the Queen had refused her consent to them all except 'Lord Monck, who has well deserved the distinction by his adminstration of Canada.'[12]

Charles no longer spoke of going home on leave. He would next cross the Atlantic in company with the delegates who were to present the Act of Union to the Imperial Government. In a letter to John A. Macdonald he said that – 'I have received in the past, and am likely to receive in the future, much more credit for the business than – I say it most unaffectedly – I feel I have any right to claim.'[13] But – 'It is of great consequence that Lord Monck should be in England during our deliberations,' Macdonald wrote to the Prime Minister of New Brunswick; he went on to say that 'only through Lord Monck' could they hope to reach a satisfactory conclusion. Macdonald knew very well that, without the Governor General, the delegates would soon be at logger-heads with each other. Formerly they had grumbled because he did not give to the interests of either the priority each thought was his due, but they could not doubt his integrity and, at a time like this, would trust him when they would not trust one another.[14]

The hope of having confederation passed during that summer grew gradually fainter, as one delay followed another. The defeat of the Reform Bill in England resulted in a change of government there, and this held up confederation plans until a new Colonial Secretary should be appointed. On 1 August the first message to be received by the new Atlantic Cable brought the good news that Mr. Cardwell had been succeeded by Lord Carnarvon. He was an ardent supporter of confederation, but admitted that it would be 'next to impossible' to pass the Act of Union before the Westminster Parliament rose, which meant that nothing could be done before February.

In the meantime, there was need for preliminary discussion, and delegates from New Brunswick and Nova Scotia had already arrived in London for that purpose. Carnarvon agreed with Macdonald that it was essential that Monck be present during these discussions. The Ambassador at Washington had heard that Charles was likely to go to England. 'I hope I may say, without impropriety, how much I regret it at the present time,' he wrote, referring to 'the good will felt towards you by Seward [United States Secretary of State], and your experience and popularity in Canada, the deprivation of which I confess I look to with some dismay.'

Of the intermittent invasion scares, which continued throughout the autumn, he wrote: 'We are not entirely safe on that score, and in the still delicate question of the prisoners.'[15] A consignment of troops was sent from England; but a warning from London stated that the regiment, the '61st', was mainly composed of Irishmen with strong Fenian sympathies. If not urgently needed in Canada, it was suggested that the ship be sent straight on to the West Indies. In reporting the incident to Lord Carnarvon, Charles showed that his many preoccupations had not impaired his sense of humour. 'Why they ever sent them here when their fidelity was suspected is a mystery to me, unless it was supposed that the Canadians were too strong and it was intended to handicap them in their contest with the Fenians.'[16]

The 'delicate question' of the prisoners referred to those Fenians captured during the June invasion who were American citizens of Irish birth or descent, and Irishmen who had not yet become naturalised Americans. The former were 'foreigners' and could be tried and convicted for felony; the latter were still technically British subjects and liable to be tried and executed for treason. The Fenians, meanwhile, regarded their comrades as prisoners of war and demanded that they be treated as such. The United States authorities were finding it difficult enough to control the Irish section of their population, without the demonstrations which would certainly ensue if any of the prisoners in Canada were executed. Between the fury of the Canadian population who demanded revenge for the casualties inflicted on their volunteers, and unofficial letters from America appealing for mercy for individual prisoners, Charles was snowed under with correspondence on the subject. He was determined not to leave Canada until he had succeeded in obtaining remission of the death sentence for the Irish prisoners, and did not relax his efforts till he received the royal sanction for this.

He confided to Carnarvon his anxiety to get home as soon as possible for reasons connected with family affairs, but that he did

not think he could sail before mid-December. 'I hear Lynch and
McMahon are moving for new trials, in which case it would not be
right to commute their sentence until after their appeals have been
heard and tried.'

On 16 November the Cunard mail brought him Lord Carnarvon's
official permission for leave, and removed all doubt of his being able
to spend Christmas with his family.

Notes to Chapter Fifteen

1   *North America* by Anthony Trollope. 1869.
2   Brown to Macdonald, 15 August 1864, quoted in Joseph Pope, *Sir John Macdonald* (London, 1894). Feo Monck and her husband had visited Ottawa in 1864 while on tour as the guests of Lord Lyons and his staff. 'We were disgusted by the squalid look of Ottawa, though we only saw it by lamplight which was scarcely any light, such *wretched* gas. The streets were so rough, like dirt roads. I went on wondering how we could ever live there, when the seat of Government is moved there,' she wrote; and later added, as a footnote to her published diary: 'I little knew how happy I should be there, after all.' *(My Canadian Leaves* by Frances Monck).
3   J. M. S. Careless, *Brown of the Globe*.
4   Bruce to Monck, 11 March 1866. Private letter. Monck Papers.
5   Bruce to Monck, 9 April 1866. Monck Papers.
6   Monck to Cardwell, 4 June 1866. Public Record Office.
7   Donald Creighton, *The Road to Confederation* (Toronto).
8   Monck to Cardwell, 14 June 1866. Public Record Office.
9   Copy of telegram in Monck Papers in possession of Mr. J. J. McCann.
10 McGee to Lady Monck, 4 June 1866. Monck Papers in possession of J. J. McCann.
11 Cardwell to Lady Monck, 30 June 1866. Monck Papers in possession of J. J. McCann. *Note:* until now, Monck had been an Irish peer; an English peerage would make him eligible to sit in the House of Lords.
12 Queen Victoria to Lord Russell, 28 June 1866. Letters of Queen Victoria, British Museum.
13 Monck to Macdonald, 22 June 1866. *Sir John Macdonald* by Joseph Pope. Vol. I p. 303.
14 Macdonald to Tilly, 8 October 1866. Copy in Monck Papers.
15 Sir Frederick Bruce to Monck, 26 September 1866. Monck Papers.
16 Monck to Carnarvon, 8 October 1866. P.R.O.

16

The Dominion of Canada

Charles had told Lord Carnarvon that he was anxious to get home to attend to private affairs, and details of some of these emerge from family correspondence. Henry had originally been entered for Christ Church, Oxford, for the current term. The boy's new tutor, Mr. Thackeray, had considered that he was not yet ready for Oxford, and should have another year at Eton. Charles had given in, though unwillingly, and nearly all his weekly letters to his son contained injunctions to work hard and not to yield to the temptation to spend the extra year at school in idleness. 'I am glad you are reading Sir W. Scott's novels,' he had written in the spring, 'but I advise you to make a rule with regard to them, as well as all books of *light* reading, not to take them up until you have finished all your serious work for the day.'

Elizabeth's letters to Henry were also full of exhortations: 'Remember "Excelsior" – always aim at the *highest* in *all* things. If you say – "there is no use in *trying,* for others are cleverer than I," you will never do great things.' She and Charles shared a capacity to concentrate on whatever they happened to be doing, being thorough in their work, yet whole-heartedly enjoying their times of recreation. They were endlessly patient with Henry, but found it hard to understand his lackadaisical attitude to life.

A further family problem had arisen through the death in Paris of Charles' sister Isabella, which had taken place in August. Charles and Dick being in Canada, young Henry had cut short his visit to the Fifes at Mar Lodge for the Braemar Gathering, and went over to Paris to his father's other sister, 'Aunt E.' He brought her back to Ireland where she stayed alternately at Summerton with her sister Henrietta Brooke, and at Charleville; but surrounded though she was by affectionate relatives, it was high time that one of her brothers came home to advise her on her financial affairs. As a 'charge' on the Charleville estate, quarterly payments were paid into her account by Flood, the family solicitor, whose records show that she invariably asked for her money in advance.

At Charleville, preparations for Christmas always began early in the autumn. There were presents for everyone on the place, warm petticoats for some of the old women and 'frieze coats' for the men, and a Christmas Tree party in the house for the children. In October Elizabeth had taken Fan and Puss to London to see Henry, soon after which they heard the delightful news that 'Papa' had actually booked his passage on the *Scotia*, to sail on 12 December, and expected to be at Charleville in time for Christmas. Elizabeth's happiness in the prospect of Charles' return was mingled with her desperate fear for his safety. In this she was not alone. On 15 November, Consul Edwards wrote from New York:

> . . . I trust that Your Lordship will not consider it impertinent if I offer a suggestion which has occurred to me in reference to your proposed going to New York en route for England. In the present state of feeling among the Irish population it seems to me – if you have decided to come this way – that Your Lordship's stay in the States should not be prolonged beyond what is necessary, and that undue publicity ought not to be given to the fact.[1]

In Ireland, alarming rumours were being circulated. It was said that 'almost every ship that crossed the Atlantic brought to Ireland men of military experience, the motive of whose coming was scarcely concealed.'[2] At the end of November, Elizabeth wrote to Henry:

> . . . My dearest Child, – I fear that you will be vexed at the contents of this letter, but I cannot but feel that you will think me right. Your Papa told me if I heard of a good house in London within his terms to take it from January 1. I have almost concluded for one in Hill St. Berkeley Square. He speaks of all being quiet in Canada as far as the Fenians are concerned, but the accounts in Ireland are fearful, there is no doubt a rising is at hand. *He* is a marked man on account of his proceedings against them in Canada. You know how rash he is, that no one could prevent his being on the roads after dark. The

203

country is becoming *full* of suspicious-looking Americans, and I feel terrified as to what *may* occur, if he land in Ireland at this time. I have therefore almost decided, if I can get the house on the 19th of Dec., to go over *then,* and I am saying to him today (my last letter!) not to be surprised if he finds a letter from me at Cork telling him not to land, but to go on to Liverpool ... I do not feel that I *could* bear the terror, and it is *only* a few days' difference.

Charles did not pay the smallest attention to any of these suggested precautions for his safety. He had said that he would arrive at Charleville in time for dinner on 21 December; and it was from Charleville that he wrote to the Colonial Secretary on 22 December to report that he had arrived there on the evening before. He wrote again on 27 December to thank Lord Carnarvon for his kind invitation to stay with him at Highclere, near Newbury – 'to talk over N. American affairs, perhaps with more leisure than is possible in Downing St.'[3] – but explained that he would like to have a little time at home before going over to London. His subsequent letters show that he stayed at Charleville until 7 January 1867, when he and his family moved into 24 Hill Street which remained his base until the passing of the British North American Act.

With his wife assuming that he would go straight to London and Lord Carnarvon expecting him to come to Highclere, his homecoming, like everything Charles did, took place with the minimum of fuss and ostentation. It was several days before it became known that he had arrived, and poor Lord Carnarvon found himself in Queen Victoria's black books for not having 'announced Lord Monck's arrival in England.'[4]

The process of hammering out the resolutions comprising the Confederation Act became known as the Westminster Palace Conference, because the preliminary discussions took place in the Westminster Palace Hotel. The Conference is commemorated by a 'conversation piece' painted by J. D. Kelly, in which Charles Monck stands with Lord Carnarvon at the head of a long table round which the delegates are informally grouped.

He was meeting the delegates and the Colonial Secretary nearly every day but he and Elizabeth went down to Portsmouth, his old constituency, for a banquet given in his honour on 29 January 1867.

Among the 320 guests were some of the Canadian delegates, including Macdonald and Cartier.

Henry came up from school to attend the opening of Parliament on 5 February; but Elizabeth and her daughters went over to Ireland immediately after the Portsmouth banquet, to be near Charles' sister Henrietta, whose husband, Francis Brooke,* was seriously ill. While Elizabeth stayed at Charleville, with a still further reduced household, she was missing all the great doings in London during the presentation of the Confederation Bill to Parliament. Of the disturbances in Ireland at that time, Charles wrote to Henry on 15 February: 'You will have seen in the papers that there has been a sort of rising in Kerry.' But every day brought news of risings in different parts of the country, and in March there was a 'skirmish' at Tallaght – only a few miles from Charleville. 'The K———s are gone to London. Lord K——— is so afraid of the Fenians', Elizabeth wrote to Henry. 'I am so afraid of the Fenians, that I have Tom Quin and his gun to sleep in the house. Naturally, he comes just in time for supper. I have the back door locked, so he has to come thro' the hall, when we are at tea and that amuses Fan.' Henry, too, was amused by this description of the old gamekeeper, always considered a farcical character, as the sole defender of Charleville.

On 19 February Charles, now a peer of the United Kingdom, made a short speech in the House of Lords following Lord Carnarvon's introduction of the Confederation Bill. Hansard's report quoted him as saying that

> . . . these colonies had so much increased in trade, in wealth, and in commerce that, taking into consideration also their peculiar geographical position, they had interests connected with questions of foreign policy, he would not say antagonistic to, but at all events, distinct from those of the mother country. We had, and he thought very wisely, conceded to these Provinces the management of their own affairs, and it would not be politically wise or just to dispose of every matter connected with the foreign relations of these Provinces without consulting the people interested.

---

* Francis Brooke of Summerton, County Dublin, died in March 1867.

Those who knew him intimately would have detected an echo of the 'leading strings' motif, when he hinted in his speech that self-government should be conceded to Canada in fact, and not only in name.

On 8 March the Act of Confederation was finally passed, uniting the provinces of Upper and Lower Canada, New Brunswick and Nova Scotia into the Dominion of Canada. The Act provided for the entry of Newfoundland and Prince Edward Island into the Union if and when they desired, also for the inclusion of British Columbia, the North-West and Rupert's Land. It received the Royal Assent on 29 March, after which the Canadian and Maritime delegates recrossed the Atlantic.

By the express wish of the Duke of Buckingham and Chandos, who had succeeded Lord Carnarvon as Colonial Secretary, Charles Monck was commissioned at the first Governor General of the Dominion.

His term of office had already lasted longer than was usual, and after accomplishing the task of 'setting the coach in motion', as he himself expressed it, he hoped to be replaced as soon as a successor could be appointed. His duties as an Irish landlord and his family commitments all pointed to the necessity of returning home on the earliest possible date and now, by remaining in Ireland until 14 June, he was allowing himself only the barest minimum of time in which to reach Canada for the ceremony of inauguration on 1 July. Fortunately the *Peruvian* made a reasonably smooth passage, and Monck and his family arrived at Spencer Wood on 25 June.

Their voyage was described by Monck as having been 'a little rough at first, but afterwards as smooth as a millpond', and by Elizabeth as 'tedious, rough, sick, wretched, and *so* slow.' To make matters worse, the ship stopped at two a.m. in mid-ocean, owing to the engine having become over-heated with the 'continual tossing', and they had to wait four hours for it to cool.

The Captain had given up his 'charming' cabin to Elizabeth for a sitting room and, after a few days of sea-sickness, she was revelling in the sea air and in having plenty of time to read. She and her family made friends with the other passengers and enjoyed the community-singing and the games on deck. When the *Peruvian* docked at Point Levi, Denis Godley and other members of the staff came on board. There was a guard of honour to welcome the Moncks. Addresses were presented, guns fired, the band played and the crowds cheered.

'So lovely this place looks, and feels so still and cool,' Elizabeth wrote on arriving at Spencer Wood. On the same evening Puss drove her out in the pony carriage to call on some neighbours, and the whole family went to 'early Church' next morning.

From this time the tone of Elizabeth's letters shows that she now shared her husband's love for Canada. Spencer Wood was not Charleville, but they had all grown extremely fond of it. It would not be long, so they thought, before they would all be going home for good; and meanwhile the family were reunited, or would be when the boys joined them. Stanley and Fräulein Denneler had been left behind, but were to follow when the hot weather was over, and Henry would come out in the *Peruvian* immediately his holidays began.

In the new Parliament buildings in Ottawa, on 1 July 1867, Charles Monck signed the document inaugurating confederation, and was himself sworn in as Governor General of the new dominion. 'My Parliament is to open on the 7th [November],' he wrote to Henry, 'and I believe it is to be no end of a function. They are bringing up the Governor General's bodyguard as a Cavalry escort for me'; and, four weeks later: 'We have had people staying here [Rideau Hall] for the opening of Parliament all this week. Dinner parties every evening, and tonight Mama is to have an evening party. The weather has become very cold but fortunately very little snow, so we were able to drive in the carriage today to the opening of Parliament... I made all the ladies who came to the body of the house come in evening dress, and there were a great many there and very well got up, and the whole thing looked very pretty ...' He himself wore court dress, as did the Prime Minister now Sir John Macdonald, K.C.B.

If Charles' notions of pomp and display fell short of what was required, he was kept up to the mark by Brock, the faithful but exasperating house steward. 'Brock has taken it into his head to make the footmen wear powder,' he told Henry. 'You should see Carbury, who officiates as a footman, in his powder! He is something quite wonderful.' The promotion of 'Carbury' to footman from whatever his normal duties may have been, was caused by yet another vacancy in Brock's department. Failing to find anyone in Canada to suit her exacting house steward, Elizabeth

Rideau Hall, Ottawa.

decided to import a footman from England. She wrote to ask Henry to interview the man, at the same time replying to her son's questions about the High Church practices which were becoming fashionable in Oxford, confusing the two subjects in her usual manner and leaving Henry to sort them out as best he could:

Sunday, Oct. 28. St. Simon & St. Jude.
My dearest Child, – Will you look after this footman. Ask him his terms. Get his character from Mr. Hales, make him read this list & say if he would feel equal to the duties. Send the list back to me, & tell me about him as soon as you can . . .

About the vestments. I think every thing should be done to make the worship in the Church whatever seems beautiful and attractive to those who have the arrangement of it. *I* do not admire the coloured vestments, because perhaps that I am old & it is too much of a *novelty,* but I do not the least object to

208

them, nor mind their being *like* Roman Catholics, if we do not share the *errors* of the R.C. Church.

> Your fondest Mother, – E.L.M.M.

Tell what he *looks* like.

She and Charles were in an agony of anxiety over their daughter Louise ('Puss'), who had been taken seriously ill soon after her arrival in Canada. At the time it was thought that she was suffering from sunstroke, but the doctor finally diagnosed tuberculosis, and warned her parents that the Canadian winter might be fatal to her. All this had happened before the Moncks left Spencer Wood for the new Government House, and Elizabeth had been torn in two between the claims of her husband and those of her sick child. Eventually it was decided that Henry should escort his sister to Ireland and, before going up for his first term at Oxford, hand her over to one of her aunts, who took her first to Torquay then, escorted by Henry during the Christmas vacation, to Cannes.

The family party at Rideau Hall though reduced by two, was enlivened by the Richard Moncks – Dick and Feo – with their child Cecil. 'Feo is expecting a baby any day now, *entre nous,'* Fan wrote in one of her delightful letters to her brother Henry. By her contemporaries, Feo's round face and rotund shape could never have been mistaken for the slim figure of Elizabeth, who was twenty years her senior. Yet, in later accounts of that period, the two have often been confused; e.g. in the family group photographed outside Rideau Hall, in which the central and most prominent figure is Feo. Feo, not Elizabeth, was 'the soloist at the first concert held at Her Majesty's Theatre at Ottawa in aid of St. Bartholomew's Church.'[5] And it was Feo, not Elizabeth, who gave offence by speaking slightingly of the women of Canada.

In all his letters home, Charles Monck emphasised the advantages of Rideau Hall; but Lady Amberley, when she and Lord Amberley stayed there, criticised Elizabeth for 'grumbling' about Canada. Lady Amberley herself noted in her diary that Ottawa was 'a horrrid, out of the way, rough place to live in and quite unfit for the seat of a govt., the streets are unpaved and there are neither houses nor hotels fit to live in.' On the whole, their visit was not an unqualified success. Charles Monck, usually the most tolerant and charitable of men, allowed himself to criticise Lady Amberley's

Foreground left to right: Lady Monck, Hon. Frances 'Fan' and Hon. Stanley Monck, Cecil Monck, Hon. Mrs. Richard 'Feo' Monck and Lord Monck outside Rideau Hall.

appearance in his letter to Henry. She wore, he said, 'a very funny sort of dress which made her look as if she had forgotten to put on all except her first garment.'

A. E. Meredith, the diarist, received Elizabeth's 'grumbles' in a different spirit. 'Lady Monck was most gracious . . . she came up to me in the evening to chat . . . and when I was leaving, thanked me for having made her laugh so much! She promised to send me a card whenever she wished to have a *growl* about Ottawa, putting *"growling'* instead of "music" or "dancing" in the corner.' On another occasion, Meredith described Elizabeth as having been – 'very pleasant and agreeable, full of gossip and very confidential.' According to contemporary reports, there were few who did not growl about Ottawa. 'The members are so angry at being brought here – no wonder,' wrote Elizabeth.

The Governor's public despatches and personal letters to the Duke of Buckingham, the Colonial Secretary, dealt with the proposed inclusion in the confederation of the North-West Territory,* the large following gained by Joseph Howe in Nova Scotia for the repeal of the confederation, and with reports that the Fenians were planning another invasion of Canada. He forwarded a copy of a letter from a George Kelly, one of the orderlies in the office of a Fenian commander, warning him that a party of Fenians had embarked from New York, intending to land 'somewhere in the Bristol Channel' and to assassinate Queen Victoria, the Archbishop of Canterbury and several prominent members of the British Government. The report could not be ignored at a time when many 'outrages' were being committed in England but it was eventually proved to be without foundation.

Charles was the reverse of an alarmist. Though it was his duty to sift any rumours of plots and invasion scares, and to pass on the more definite reports to the Colonial Office, he usually assured the Duke that he, personally, suspected them of being false alarms. When reporting George Kelly's letter, he wrote: 'I shall be very glad to bear the ridicule of having been taken in if the story shall prove to be a hoax.' There was no question of ridicule. As the result of a series of acts of violence, security officers in England were continually on the alert at that time, and the Colonial Secretary relied on Monck to keep him informed of all assassination rumours, probable or improbable. He in his turn passed to Monck anything heard in London regarding the ever-recurring threats of invasion of Canada. Charles Monck would have been the first to be amused could he have foreseen the comments made, more than a hundred years later, by the author of a book about Queen Victoria: 'Where Lord Monck got his information [on the assassination plot] is not clear. ... What is clear is that His Lordship was recalled from Canada, his career resting under a cloud, before another twelve months were out.'[6] So legends are born. Monck 'got his information' from Sir John A. Macdonald, the Canadian Prime Minister, who had been alerted by Edward Archibald, the British Consul in New York. It is true that Charles left Canada eleven months after the above incident, in the

---

* The North-West Territory was included in the Confederation in 1870; Prince Edward Island in 1873; and Newfoundland in 1949.

face of the urgent entreaties of the Colonial Office that he would stay longer. There was no 'cloud', unless warm tributes from the governments in both London and Ottawa, and from Queen Victoria herself, could be so-called.

Charles and his friend Adderley, who was Under-Secretary for the Colonies, regularly exchanged personal letters. In the course of their correspondence Adderley put out a feeler as to whether Monck would be prepared to stay 'over his year'. In his reply and in many subsequent letters to the Colonial Office, Monck said that he would like to go home as soon as a successor could be appointed to relieve him.

Living in daily expectation of his release, his weekly letters to Henry convey a sense of 'marking time', while he wrote serenely of such day-to-day events as he thought might amuse or interest his son. An old Indian chief had attended a levée – ' in *full dress* and with his head all stuck about with feathers'; Elizabeth had held a large evening reception at which the band of the Rifle Brigade played. 'They gratified our *ears* very much, but I cannot say much for the effect on our *noses* as the *esprit de corps* was rather strong.' Feo had had her baby; Elizabeth and Fan had never been better; while Stanley was actually putting on weight and had taken to skating. 'Stanley has put his pony into the red cariole . . . he drives into Ottawa sitting on the knifeboard, with Brock sitting in the body of the sleigh. To my astonishment I saw him yesterday driving Col. Hawley about Ottawa.* Charles also confided to Henry his intention to send Stanley to school after the summer. 'Between you and me, I think he is getting a little beyond petticoat government.' There was no question as to which preparatory school he would be sent. Mr. Wilkinson's services as holiday tutor to Henry being no longer required, he had started a private school of his own at St. Leonards-on-Sea. His venture was enthusiastically backed by Charles and Elizabeth who never spared themselves in their efforts to help their friends. Neither did they spare other people, and all their acquaintances were urged to send their sons to 'Quebec House', as the school was nostalgically named.

To amuse his father, Henry forwarded to him two letters he had received from the Charleville keeper, Tom Quin:

* Colonel Hawley commanded the Rifle Brigade.

Dear Sir, – I write to let you know that their is no sign of the corn been sown for the pheasants yet the time is getting late some time ago hobson [gardener] was talking about sowing buck wheat there is no use to sow buck wheat in Charleville the ground does not answer for it oats or barley is the best – he have cut down all the big lorrels in the garden and pleasure ground the are going to cut the burnt house this season agen everything is going on very well here.

I had a Letter from Mr Stanley asking about his rabbit and pidgeons I was glad to hear that the family is all quite well dont let on to Mr Sandys that I rote about the corn

I am dear Sir your humble and obedient servant

Tom Quin

The next letter, written later in the season, reported that 'the young Phesants is going on very well so far,' and that he had sent three 'nicely taned' (tanned) setter puppies to the Clancartys at Garbally. 'Norah never proved to be in pup, I think she was to fat when I Brought her to the Dog.'

There was great rejoicing when Henry wrote that he had won the Christ Church two-mile race, and had come in third in the mile race; but his next letter brought the unwelcome news that he had failed in 'Smalls' – the first of his Oxford examinations. He told his parents that he was deeply sorry to have disappointed them, and promised to work harder next term. 'Of course I am sorry you did not pass the examination, but I am sure you worked for it, and please God you will have better luck next time,' replied his indulgent father. 'My principle all through life has been never to spend time "crying over spilt milk", and I am sure you will work hard next term.'

Elizabeth expressed herself more strongly, having perhaps heard something of her own father's inglorious career at Eton – 'nearly at the bottom of the school.' 'The *great* secret of success in *any* mental undertaking is to acquire the habit of *firmly* fixing your attention on whatever you have to do. You have a bad habit of undervaluing your own powers, of thinking you are not clever, & cannot do things, whereas if you *determine* on any success, & bend your whole mind to it, you will achieve it. Get your mind into a *habit* of hard study.'

Family triumphs and failures were eclipsed by a tragedy which took place in Ottawa on 8 April 1868. Rumours of a great Fenian conspiracy culminated in the murder of d'Arcy McGee, who was shot in the back on reaching his home after attending a parliamentary session. Thomas d'Arcy McGee, poet and historian, had in his early days been an Irish patriot and escaped to America after the rout of the Young Ireland Party in 1848. He subsequently settled in Canada, where he became one of the earliest and most enthusiastic supporters of confederation. At the time of his death, he was member of Parliament for Montreal West, and Minister for Agriculture and Emigration.[7] His murder was the consequence of his open denunciation of the Fenians. 'I cannot doubt that you have heard of the fearful tragedy which has filled us with horror,' Elizabeth wrote to Henry on 9 April. 'Poor Mr. d'Arcy McGee's murder. I send newspapers. Never was there a more *fearful* occurrence, I never was more shocked! As you know, I always liked him *so much.*' The liking appears to have been mutual. In writing to one who did not know his 'Governess General', as he called her, McGee had said: 'If you see her, mark her – she is one of my best friends.'[8] Ten days later, Charles wrote: 'Mr. McGee had a very large public funeral at Montreal on Monday last . . . They actually *cheered* in the Church when the Priest, who was preaching the funeral sermon, denounced the Fenians.'

Notes to Chapter Sixteen

1   Pierrepont Edwards to Monck, 15 November 1866. Private letter. Monck Papers.
2   *A Short History of the Irish People* by M. Hayden and G. Moonan. Hayden Press, Dublin.
3   Carnarvon to Monck. Private letter. Monck Papers.
4   Lord Grey to Lord Carnarvon, 5 February 1867. Letters of Queen Victoria. British Museum Reading Room.
5   Cowan, John, *Canada's Governor Generals* (Toronto, 1952).
6   Cullen, Tom, *The Empress Brown* (London, 1969).
7   *D.N.B.*
8   McGee to Mrs. Ferguson, 16 June 1866. Quoted in Lady Ferguson, *Sir Samuel Ferguson and his Ireland* (London, 1896).

17

Packing Up

The Moncks began to make their preparations for the journey home. Horses and carriages must be shipped back to Ireland; furniture, linen, silver and china must be crated up ready for transport. In June, Charles made the first stage of the journey by removing the whole of his establishment to Spencer Wood:

> ... The day was very fine and it was a very pleasant excursion... We are so far on our way home. I mean to stay here till my successor arrives . . . I am glad you are working so well for 'smalls', and I do trust that by this time you are all right, but you need not be afraid that I shall be annoyed with you if you do not succeed, as I am sure you are doing your best and no man can do more than that.

As soon as he heard the welcome news that Henry was 'well through "smalls"', his letters were full of advice about preparing for the next hurdle. Henry, however, felt that he owed himself some relaxation, and went to Ascot with a party of friends. Going down from London in the Ascot 'special', he was surprised to find himself travelling with his 'Uncle Croker'. His parents were even more surprised when they heard of it, Elizabeth having received a letter from her sister Georgina saying that poor Edward had had to go over to London on business connected with their eldest son's army commission. It had been clear from her letter that Georgina knew nothing about the visit to Ascot.

No sooner were Henry's parents relieved from their anxiety about his examination, than they heard that they were not to go home after all. Lord Mayo, who had accepted the post of Governor General, changed his mind on hearing that the Ottawa Parliament had passed an act reducing the salary. This put the Colonial Office in an embarrassing position. It was an awkward moment in which to offer the post to anyone else, and the Duke of Buckingham asked Charles if he would consider staying on, at least for a few months. Charles sympathised with his predicament and agreed to stay till November, on condition that he should not be asked to stay longer. When writing to break the news that he, Elizabeth and Fan would not be sailing till 14 November, Charles asked 'Puss' not to express disappointment when she wrote, 'as Mama is rather distressed about the postponement of our going home, and I don't want to have her additionally vexed about it.' Poor Elizabeth had good reason to be vexed. All plans were thrown into confusion. They were, to a certain extent, 'living in their trunks', having packed all but bare necessities, and Stanley and Fräulein Denneler had already sailed, escorted by Francis Burrowes who was going home on leave. The boy was to spend a few weeks in the 'bracing air' of Llandudno, at the end of which time his parents had expected to be in Ireland. It had been arranged that he should go to Mr. Wilkinson's school in September, but this must now be postponed until after Christmas.

To make matters worse, Puss was due to arrive home from Switzerland where her doctor had ordered her to 'drink the waters' at Bex. Her parents had not seen her since the previous autumn when she had developed a patch on her lung; and though, after spending the winter and spring at Cannes, the cure was nearly complete, they had counted on being at Charleville to look after her when she returned. Charles wrote imploring her not to over-tax her strength. He seemed almost equally anxious lest she should override her horse, who had been put out to grass during the summer. Henry, too, was given instructions about two horses which had already been sent home in the *Nestorian,* and warned not to ride them until they had been given a week or ten days' rest.

While Henry went to stay with the Fifes in Scotland for grouse-shooting and the Braemar Gathering, Puss paid a visit to her mother's sisters at Barbavilla. Her parents approved of this plan, knowing that she would be in good hands. Elizabeth might be Lady Monck and the mistress of Charleville, but she still regarded her beloved elder sister Anne as 'mother superior' in the Monck sisterhood. Puss would go back to Charleville in time to welcome Stanley and 'Denny' when they came there from Llandudno. But instead of the news of their safe arrival, the next mail to reach

216

Spencer Wood brought a letter from Fräulein Denneler to say that Stanley had 'the whooping cough', the one illness which Elizabeth dreaded above all others, at least one member of the family having died of that illness. 'You may suppose that Mama was at first rather uneasy and had made up her mind to go home next week,' Charles wrote with his usual mastery of understatement. 'But today brought us so good an account that she has quite given that up, and is reconciled to remaining until I am relieved.' He was soon able to write that 'The accounts of Stanley are very good. He appears to have the whooping cough very lightly, and it is a good thing for him to get it over before he goes to school.'

At the end of September, letters from home reported that Puss was able to lead a perfectly normal life, and that Stanley had arrived at Charleville with his cough 'nearly quite gone'. Charles and Elizabeth had become as serene as it was possible to be while the Atlantic divided them from three of their four children, when the peace of Spencer Wood was shattered by startling news from Henry. During a visit to the Fifes at Mar Lodge in Scotland, he had fallen in love and returned to Charleville an engaged man. He realised, or perhaps Puss reminded him, that at the age of nineteen he must first gain his parents' permission before being officially engaged or even making a formal proposal. This permission he now asked, in letters that he afterwards discreetly destroyed as well as the first replies from Charles and Elizabeth. Later, Charles referred to the object of Henry's devotion as 'Lady Alexina'; and as she was aged seventeen, she can have been none other than the Fifes' youngest daughter, whose brother Macduff had been Henry's great friend both at Woodcote and Eton.

More than thirty years earlier, Louisa Monck had written that 'Love, Lovers and Lizzy seemed to belong to each other'; and although there was never the slightest hint that Elizabeth ever stepped out of line after her marriage, a romantic love affair was to her as the smell of battle to a war-horse. Never was there a more sympathetic 'confidante'. 'Captain Webber comes here almost every day to talk to Mama about his bride!' Fan had written to Henry from Spencer Wood. Now that her own darling son was in the toils, Elizabeth's letters were all passionate interest and sympathy. They were sorrowful, too, for of course she supposed that Charles was right in saying that Henry and Alexina were both too young to bind themselves; that Henry had only completed one year at Oxford; and that he had not yet decided on a career, which must depend on his taking a good degree – or on his taking any degree. She also knew that the family finances were in an unsatisfactory state, and that the greater part of the debts left by her own father were still unpaid.

She left it to Charles to write wise counsel, imploring his son to 'resist the temptation to act with haste and want of due consideration.' He went on to explain that his 'principal object' in accepting salaried appointments had been that 'money obstacles' should not prevent Henry from marrying; but that owing to 'various causes' he was returning from Canada no richer than when he left England. He hoped, however, to get employment in England, in which case 'one of the greatest gratifications will be that it will enable me to do what you wish.'

There is a fragment of a note from Elizabeth: 'You *well* know how very near my heart is in *all* connected with *you*.' Letters came and went by every mail, but in none of them are Alexina's parents mentioned and one wonders what they could have been about to have allowed matters to progress so far. To be photographed was still an event, but Henry was able to send a photograph of Alexina to Canada, as well as some new ones of himself.

> My dearest Child. – I return the sweet innocent-looking nice-looking photo: without loss of time. She must indeed be just what you describe her . . .
>
> My child, I do not like yours *at all,* it quite distresses me even to *look* at them. I do not *at all* like a beard on you & I do not like the way your hair is settled in these photos. I used *so much* to like the *Eton way* in which you used to have it, very short & divided down the middle. These do not bring *you* at all to my mind, but something *so* different.

Elizabeth must indeed have felt that it was high time she went home, as much to deal with her son's altered appearance as with his love-sick condition.

'Henry is never out of my thoughts,' she wrote in a letter to Puss, saying again how charmed she had been by Alexina's photograph. She seldom if ever disputed Charles' judgment; but had it been left to her, it is possible that she might have seen no reason why her 'dearest child' should not be allowed to marry his first love and live in a corner of Charleville, as two of her sisters and their husbands had done, and as – many years later – Puss was to do. After the first week in November there were no more letters about Alexina – or, if there were, Henry did not keep them. He fell in with his father's suggestion that all 'further discussion' be postponed until they were able to meet; but there is no record of what then took place, nor of how long Henry remained inconsolable after the faithless Alexina married Henry Coventry during the summer of 1870.

The next mail brought good news from the Colonial Office. Sir John Young,* lately Governor of New South Wales, had definitely accepted the post of Governor General of Canada. It also brought permission for Charles to sail on 14 November, whether or not Sir John had arrived. Meanwhile Sir Charles Windham, K.C.B., Commander of Her Majesty's Forces in British North America, was to act as administrator.

The next weeks were a whirl of farewell parties given by and for the Moncks. 'We are just beginning the bore of packing up,' wrote Charles, adding that Fan was driving herself about with a pair of ponies in the pony-carriage, paying last visits to their neighbours. She had also attended a luncheon-party on board ship, and the Burstals' dance. She had greatly enjoyed all the dances in Quebec, and this was the last she would ever attend. Though devoted to Charleville, she had developed a great love for Canada where she had been treated with so much kindness and consideration. Besides the parties given to and by their friends, there were many formal dinners and other functions; also an official farewell to the Canadian volunteers for whom Charles Monck felt so much pride and affection.

Shortly before he sailed, Charles Monck received an official despatch from the Duke of Buckingham:

> ... The Queen desires me to convey to you Her approval of the manner in which you have discharged the duties which have been confided to you. The period of your administration has not been uneventful. The relations between Canada and the United States, before and after the termination of the civil war.

---

* Lord Lisgar.

... have presented questions of much moment and delicacy and it has been your fortune to bear a distingished part in one of the most important events which have occurred in the history of the British Colonies – the Confederation of the three leading Provinces of British North America.

In all these matters you have exhibited a discretion, an uprightness of judgment, and a considerate and vigilant regard for the public interest, with which Her Majesty is entirely satisfied . . .

I am to authorise you to communicate this despatch, in the most fitting manner, to the people of Canada.

'The house is getting a very *packy* look,' Elizabeth wrote. 'I dread the voyage and wish we were safe over. I have 3 evening receptions next week for farewells.' To add to the confusion of their last weeks, she had insisted on sending home her great red cariole, although Charles had advised against it. 'I do not think she will have much use for it in Ireland,' he told Henry. The result was that they had to hire a cariole from Gringras, the sleigh-maker, for their ceremonial departure on 14 November, as the snow came early that year, and wheeled vehicles were already laid up for the winter. 'The sleigh we got at Gringras would not do for 4 horses,' Elizabeth wrote, 'so we had to go down with 2. Streets lined, guard of honour, guns, band, etc. etc. *Everybody* you can think of came on board to take leave. Very fine, calm & bright.' They were escorted to the place of embarkation by members of the dominion and local cabinets, with other officials, both civil and military; while a guard of honour from the 53rd Regiment received Monck on the wharf. As the steamship *Nestorian* left the shore, a salute of seventeen cannons was fired from the citadel.

Elizabeth began writing an account of their last voyage home during their first evening on board the *Nestorian*. The weather changed as they passed the Gaspé coast, entered the Gulf of St. Lawrence, then the Straits of Belle Isle, where they saw '2 or 3 large icebergs'. After 'November 18th – into the Atlantic', there were no more entries until the 22nd when she wrote that there had been a desperate week of rough weather . . . Your Father, who has crossed so often, says it is the worst *he* ever had.' It was just over seven years since their first crossing of the Atlantic, and during that time Charles had spent a total of only nine months away from Canada.

On the evening of Tuesday 24 November 1868, Elizabeth triumphantly wrote her last entry: 'Just going to land!'

PART III

IRELAND: 1868-1894

18

Irish Land Acts

It had always been a wonderful place to come back to; taking no account of time, it was serenely welcoming whether the absence had been of days or of years. Charleville never changed, and something of the place went with her children no matter how far they travelled; yet they experienced a strange shock of pleasure each time they returned. Often as they had thought of their home, it was always more beautiful than they had remembered: the roughness of silvery-grey limestone as their hands rested on the low walls bounding the wide, curving steps to the front door; the accoustics of the hall, and of the gallery at the head of the staircase, which gave to voices and footsteps the special 'Charleville sounds'; the scents of the many aromatic shrubs and trees; all were part of the blessed familiarity of home-coming. Late November might not be the most attractive season of the year, but this mattered nothing to Elizabeth, renewed and rejuvenated, filled with fresh vigour and vitality by the famous 'Charleville air'.

Reunited with Puss, Henry and Stanley, and with all their friends 'on the place' and in the neighbourhood, Elizabeth and Charles must also see their sisters: Fanny Cole in Dublin, the four at Barbavilla, Henrietta Brooke and 'Aunt E.' at Summerton. There was Christmas to prepare for, with the party and Christmas tree for the children on the estate. These would be invited again, a fortnight later, for a tea and magic lantern show on Henry's birthday, which had been celebrated in this way ever since he was a little boy.

Charles went over to London before Christmas; Parliament had been dissolved three days before he left Canada, and the general election had resulted in a great victory for the Liberals, led by Mr. Gladstone. Nearly all the members of the new cabinet were Charles' personal friends, and he hoped and expected to be given some kind of government appointment. 'I have not yet been offered any office,' he wrote to Henry on 10 December, 'but I see the *Times* of this morning says it is likely I shall be Under-Secretary for War. I should like that office very well as it is very interesting and I should be with Cardwell whom I like very much.*

The under-secretaryship was not given to Charles. Instead, he had been earmarked for an appointment which was about to come into existence for the first time, that of Commissioner for (Irish) Church Temporalities. Owing to its newness, the significance of the post was not immediately apparent. In fact, the disestablishment of the Church of Ireland was the chief question of the day, and with the Liberal party in power, it hit the headlines of the London newspapers. Gladstone had introduced a resolution for Irish church disestablishment in March 1868, when it was passed by the Commons but defeated in the Lords. Upon taking office as Prime Minister, he immediately brought it forward again and, after several months of controversial debate, it became law in July 1869.

To the general public, the storm created by the controversy somewhat obscured the complications involved in putting into effect the results of the Act: the administration and re-allocation of the immense property of which the Church of Ireland was disendowed.** The difficult and extremely delicate problem of redistributing this great wealth created the need for a new government office. For this, Charles Monck was the obvious choice, and that not only because he had proved himself to be a capable and trustworthy administrator, had been a Lord of the Treasury, and was known to be an ardent supporter of disestablishment but also, chiefly, because of his possessing detailed knowledge of the system by which the Anglican Church in Canada had been organised, since its disestablishment by the Clergy Reserves (Canada) Act of 1853. It was intended to adopt the outlines of that system in Ireland, and though here it would be considerably more complicated, the general principles were to be the same.

As early as 1867, while he was still in Canada, Charles had received private letters from his political friends in England, asking for information on the subject. After corresponding with Canadian

*   Edward Cardwell had been made Secretary of State for War.
** There were, and still are, differences of opinion about the exact capital sum involved.

bishops and other leading churchmen, he summed up his findings in his reply to William Monsell. His letter, giving details of statistics and method of organisation, ends with an expression of his approval of the system, and his conviction that its effect on the clergy was favourable, while 'unalloyed benefit' to the laity was produced by 'the sense that the Church is *their own.'*[1] To put the effect at its lowest, he believed it inconceivable, he said, that a man would give up his time, as an active member of Synod, and his money as a regular contributor, without being brought 'almost unconsciously, through his zeal for the externals of religion, to a thoughtful consideration of its deeper and more important objects.'

'I am looking with a good deal of curiosity for the report on the proceedings in the House of Commons on Gladstone's motion about the Irish Church,' he wrote to his son in March 1868:

> I have always thought that it is a great injustice that the provision which the State makes in Ireland for the support of religion should be given exclusively to maintain the Church of a small minority of the population, and that minority by far the richest portion of the people of the country, and I am therefore very glad that there is now a prospect of seeing that injustice redressed.[2]

His detailed information on the practical side of Canadian Church management gave valuable assistance to Gladstone when he was drawing up the Irish Church Bill. Chichester Fortescue, at that time Chief Secretary for Ireland, told Gladstone of the view held by 'so good a judge as Lord Monck . . . that a compulsory settlement of rent by a public authority was an essential reform. This was a revolutionary proposal, breaking against all the most firmly fixed English ideas.[3] The Bill was presented when Parliament assembled in February 1869, and Charles Monck took a prominent part in the debates. He was now in the House of Lords* and, in seconding the Speech from the Throne, he expressed himself forcibly on the injustice of confining state provision to the Church of the Protestant minority at the expense of the Catholic majority:

---

* He had been created a peer of the United Kingdom in 1866.

Even if the measure were injurious to the Church, I would wish justice to be done at whatever cost. But I am firmly convinced that the true interests of the Irish Church concur with the demands of justice and policy . . . I say it with all reverence, I have too firm a faith in the vitality of my own religion, and in the Source from whence its vitality is derived, to doubt for a moment that the necessary funds will be forthcoming.[4]

His only fear, he continued, was that the opponents of the Bill, while unable to defeat its main objects, should be sufficiently powerful to 'diminish the beneficial effect of the measure' by an amendment. His wife's cousin, Lord Clancarty, was one of numerous Anglo-Irish landlords who were antagonistic to disestablishment; and before the Irish Church Bill was passed during that summer, they had introduced the expected amendment which Charles vigorously opposed. 'All the misgovernment of Ireland which followed the relaxation of the Penal Code' had been, he affirmed, the result of 'refusal to give practical effect to the logical result of adopted principles.'[5] On 23 December 1868, he had written to William Monsell:

I think I see in the writing on this question in the public press a tendency to 'make things pleasant' to the supporters of the (Protestant) Church even at the expense of risking some of the benefit to be derived from the disestablishment.

Undoubtedly it is of great importance that the change should be attended with the least possible aggravation of feelings, but I trust the desire for this may not go so far as to affect the settlement of the question with the same vice which has damaged every previous concession of justice to Ireland, namely the refusal to base your acts on principle and to carry out that principle to its legitimate consequences.[6]

The Commission of Church Temporalities, formed to administer for the benefit of the country as a whole the large resources of the disestablished Church, consisted of Charles Monck and two other **Commissioners. Mr. Justice Lawson, like Monck, supported** disestablishment, while George Alexander Hamilton, who had opposed it, was 'obviously appointed as a guarantee of fair play.'[7]

The Church of Ireland was not left without any resources, the large proportion retained by them being presumably due to the 'amendment' disapproved of by Monck. The remainder was divided between such public works as national education, the relief of distress, the covering of payments under the Arrears of Rent Act (1882) and sea-fisheries.[8]

During the early years, the work of the Church Commission was often arduous and frustrating, partly owing to the clashes between the Treasury's Comptroller and Auditor General and the Commissioners' own solicitor. The latter eventually had to be sacked for his 'irregular' conduct of affairs. Another source of friction arose through Monck's having appointed Denis 'Almighty' Godley as secretary to the Church Commission, keeping him on in that post when the Irish Land Commission was formed. Godley's health had been impaired by the shooting accident already referred to, when he had lost the sight of one eye. He had, however, retained sufficient vitality to be up to his old tricks, and complaints were laid against him during parliamentary debates. The main grievance was that Godley inflated the importance of his own post by trying to prevent direct access being made to his chief, even at the highest level.

The work of the Commissioners was not confined to the distribution of hard cash. The historical significance of the Irish Church Act lay in the fact that a large part of the Church property had consisted of land. This was now used by the Commissioners for an experimental scheme of state-aided purchase of the land by the tenants, who were given first refusal before it was offered for sale elsewhere. The significance of their scheme has, in retrospect, been obscured by the prominence give to the tenant purchase provisions of the 1870 Land Act, which has been described as 'a much less successful and less extensively applied measure.'[9] In fact, the Church Commissioners paved the way and laid the foundation for both the 1870 and the 1881 Land Acts.

The partial failure of tenant purchase under the 1870 Land Act was caused by the complicated nature of the presentation of the 'Bright Clauses', so-called because they were drawn up by John Bright. A large number of the small-holders, who were illiterate and spoke no English, were unable to understand the conditions of conveyance of property, with the result that they were blamed for being uncooperative. Monck and his colleagues on the Church Commission had regarded the conversion of small tenant farms into peasant proprietorships as 'a special trust and duty . . . The extent and success of the scheme was due very largely to the sound business methods of the Commissioners and their sympathetic appreciation of the people with whom they had to deal.'[10] By taking an immense amount of trouble, they reduced the terms of all transactions to the simplest possible form. To accept an offer of pre-emption (first refusal) the tenant merely had to sign his name or make his mark, write or cause to be written about five words on a questionnaire, and produce one quarter of his purchase money. In due course, by payment of instalments in place of his former rent, he became the absolute owner of his land. The Commissioners made a second offer to all tenants, carefully explaining the terms personally, so that those who had misunderstood the first might have another chance.

Some of their reports show the amount of work involved. On $3\frac{1}{2}$ acres in County Mayo were 120 cabins in a ruinous condition, while in County Armagh 'the farms of individual tenants consisted of small separate fields scattered here and there and unconnected by any definite right of way.'[11] It was necessary for the Commissioners to provide a map in their report, showing the allocation of land to different tenants; but conveyances of land to the tenants were made by description, since there was no power to make maps binding in case of disputes over boundaries.

The Land Commission, formed in 1881 to put into effect the provisions of the first and second Land Acts, evolved directly from the Church Temporalities Commission; and as Land Commissioners, Monck and some of his colleagues continued the work for which, as Church Temporalities Commissioners, they had already laid the foundations.

Charles Monck was also appointed Commissioner for National Education in Ireland following the passing in 1870 of the Elementary Education Act which provided for state-aided, non-sectarian schools; and in 1880, he became one of three official Visitors to the Convict Prisons of Dublin, who were given 'free access to all prisoners and all parts of the prisons.'

Although his work for both Church and Land Commissions was employment after his own heart, his letters show increasing dissatisfaction with the government's dilatory treatment of Irish affairs. While he agreed that, in some circumstances 'half a loaf was better than no bread,' he openly denounced the pretence of offering the whole loaf when the intention was to give half. The Land Act of 1870 had provided for Courts of Arbitration to settle landlord-tenant disputes, 'restraint' on evictions other than for non-payment of rent, for state loans to tenants wishing to purchase their holdings, for compensation to evicted tenants for 'disturbance' and for improvements they had made. The original Act was amended by the House of Lords, leaving it with far too many loop-holes which were taken advantage of by unsympathetic landlords. Monck had made a long speech in support of the Bill in its original form, and protested strongly against the amendment which, he said, would have the effect of 'mutilating' the Land Act. He described his own county of Wicklow which now contained some of the best farms in Ireland, but which had once consisted of dense forest:

> It was said that, in old days, a squirrel could pass from one end of the county to the other without touching the ground. The land in Ireland has been brought under cultivation almost exclusively by the labours of the tenants, and that gives them a claim to consideration totally irrespective of specific improvements they might make.[12]

He was able to tell them truthfully that his relations with his own tenants in five counties * had always been satisfactory, only two cases having been brought to court. 'Of course I shall not press them,' he wrote to his son, when telling him of personal economies he was making owing to his Kilkenny tenants' being unable to pay their rents.

The Land Act with which Gladstone hoped to 'pacify Ireland', unfortunately coincided with demands for strong measures to repress 'outrages'; and at the opening of Parliament in February 1870, the Speech from the Throne recommended 'special provisions against agrarian crime'. Monck's reply to the speech was not of a kind to make him popular with members of the government. He told them it was time they faced the fact that there was enmity between

---

* His property in County Meath had already been sold.

the Irish people and British law. 'Can Parliament,' he asked, 'with a clear conscience pass extra-constitutional and repressive measures for the prevention of crime which was directly due to their own neglect?'[13]

A succession of good harvests during the late sixties and early seventies had not improved the relations between tenants and landlords. Many of the latter made the resulting comparative prosperity an excuse for raising their rents, the non-payment of which was followed by eviction. The first Land Act, as originally drawn up, had contained a clause to prevent 'rack-renting', that is, the forcing up of rents. The amendment removing this clause had, as Monck prophesied, so mutilated the Bill that it went a long way towards cancelling out the provision against eviction other than for non-payment of rent. By this provision the Act aimed to abolish the age-long grievance of insecurity of tenure or tenancy-at-will, whereby a man could be turned out of his farm when it suited the landlord's convenience. Without fixed rents, this clause of the Act was to a great extent ineffective. The tenant moreover would not be entitled to 'compensation for disturbance' if it could be proved that he had not paid his rent; in any case, a sum of money, however large, would not compensate an Irishman for being driven from the plot of land on which he and his fore-fathers had lived and worked.

In their ignorance of Ireland and the Irish, Gladstone and his colleagues had not taken into account the Irishman's passionate attachment to his land. To deprive him of it in exchange for compensation was like asking him to sell his child or abandon his mother. Rather than be dispossessed, many of the small-holders borrowed money to pay the increased rents, only to find themselves unable either to repay the loan or to meet the next year's rent. Destitution followed the inevitable eviction for non-payment, and the situation became still more desperate when, in 1876, the period of good years came to an end and was followed by a succession of wet summers and ruined harvests. The failure of potato and corn crops coincided with a drop in prices of livestock. As the result of the sudden growth of the American livestock market, cattle were unsaleable, and a state of near-famine existed in many districts.[14]

Thousands of landlord-tenant disputes were dealt with in the special courts set up by the Land Commission. Charles Monck set a personal example by voluntarily reducing his own rents where necessary, refusing to evict for non-payment, and encouraging his tenants to purchase their own land at a rate agreed upon between them and himself.

If from the Government's viewpoint he was the ideal man to fill the office of Land Commissioner, the appointment was equally the answer to his own personal wishes, both on public and on private grounds. From the time of his boyhood in County Tipperary where his father had worked for poor relief, through his early manhood when he had devoted himself to works of relief during the years of the Great Famine, he had aimed at a position from which he could attack the basic causes of distress in Ireland. His travels throughout the country, in connection with the Land Commission, enabled him to speak with authority on conditions existing in different parts of Ireland; and the experience gained by these tours, and from the findings of the Land Courts, caused him to revise some of the opinions he had formerly held. His own county of Wicklow comprised, as he had said, some of the best farming land in Ireland, but he had long been aware that very different conditions prevailed in other parts of the country. Of this he had personal experience from the supervision of his estates in Westmeath, Wexford and Kilkenny; also through his work for the Agricultural Improvement Society. In his early years he had seen the wretched state of the poorer tenantry in Tipperary, having been born and brought up at Templemore in that county. His grandmother, Anne Viscountess Monck, had married as her second husband, Sir John Carden, the owner of the Templemore estate. Sir John had had the reputation of being a good landlord, but one of his descendants by a former marriage earned the nickname of 'Woodcock' Carden 'because he had been shot at so often.' Before going to Canada, Charles and Elizabeth had been in the habit of paying regular visits to their numerous relations who were scattered all over Ireland and who, with one or two exceptions, were exemplary landlords. In consequence he had held a slightly over-optimistic view of the landlord-tenant relationship as a whole.

In 1846 Charles had written to Sir George Hodson that they must not expect an immediate response to their efforts to better the condition of the farmers by means of the Royal Agricultural Improvement Society owing to the small-holders' suspicion of anything in the nature of 'improvement', bitter experience having led them to believe that it was inseparable from dispossession; yet, when on leave from Canada in 1865, he had written enthusiastically to Henry of a model estate in County Galway. He now learnt that the owner was one of the dreaded 'improver landlords', and had caused intense misery in the district by wholesale 'clearances' having, so it was said, 'dispossessed a thousand families.'[15]

One of the apparently insoluble problems which confronted the Land Commission was the difficulty of being fair to both sides. Far too many of the landlords were ruthless and indifferent. In the 1880's, a landlord in County Clare mustered a large force of police and two detachments of regular troops in order to evict twenty-two of his tenants. The families to be dispossessed barricaded themselves into their houses, and poured from the windows hot water and 'stirabout' (porridge) on to the heads of the invaders, who made breaches in the walls with a battering-ram in the form of 'a huge beam with an iron ferrule supported on a tripod.'[16] Other landlords, however, were as humane and conscientious as Monck himself. During the run of bad seasons which succeeded the year 1876, they gave help which they could ill afford to their poorer tenantry. One of these, the proprietor of over 12,000 acres in County Galway, was George Henry Moore, M.P.,* to whom Patrick Lavelle dedicated a book on the Irish land question, addressing him as 'a true and constant advocate of the Irish tenants' rights, and a practical tenant-righter yourself.'[17]

These landowners whose predecessors had been absentee landlords, inherited estates which had been subdivided into holdings of an acre or less, this being an agent's usual method of getting a quick return from his employer's estate. A landowner whose entire income was derived from rent, must either go bankrupt when these were not paid, or else evict the tenants, consolidate the holdings, and farm the land himself. It was frustrating for a well-meaning landowner to know that, with the help of expert advice supplied through the Agricultural Improvement Society, he might farm his land successfully by consolidating the numerous small-holdings into an estate of a workable size. One of these, the English owner of a large estate in County Cork, believed he was dealing justly by his tenants when he took their farms in hand and offered to employ

---

* G. H. Moore, M.P., was father of the author, George Moore.

233

them as labourers. He could not understand their reluctance to be employed on a prosperous and well-run estate in return for a regular weekly wage, preferring to scratch a bare living from their own small plots. A man might possess no more than a potato-patch and a pig while the more fortunate kept a cow which grazed on the grass verges beside the road; yet neither would willingly exchange this precarious livelihood for regular employment, however well paid. When forced to do so, he was unable to adapt himself to the unaccustomed routine of working to rule, for set hours, following unfamiliar methods imposed by his employer.

The Land Commissioners and their courts had to distinguish between the heartless, rapacious landowners and the benevolent ones whose tenants took advantage of their leniency; between the thrifty, industrious small-holder struggling under impossible conditions, and the improvident layabout whose farm was a disgrace to the district, who allowed weeds to grow unchecked, seeding themselves over neighbouring farms; or who divided his holding into even smaller plots and sublet them, rather than work the land himself. In Parliament, in his correspondence and in discussions at the Athenaeum, Charles Monck continually strove to refute the general impression that these undeserving tenants were typical of the whole of Ireland. He also tried to convince the government that, if many of the Irish were shiftless and unenterprising, it was because neither they nor their forefathers had had any inducement to be otherwise. During the penal times, every attempt was made to create an illiterate peasantry. Catholic schools and colleges were forbidden by law, and the Foreign Education Acts forbade the sending of children to colleges abroad.[18] The deliberate crippling of many Irish industries by embargoes and restrictions on commerce, gave foundation to the saying that 'England was enriched at the expense of Ireland.' While, on the land, insecurity of tenure and the hopelessnesss of making ends meet, were not conducive to hard work and planning ahead; and there were plenty of agitators to convince the farmers, often with justice, that the landlord class was responsible for all their suffering.

The second Land Act, passed in 1881, gave the Land Courts power to reduce rents where necessary, and to forbid raising of rents by the landlords for the next fifteen years. Owing to parliamentary delays, this Act, like its predecessor of 1870, was passed too late to prevent outbreaks of violence as reprisals for unjust evictions. Charles Stewart Parnell, an Irish member of parliament, had become leader of the Home Rule League in 1875; the Land League – 'to oppose landlords' – had been formed; and the passing of the Coercion Act – 'for the protection of life and property, and to suppress murders and outrages'[19] – preceded the passing of the second Land Act.

On 17 January 1882, Lord Acton wrote that he had seen Charles Monck in London and that he was remarkable 'as the one happy Irishman'.[20] Charles' apparent cheerfulness can only have been due to his habit of keeping a 'stiff upper lip' as he had good reason to feel harassed and depressed. In August 1881, when Gladstone's second Land Act was being shuttled back and forth between the two Houses of Parliament, passing in the Commons and being amended in the Lords, Charles wrote to his son Henry:

> I don't think the English people care much about the Land Bill, but I think they care a great deal about the fact that the House of Lords has over-ruled the decision (to pass the Act in full) to which the House of Commons has come by majorities of more than two to one. It is very hard in argument to defend the House of Lords as a portion of our Constitutional arrangement. The best thing that could be said for it was that it worked well, but if it is found that this is not true, I fear its days are numbered.[21]

He was a staunch supporter of those provisions of the Act **which** were commonly called 'the 3 F.s', and stood for Fair **Rent, Fixed** Tenure and Free Sale, Free Sale giving a tenant the right to dispose of his holding. He had secured a hearing in Parliament, and although his views were not always complied with, they were listened to with respect by many statesmen, including Gladstone, Granville and Spencer. This is shown in their private letters, to himself and to each other, in which they frequently sought his advice or suggested that his opinion be asked. His present post, being a newly-created office, was neither glamorous nor spectacular; its importance became significant in retrospect, and then only to those who were politically well-informed. He had been offered alternatives; nothing came of Granville's suggestion that he should be sent as Ambassador to

Constantinople, and when offered the governorship of Madras, he turned this down on the grounds that a hot climate would be injurious to his wife's health.[22] An equally strong reason for refusing the latter was that it would have entailed another long absence from Ireland, against which he was determined.

During the year 1869 he was called to the Privy Council and received the Grand Cross of St. Michael and St. George. There had been warm and unqualified praise in the British press, by statesmen both Liberal and Conservative, and by the Queen herself, for his governorship of Canada. Consequently in that country, at least, it had been expected that he would be transferred to another senior colonial governorship, and one of their writers noted that – 'his subsequent career has been in no way remarkable.' In later years, Canadian historians have sought a reason for the return of the 'Unknown Irishman' to the obscurity from whence he came; in their eyes, the office of land commissioner was a come-down after being Governor General of Canada.

There is a striking similarity between the political careers of **Charles Monck and Trollope's hero 'Phineas Finn'.** The similarity must be a coincidence, however, *Phineas Finn* was published in 1869, before Charles had even returned from Canada. 'Finn' was denied government office, because, though well-liked as a man, he could not be trusted to vote against, for instance, Irish tenant rights, if the claims of his party required him to do so. Like Charles, he was an Irishman first and a party-man second, and he, too, was given a job in Ireland, perhaps to get him out of the way. But Charles Monck had the advantage of a seat in the House of Lords, so his voice could not be so easily silenced. And there may have been no ulterior motive in his case. He was the obvious man for the Land Commission, and all his letters show that he was well content with it. He was doing the work nearest his heart, in a salaried appointment which would take him no further from home than London, and would enable him to spend the greater part of each year in Ireland.[23]

An entirely fictitious rumour was circulated, many years after his death, to the effect that he impoverished his family by spending lavishly on the aggrandisement of Charleville, in order to persuade Gladstone to visit him, with the object of being offered the Viceroyalty of India. Also that his subsequent disagreement with

Gladstone was the result of his disappointment on that score. 'Hopes of India were his [Monck's] , but they were never realised, and the family finances suffered somewhat in the process of casting bread on ungrateful waters.'[24]

It is quite certain that Charles would never have consented to go to India even if the Viceroyalty had been offered him – an unlikely event when the post was not vacant. As for Gladstone, Charles was Lord Lieutenant and Custos Rotulorum of the County of Dublin from 1874 to 1892, and could do no less than invite Gladstone to Charleville when, in 1877, Gladstone paid his first and only visit to Ireland. Gladstone had known the Monck family for more than forty years, and needed no special inducement to visit them. The *Pinus insignius* which he planted on that occasion, can still be seen in the 'pleasure grounds', disproving the further rumour that Monck 'uprooted it after falling out with Gladstone.'

Charles belonged to the Liberal party, but his private correspondence and his speeches in the House of Lords show that he was never in complete agreement with its leader. His lack of confidence seems to have dated from Gladstone's famous pronouncement on first becoming Prime Minister: 'My mission is to pacify Ireland'. During the next twenty years Charles fought a losing battle against the administering of palliatives to Ireland, rather than the removal of injustices. He was severely criticised for his views which, forty years later, would have been labelled 'Bolshie', and to-day might be stigmatised as extreme left-wing.

The House of Lords was then largely composed of landowners on a big scale, and the greater part if not all of their wealth was derived from land rents. Besides those who were resident, or nominally resident, in Ireland, there were many who owned land in that country in addition to estates in England or Scotland, and yet others who had no stake in Ireland but objected to the second Irish Land Act (1881) on principle. The Duke of Argyll was one of many who considered that the second Irish Land Act threatened the rights of property. He resigned from the Cabinet, and afterwards wrote an indignant personal letter to Monck in reply to one that the latter had written to *The Times* defending Irish tenants' rights and giving detailed statistics in support of the defence. Argyll's main grievance was that the provisions of the Act were to be paid for 'not by the State out of its own funds, but out of the Property of one class which

237

happens to be in the minority . . . the most demoralising transaction to which the British Parliament has ever been committed . . . the consummation of humbug.'[25]

Only a few of Monck's friends shared his views and aim; most of them agreed with Argyll that 'the rights of property' were threatened by the Land Act, in spite of the pruning it had received before being passed in the Lords.

Among those of Charles Monck's letters which have survived to the present day, there are several which prove that he wrote and spoke in defence of the landlords when it was possible to do so with justice. If the majority of his letters seem to imply that he was unfairly prejudiced in favour of tenants' rights, this was because they were written to prominent members of the government and owners of large estates, whose correspondence is preserved in museums and archives, and therefore accessible today. These men were usually heavily biased in the opposite direction, and none was more so than his eldest son, Henry. Unlike his father, who had been educated in Ireland, Henry had been sent to Eton and Christ Church, Oxford, and was now in the Brigade of Guards. He idolised his father and deferred to him in all personal matters, but in politics he was as rigid a die-hard Tory as his namesake and maternal grandfather, Henry Rathdowne, who had received the same education.

To young Henry, all Irish patriots were rebels, while the formation of nationalist movements was an act of disloyalty to the British Empire. That the Irish had never accepted British rule, that they considered their country to be under enemy occupation, that to them every act of violence was justified in being a blow struck in the cause of freedom – all this was entirely beyond the scope of Henry's comprehension. Charles did not mince his words when speaking in the House of Lords, and expressed himself forcibly in letters both personal and official; but when writing to his son, he often adopted an apologetic tone, pleading the bad harvests and falling prices as an excuse for reducing his own rents, pointing out that it was to his own financial advantage to help his tenants to purchase their land.

Notes to Chapter Eighteen

1 Monck to Monsell, 24 October 1867.
2 Monck to Henry Monck, March 1868. Monck Papers. Canadian Archives.
3 J. L. Hammond, *Gladstone and the Irish Nation* (London, 1938).
4 Hansard Parliamentary Reports, 1869. Institute of Historical Research.
5 *Ibid.*
6 Monck to Monsell, 23 December 1868.
7 The Rev. Canon A. Stokes in an article in *The Irish Times,* 1970.
8 Between 1871 and 1882, £1,000,000 was given to Irish intermediate education; £1,300,000 to a pension fund for National School teachers; £1,271,500 to distress works; £950,000 to cover arrears of rent payments; £250,000 to sea-fisheries. By agreement with the Catholic Church, the existing grant to Maynooth Theological College was discontinued in return for compensation. Sir Llewelyn Woodward, *Oxford History of England, 1815-1870.*
9 Hugh Shearman, *Irish Historical Studies, 1944-45: state-aided land purchase under the Disestablishment Act of 1869.*
10 *Ibid.*
11 *Ibid.*
12 Hansard Parliamentary Reports.
13 Hansard Parliamentary Reports.
14 The Rev. Patrick Egan, *Ballinasloe. A Historical Sketch.*
15 *Ibid.*
16 G. Shaw Lefevre, *Incidents of Coercion in Ireland.*
17 Rev. Patrick Lavelle, *The Irish Landlord since the Revolution.*
18 Hayden & Moonan, *op. cit.*
19 J. C. Beckett, *A Short History of Ireland,* (London, 1952).
20 Paul Herbert (ed.), *Letters of Lord Acton to Mary Gladstone* (London, 1904).
21 Monck to Henry Monck, August 1881. Monck Papers.
22 A letter from Sir Mountstewart Grant Duff to Monck, from Government House, Madras, 18 October 1886, refers to Monck's former refusal of the post. Monck Papers.
23 'I shall now, I hope, be pretty constantly resident at Charleville,' he wrote in February 1870, to Sir George Hodson, after thanking him for having deputised as manager of Callary School, and confirming his intention of 'resuming his former position.' In the same letter he accepted an invitation to join a 'Literary Club' in Ireland.
24 *The Irish Times,* 8 January 1963, in an article on Charleville.
25 Argyll to Monck, 3 January 1882. Monck Papers.

19

Three Weddings

Far from 'spending lavishly', schemes for retrenchment formed the theme of all Charles' letters to the family after his return from Canada. His own father had died at the age of fifty-eight, and Elizabeth's father at sixty-three; having passed his own fiftieth birthday, Charles was looking ahead with some anxiety to the time when Henry would succeed him. Mainly by selling property, he had already reduced the debt of £90,000 inherited from Henry Rathdowne to £27,000, but he would not feel easy until the estate was solvent. In a letter written in 1874 he told Henry that, with one exception, the only expenditures he had made in the past five years had been on the water-supply for the house and farms, and on farm out-buildings.

The one exception was a dreadful act of philistinism, typical of the period in which aesthetic taste was still influenced by the erection of the Crystal Palace in 1851. Charles had been naïvely proud of the domed conservatory he had built on to Spencer Wood in 1863, and of another, in the same style, added to Rideau Hall. Charleville was saved from the same fate by his determination to economise, and he contented himself with concealing the front door by a large glass porch.

A few changes had been made in the Charleville personnel. Brock still ruled the menservants, but Agga had died. Hobson had been allowed to stay on as head gardener long after he had lost the use of his limbs and could not even supervise the work. But now Charles installed a young steward, James Douglas, who would be responsible for the gardens, demesne and home farms. A hypochondriacal sister lived with him in the charming little house built into the wall surrounding the kitchen garden; self-centred and exacting, she was perhaps the reason why Douglas never married. Henry Sandys was first assisted and, later, replaced by a young agent called John

240

Macdonald Royse, as handsome as he was efficient.

The death in 1871 of her sister, Fanny Cole, was a great shock to Elizabeth. They had been very close and had, to a certain extent, 'shared' their children; Elizabeth treating Feo and Frank as if they were her own, while Fanny had taken charge of Stanley when he was sent home from Canada without his parents. Fanny had been regarded as an object of compassion by her sisters who had no use for Owen Cole. He, however, appeared to be prostrated with grief when she died, and celebrated the occasion with one of his elegiac poems. Louisa Monck had died at Barbavilla during the previous year and, though this was the first break in the 'sisterhood' since 1837, she had been very ill for so long that her end was what was then called 'a happy release'.

It was hard on Puss to have her gaieties curtailed by two periods of family mourning. She adored parties, and had only lately escaped from the bondage of her long convalescence. She usually managed to get her own way, but for several months after her aunt's death, even her indulgent parents drew the line at attendance at balls in London or Dublin. So she was thrown back on the resources of the neighbourhood, where she enjoyed riding the young horses and driving herself about to visit her friends.

Before the black-edged period set in, there had been a great gathering at Charleville for Henry's coming of age in January 1870. His own generation of cousins was represented by two of the Croker girls; Grace, the young Duchess of St. Albans; Frank Cole; and, of course, George Brooke. Frank was eleven years older than Henry and George, but he joined these two inseparables as often as his military duties permitted, thus forming a trio whose chief preoccupation was field sports.

If Charles had wanted a boy with his own strength of character and capacity for hard work, he should not have married his first cousin. Henry had not been long at Oxford before his father accepted the fact that his schemes for a brilliant political career for his son were a waste of time. He had foreseen this possibility while Henry was still at Eton, when long and effusive letters from Mr. Walford – representing Henry as a paragon – were succeeded by Mr. Thackeray's brusque and more realistic reports:

His Composition is deficient in Imagination, but if he will

secure accuracy, I have no doubt that allowance will be made
for his lack of style. His Mathematics are not as good as they
should be. He is a very steady trustworthy lad.*

Charles had written then to the Duke of Cambridge, and
provisionally arranged for Henry to have a commission in the
Coldstream. Since Dick belonged to the same regiment, he and Feo
could continue to keep an eye on Henry, who would find many of his
former school-friends among his brother-officers. An added advantage, in the eyes of his parents, was that regiments of the Household
Brigade were stationed alternately at Windsor, Aldershot and in
London, and the long periods of leave could be spent at home. By
the time the Moncks returned from Canada, it was regarded as a
settled thing that Henry should enter the Coldstream when he left
Oxford after, it was hoped, taking his degree. 'I will gladly pay for
your coaches,' Charles had written; and with their assistance,
supported by exhortations from home, that end was eventually
achieved.

Meanwhile Henry did not allow his studies to weigh on his mind,
judging by his correspondence with George Brooke and Frank Cole
which was exclusively concerned with their respective horses
and dogs. Among the many dogs at Charleville, the speciality had
always been Irish Setters, both the ordinary red variety and the less
common black-and-tan breed. Tom Quin, the keeper, had referred
to the latter when he wrote of having sent a 'nicely-taned pup' to the
Clancartys. There were also at least eight terriers, and some
Newfoundlands, the stock of which had been increased by Henry's
taking home a puppy each time he returned from his summer
holiday in Canada. 'Shall you be bringing the Newfoundlands?' a
friend wrote to Henry whom he had invited to stay for a shooting-
party, implying that there had been at least an attempt to train them
as gun-dogs. Henry was later described as 'the best shot in Ireland',
and whether or not it was true, he was very much in demand, and
shooting visits in Ireland and Scotland occupied a large part of his
vacations. There was then good trout-fishing in the Dargle river, and
a letter to his father describes a day in which he and Tom Quin
caught eighty-four 'good-sized fish' between them, one of them

* Thackeray had succeeded Walford as an Eton house-master.

Capt. Hon. Henry Monck, Çoldstream Guards, in 1874.

weighing 2½ lbs. A letter referring to his hunting does not state the name of any particular pack. There was still no hunting in the immediate neighbourhood of Charleville, but George Brooke had had his own pack of harriers since 1869. Known as the 'Brooke Harriers' they subsequently became the Kildare Harriers.[1]

The family letters covering the period during which Henry left Oxford and joined his regiment, have been intentionally or accidentally destroyed. His next appearance on the scene is in the winter of 1873-74, when he became engaged to Edith Scott. Charles and Elizabeth had always found it hard to deny their children anything on which they had set their hearts, but in this case Henry's wishes coincided with their own. Edith was everything they could wish; Henry's young cousins described her as 'very pretty and great fun', and James Douglas, the steward, wrote that 'Lady Edith has

243

Lady Edith Scott, daughter of 3rd Earl of Clonmell, wife of Henry Monck.

won all hearts'. She was an orphan and the youngest survivor of a large family. During the two years since her mother died, she had lived in London with one of her sisters, Lady Maria Fitzclarence, who had a house in Warwick Square. But her girlhood had been spent in the country at the family home, Bishopscourt, near Straffan in County Kildare, and she had no difficulty in adapting herself to the Charleville way of life.

The head of her family was her eldest brother, known to his intimates as 'Earlie' Clonmell; not, as might be supposed, because he was an earl, but because he had borne the courtesy-title of Earlsfort during his father's lifetime. 'Earlie' was inclined to be tiresomely pernickety over details of the marriage settlement, and Charles gave way to him rather than cause embarrassment to the young couple. He and Elizabeth were delighted when the wedding, to take place in

London, was fixed for 23 July, their own wedding-day.

It did not matter to Henry that 'darling Edith' was not intellectually inclined. She was beautiful, merry and kind, passionately fond of horses, dogs and gardens. She had a talent, unusual at that time, for arranging flowers, and her services were much in demand for the making of funeral wreaths. Though with plenty of originality and a strong will of her own, she was accustomed to doing as she was told and to adapting herself to the convenience of her elders. Since her father died, she had implicitly obeyed 'Earlie'; from now on, she would obey Henry, even to the extent of asking a cousin of his friend Macduff to be one of her bridesmaids. During the weeks before her wedding, she was often with her future in-laws who were spending that summer in London.

> My dearest Henry I was so glad to get your letter this morning. I am longing for tomorrow to come, what a bore this wind is, I am afraid you won't be able to shoot either. [The month being June, she must have been referring to an army exercise or contest.]
>
> Louise [Puss] and I lunched with the Howards yesterday, and I dined with your people in the evening, and I think got on very well with Fan. You must teach me to talk on my fingers.
>
> I am very glad dearest Henry you will be able to go on Thursday [to Ascot], of course I shall go if you do, I only said I did not wish to go as I thought you would be at Aldershot. Come here tomorrow soon as you arrive, you will be sure to find us at lunch.
>
> Ever dearest Henry, – Your very affecate
Edith Scott
> I hope dearest you are feeling all right again.[2]

Henry had not been able to get leave for more than a very short honeymoon, allowing no time for a 'wedding tour' on the continent. There was a suggestion that they should go to Bishopscourt as 'Earlie' was not then living there, but it was decided that the journey to Ireland for such a short time would be tiring for Edith. The final choice of Tunbridge Wells* was perhaps due to that lack of

---

*   Tunbridge Wells was then a very fashionable watering place.

imagination of which Henry's Eton tutor had accused him.
'Tuesday, July 21st [1874]. Edith gave a tea-party in Warwick
Square, to show her presents to her friends,' Elizabeth wrote to a
relation, probably her sister Anne, who had not been able to come
over from Ireland. 'Such a number and variety of beautiful things I
never saw, and all so well-chosen and useful. Thursday, July 23rd.
The Anniversary of *our* wedding day. We were at the Church [St.
Paul's, Knightsbridge] at 11, and soon the bridesmaids and friends
arrived also.' Here followed a list of guests – 'as many as I can
remember,' and of the seven bridesmaids – '4 in pink and white and 3
in blue and white.' Henry's two sisters were bridesmaids, and the
others were his cousins and Edith's.

> It is a pretty Church and quantities of flowers growing round it,
> which made it all look pretty, or rather *helped* to make it so.
> Many Sergeants of the Coldstream Guards lined the wall from
> the gate to the Church. Lord Hawarden whispered to me: 'I am
> glad the sergeants are there to seize Henry if he wants to be off
> at the last.' At last the bride arrived with her brother, Lord
> Clonmell, and indeed it would not be easy to see a lovelier.
> Dressed in thick white silk and lace, long veil, and wreath put
> on to perfection. Both behaved very well. Stanley had prepared
> us for Henry's acquitting himself properly, for he amused us
> much by announcing when he arrived with George Brooke
> (Henry's two caretakers): 'Oh, we have brought him up *very*
> fit.' Officiating Clergy: The Hon. & Rev. H. Liddel [Dean of
> Christ Church], and The Hon. & Rev. H. Mostyn [Edith's
> cousin]. The service was beautifully read. After signing, etc.,
> we all went off to a déjeuner at Col. Scott's, Eaton Square
> [Colonel Scott was Edith's uncle]. The Bride and Bride-
> groom's health was proposed by Lord Clonmell, and Lord
> Headfort led a *tremendous cheer*. Edith changed her dress for
> an exquisite one of Eton blue, and bonnet to match, and they
> went off with a shower of old shoes after.
> I just add, Feo was in green, Nina [Cole] in grey and pink. I
> in violet silk, with bonnet to match, with white feathers and
> point lace, and point lace shawl.

Before the summer ended, Henry was given a sufficient period of leave in which to make a long visit to Charleville with his bride. On the day they arrived, all tenants and employees were invited to a reception at Charleville, and Elizabeth made the occasion an excuse for assembling a mammoth house-party of relations. The Charleville carriage, and two other conveyances for their servants and luggage, met them at the Carlisle pier, and the coachman delivered a note from Charles welcoming Henry and Edith and preparing them for what was in store. 'They wanted to take the horses out and draw the carriage up the drive, but I have said it is my particular wish that this should not be done. I do not like to see men doing the work of beasts.' A local paper described their arrival and progress:

> The happy pair and suite were rapidly conveyed through Kingstown and the beautiful scenery which this part of the country presents, towards the far-famed Dargle, where they were met by Lord Monck's tenantry on horseback who escorted the carriage to Charleville.
>
> At another part of the route, several gentry of the neighbourhood evinced their respect by attending in carriages and on horseback, as well as a host of pedestrians. At the private entrance the labourers on the estate attended in a body and lined the approach to the house. At different points along the route triumphal arches had been erected, in evergreens and flowers, tastefully decorated with appropriate mottoes and devices, under the superintendence of Mr. Douglas, the head gardener at Charleville.

The article described the ceremonies which immediately followed their arrival at the house, the 'outburst of cheering' as the family and their visitors appeared on the raised terrace, and the speeches, presentations and introductions, which lasted until darkness fell. Then – 'Bonfires were lighted on several hills, and rejoicings were kept up to an advanced hour in the morning.'

In October, Henry and Edith were still at Charleville, but long before that time Charles had gone over to London. He was now working at full stretch; to his commitments in Dublin, as Custos Rotulorum and Lord Lieutenant of the County, and to his work on the Irish Church and Land Commissions, were now added directorships and subsequently chairmanships of the National Bank in London and the Anglo-American Telegraph Company. The latter directorship occupied a great deal of his time, but it also increased his income, and this was no small consideration when the prospect of paying off the inherited debt seemed more than ever remote. He had had unexpected expenses owing to sixteen-year-old Stanley's total inability to keep within his allowance, and the provision for Henry's marriage settlement was a heavy drain on his resources.

With Edith being entirely submissive to Henry, who seldom took any step without first consulting his parents, it fell to Charles to find them a London house in which they would start their married life. 'I think I have seen a house that would suit you exactly,' he wrote. Number 78 Belgrave Road, with nine bedrooms, four reception rooms and 'capital offices' in the basement, had the added advantage of being 'close to Warwick Square' so that Edith would be near her sister, Maria Fitzclarence. It also had the inevitable conservatory 'opening off the smaller Drawing room'. Charles advised Henry to talk it over with Edith before deciding, and duly received a telegram asking him to secure the house immediately.

Edith was one of those happy and uncomplicated people to whom kindness and giving pleasure to those around her came as easily as breathing. Charles and Elizabeth grew more and more fond of her; she was their 'dearest Edith', especially when the birth of Annette Louise in 1875 was succeeded by that of Charles Henry Stanley in 1876.[3]

A few months after her brother's wedding, Puss electrified the family by announcing that she intended to marry Jack Royse, her father's extemely good-looking young agent. Owing to another gap in Henry's store of letters, the attendant circumstances can only be learnt by verbal accounts handed down from that generation to the next. If there were stormy scenes, they took place only in the privacy of the immediate family circle. It was generally supposed that Charles and Elizabeth were appalled, although not to the extent some parents would have been in those days when it was simply 'not done' for a girl to marry her father's agent. Charles was considered to be democratic to the point of eccentricity, while Elizabeth's views on marriage were romantic rather than ambitious.

Puss was a good horse-woman and a talented pianist. She was pretty and vivacious, though already, at twenty-eight, had become

Hon. Louise 'Puss' Royse, *née* Monck (1874-1913).

enormously fat. Her parents thought her a pearl among women; and
while their dear Fan was obviously cast for the role of a 'daughter at
home,' they fondly imagined that Puss had only to choose in order to
make a desirable marriage. This did not necessarily mean a distinguished match in a worldly sense. They would have welcomed as a
son-in-law any man of good character who would make their
daughter happy. The trouble was, they could see no prospect of
either happiness or security in marriage with Jack Royse, who was a
compulsive gambler and had not the means to support a wife in even
the humblest style. Nor did he show the least sign of intending to
improve his position or of putting himself out in any way by altering
his present habits. Apart from his well-earned salary, his handsome
face was his fortune, as were his tall figure and charm of manner; and

if Louise Monck liked to share his life in Dargle Cottage, he had no objection to allowing her extravagant tastes and his own to be supported by her father. Puss was not cut out to be a poor man's wife, but she had had her own way for too long, and would not yield either to warnings or entreaties. She and Jack were married in the September of 1875, and all her parents' fears for her were realised.

'Poor Puss, *I grieve to say,* is on the way to another child' – thus Elizabeth, twelve years later, informed Henry of the imminent arrival of the seventh Royse daughter. She and Charles never blamed Puss for having ignored their advice; if anything, she was dearer to them than ever, but they never arrived at the stage of calling their son-in-law by his Christian name. Charles had complete confidence in him as an agent, and his letters refer to 'Royse' only in that capacity, ignoring the closer relationship; except on one occasion when he wrote to Henry about 'guaranteeing Royse's overdraft at the bank.' In Elizabeth's letters he is not mentioned at all.

These were sorrowful years for Elizabeth. Her sister Anne died in 1876, and early in the same year Charles became seriously ill. It was said that his illness, possibly rheumatic fever, was the result of having been given a damp bed to sleep in during his travels about Ireland on behalf of the Land Commission. He recovered to a certain extent, and continued for several years in his various posts, until another onset of 'rheumatism' left him, for a time, unable to walk. His friends had been greatly alarmed about him and agreed that the chief cause of his illness had been over-work. There is no date on the letter he received from Elizabeth's sister Harriet, whose sturdy independence had caused her to lead a life of her own, returning only occasionally to Barbavilla:

Dearest Monck. – I open my letter to Lizzy to say a word to you, and do not pooh pooh it without consideration. You have sometimes talked to me a little about your affairs. I do not want [need] you to *tell* me you work hard. I have lately, specially today, been thinking much of you working away whether you feel inclined or not. I want you to let me give you £2,000 of my *own* money, which would lessen my income about £100 a year. Thanks to your excellent arrangements about my other money I have plenty and should not want that £100 a year. I do not know whether £2,000 would be any good to you but if it would I can only say what *pleasure* it would be to give it you and lighten your burden a little. Now do not ignore my plan for I really have *plenty* of income. With best wishes Ever your affect anxious sister Harriet M. Monck.

I can send you my books to show you I have plenty.

Charles wrote later to Henry on the subject of repaying his debt to 'Aunt Ha.', implying that he accepted a loan though not a gift. He would not have accepted even that, if he had not been desperate; but besides paying doctors' bills for Puss, he was being constantly besieged by Stanley's creditors. In 1878, at the age of twenty, Stanley was commissioned as 2nd Lieutenant in the 58th Regiment of Foot. According to one report, he was 'extremely lovable and had winning ways', and he was said to be universally popular. His parents, sisters and elder brother had always doted on him, servants adored him, and his friends found him irresistible no matter how much money he owed them. Part of his charm arose from his ability to live exclusively for the present moment. He was disarmingly penitent for past misdeeds, even while asserting that they had not been his fault; and the future only held reality for him in connection with hare-brained schemes which were always 'certainties'. He broke promises as easily as he made them, yet his friends continued to seek his company for the brightness and joy of living which he brought wherever he went. 'Send me a list of *all* your debts,' Charles would write, only to find, after settling them, that considerable sums were still owing. Worried to death by his own financial difficulties, he began to tire of Stanley's plausible letters, full of self-justification and of promises to reform; but the climax was reached in 1879, when Stanley was twenty-one.

Henrietta Brooke used to tell her grandchildren: 'Your cousin Stanley married a Lady we never quite cared about.' Her refined version of the event was wasted on her grand-children, who had already heard from their father, George Brooke, how Henry had burst into the room shouting: 'George! The most awful thing has happened. Stanley's gone and married a whore.'[4] Miss Alice Lymer was said to have plied her trade in Windsor, and to have 'got hold of Stanley' before he left Eton. If he did then engage himself to marry her upon reaching the age of twenty-one, it shows that he was capable of keeping at least one promise; and, as far as is known, he remained faithful to her for the rest of his short life, standing by her despite his father's refusal either to receive her or to allow any member of the family to meet her.

Charles' terrible anger and unyielding attitude can only be understood by taking into consideration the current conventions. It was then a man's duty to his womenfolk to prevent them from having even the remotest contact with one of doubtful reputation. To this end, a 'lady' did not dine in a public restaurant; if it was necessary to stay at an hotel, a private room was engaged. When Charles learnt of his son's secret marriage, his first care was to ensure that his own wife and daughters should be protected from any association with Stanley's wife. Neither would he insult his employees, tenants and neighbours by asking them to meet her. He was deeply angry with

Hon. Stanley Monck (1858-1896).

his son, who had placed him in a really frightful predicament, but the stern line he took was not through vindictiveness. He was still far from well, his daughter's marriage was proving to be as financially disastrous as he had feared; and now, as the result of Stanley's 'insane action', he found himself for the first time in opposition to his loyal wife.

Stanley was Elizabeth's youngest and favourite child, and by marrying secretly he had cut her to the heart. But he was still her son, she could not live without him, and she honestly believed that his wife should be received into the family no matter what her reputation had been. Charles remained adamant on the subject of Alice, but eventually Elizabeth wore him down to the point of allowing Stanley to come to Charleville at Christmas-time, though without his wife. Henry and Edith had not been able to get over for Christmas, and on 31 December Charles wrote:

> Stanley has, on the whole, behaved well. He asked me to forgive him, of which request I really did not understand the meaning, unless it was that I should receive his wife as my daughter-in-law, which I have no intention of doing. He has not alluded to the subject since, and no more have I. I think it right to put you on your guard, as I think it very likely that some pressure may be brought to bear on you to induce you to see the woman, and I think it would be better for you to refuse. I don't think it would be right not to mark by our conduct in that respect the sense we entertain of the ruin Stanley has brought on himself and the outrage he has committed on his family by his insane conduct. The best thing he can do is to . . . prove by a long course of steadiness that he is in some sense worthy of being restored to the place he formerly held in his own family. I am greatly afraid that this is not a lesson which he is learning here. I believe he goes back to England the day after tomorrow. I don't know what arrangement he had made about being in London, but Mama intends to go over to you on Monday next. I *cannot* leave before Monday week, but then we shall take a lodging.

This is the only letter in which Charles refers to Stanley's marriage. It shows him as a lonely figure, aware that matters are slipping beyond his control, unable to count on support from any member of his family.

A temporary solution to the problem arose through Stanley's regiment being ordered to the Transvaal where the Zulu war was in progress. Stanley fought at Ulundi and came through the Battle of Laing's Neck unscathed, although his horse was shot under him while he and his captain were leading a charge. The incident was commemorated by a painting by Lady Butler, afterwards engraved, called 'Floreat Etona'. Stanley's wife had accompanied him and slept in his tent until her ill health made it necessary for him to find other accommodation for her. 'The doctors have forbidden my wife to sleep under canvas,' was one of his many excuses for needing financial help from Charles. In acknowledging his father's contributions, he admitted that they had in one case saved him from being 'forced to leave the regiment', and in another from being 'arrested for debt on leaving the country', when the regiment was returning to England.

There is no further mention of either him or his wife in the family correspondence, except when Elizabeth wrote to ask Henry to see that Stanley's name was taken off the list of members at his club, as she could no longer afford to pay his subscription 'which is a great sorrow to me,' and when Charles said that Stanley had been to see him in London and had 'grown a great deal'. But it is still remembered at Charleville that Stanley was allowed to bring his wife home on at least one occasion, and that this was the result of Elizabeth's persuasion.

Notes to Chapter Nineteen

1   Raymond Brooke, *The Brimming River* (Dublin, 1961).
2   Edith Scott to Henry Monck, from Warwick Square, 16 June 1874.
3   Charles Henry Stanley Monck, Captain, Coldstream Guards, served in South African War, 1899-1902. In 1904 married Mary Florence Portal. Killed in action at St. Julien, France, 21 October 1914. Father of present Viscount Monck.
4   Raymond Brooke, *op. cit.*

20

Murder at Barbavilla and the Egyptian Campaign

When the Coercion Bill had preceded the passing of the second Land Act in 1881, Charles had protested against the use of force to suppress 'agitation', rather than the removal of its cause. To the Chief Secretary for Ireland, W. E. Forster, fell the ungrateful task of putting into effect the enactments of the Coercion Bill which included the suspension of the Habeas Corpus Act and caused hundreds of people to be imprisoned without trial. Forster was blamed for its desperate measures, although he was a humane and just man, and had earned the unkind nickname of 'Buckshot' Forster by his order that police should substitute buckshot for the ball cartridges they had formerly used for firing on hostile crowds.

The result of coercion was an increase in those very acts of violence it had been intended to suppress. Cattle were maimed, buildings burned, landlords, bailiffs and agents were murdered; judges feared to officiate and witnesses refused to give evidence. Reprisals also took the form of ostracising landlords, their agents, or any tenant who was rash enough to take a farm from which another had been evicted. This practice was given the name of 'boycotting' after Lord Erne's agent, Captain Boycott, had been victimised in this way in 1879. His case was by no means the first, but it was much publicised owing to British troops having been sent to relieve him and his family from what amounted to a state of siege. No labourer dared to work for a victim of boycotting, letters and newspapers were not delivered to him, and all supplies were cut off since shop-keepers refused to serve him. 'Nobody would buy from him a load of hay, nor sell him a loaf of bread.'[1] Charles Monck declared that boycotting produced 'as much actual loss and suffering, and more widely diffused, as murder, maiming and what are generally called outrage. But it is not calculated in the same degree to strike the imagination of those at a distance.'[2] The Land

League urged the people to regard landlords and their deputies as enemies, to kill whom was an act of war and no murder.

It became increasingly hard for Monck and the Land Commission to carry out the new Land Laws, when landowners could justly complain of 'atrocities'. Hitherto these acts of violence had arisen out of the desperation of men who had been evicted from their homes and had seen their wives and children starve. But in 1882 a new situation arose, proving that a state of war had been declared indiscriminately against the entire landlord class, irrespective of their individual merits. Also that shiftless and improvident small-holders were taking an unfair advantage of the relief gradually introduced by the Land Commission, and when their demands were not met, they profited by the general lawlessness and took their revenge. At the end of March a Mr. Herbert, known to be a generous and benevolent landlord, was shot at in County Kerry; and three days later, a murderous attack was made, in County Westmeath, on Monck's own brother-in-law, William Barlow Smythe.

William Smythe had been living alone at Barbavilla since Mary, the youngest of the Monck sisters, died during the previous year. On Saturday 5 April 1882, Harriet Monck came from her home in Dublin to spend Easter at Barbavilla, arriving at the same time as Maria Smythe, the wife of William's brother Henry who had been left behind in Dublin. Maria brought with her her two daughters; and 'two young gentlemen', whose names are not known, were also staying in the house. On Sunday morning, Maria Smythe and Harriet Monck were driven in the brougham the 'short half-mile' to Collinstown Church, where they were joined by William and the four young people who had walked across the fields. After the morning service, the younger members of the party returned to the house on foot, while their three elders remained for a celebration of Holy Communion. When leaving the church, Maria, who was by far the youngest of the three, politely insisted on sitting with her back to the horses, while William sat beside Harriet. The _Westmeath Guardian_ described the brougham as being 'circular-fronted with glass panels, so that the occupants of the rear seat could look out in front, and either see or be seen.' On entering the drive, where the avenue of trees was interspersed by shrubberies, a loud report and the shattering of one of the glass panels caused William to exclaim: 'Good God, I think we are under fire!' William, giving evidence at the inquest, described how, at the same moment, Maria Smythe fell forward with her head on the 'rere seat' between himself and Harriet –

> I thought she had fainted from terror, as she was a very nervous person. My attention was diverted from her as I pulled out my revolver, and held it out of the window. I did not see any person. The coachman stooped down to ask me if anyone was hurt, and I said no; I did not know she was dead at the time. He galloped the horse straight up to the yard. I only knew when we arrived in the yard that she was even wounded, she was carried in, and Doctor Carlton sent for.

According to the *Westmeath Guardian* (7 April 1882):

> The ball struck Mrs. Henry Smythe on the right side of the back of the head, shattering the skull. The unhappy lady at once fell forward, with her head between Mr. Smythe and Lady Harriet Monck. Mr. Smythe's coat was splashed with blood and Lady [Harriet] Monck's dress shockingly stained and smeared . . . investigation prompt and rapid failed to discover the murderers.

William was in the tragic position of knowing that his sister-in-law's death was the result of her having taken the seat he would normally have occupied, since there was no doubt that he had been the intended victim. His personal grief took the form of intense bitterness which increased when his demand for vengeance remained unsatisfied. The police of the district did their utmost, at the risk of their own lives, but nobody dared come forward to give evidence. Even the coroner insisted that information relating to the murder was 'a subject for investigation by a stipendiary magistrate', and not for his court which was 'for ascertaining the cause of death only'.

It was well known that William's death had been planned by friends of one of his tenants who had recently been evicted, if not by the man himself. William published the press reports of the murder and inquest, with the whole correspondence concerning the eviction – the first to take place on his property for fifty years. He declared

Cartoon published in *Citizen and Irish Industrial Advocate* three years after the Barbavilla murder. *Left to right:* 'Organising expenses' from U.S.A.; 'Innocence executed', Mrs. Smythe; the gallows are innocent people executed owing to their refusal to testify for fear of reprisals; 'No pull, no pay', the boycotting of those refusing to collaborate. 'Nationality'...

that he had been the first landlord in that county to reduce rents; and that he had in the past given financial assistance to the man Riggs, who was dispossessed of his sixty-seven acres only after he had refused offers of compromise and compensation. William had been forced to deal with the matter personally, the agent having left his employment after receiving anonymous, threatening letters, signed 'Rory of the Hills'. One of these is given below:

> This is to warn you to give up immedally Barlow Smyth's agentcy if yo expect to live long let him do his dirty work himself as he is going to be a tyrant the same hand is ready for you as took down Crawford. If you disregard this warning, If you mention this letter to anyone except your wife yo sale your own Death Warrant. I'll hear if yo spake of it to peelers or any one else and if I do remember rory. death to Tyranny.[3]

William had been bewildered and hurt, as well as indignant, by the hostility of his dependents. After the tragedy on 2 April, the local paper described him as 'the most generous landlord in County Westmeath . . . So far as is known, he was popular with his tenantry.' He claimed to have 'acted with moral equity' throughout the eviction case; yet apparently nobody seemed to care that an attempt had been made on his life, and that it would probably be followed by another. His letters, both before and after the murder, suggest that his weakness lay in the fact that, while acting with justice and even with generosity, he did not really like the Irish people. His antecedents, he said, were Celtic as well as Saxon; yet he wrote of 'this wretched country', and while doing all the right things, he felt no real friendliness or sympathy for the Irish, either collectively or individually.

After 'Rory's' revenge had been taken on the wrong person, William received many hundreds of letters. The majority of these were sympathetic, but some were abusive. 'Treat the people better and you'll be treated better yourself,' wrote an ex-employee who had emigrated to America. The same writer expressed an earnest hope that Lady Harriet Monck had suffered no harm; while the Queen, who was at Mentone, directed the Lord Lieutenant to 'enquire for the health of Lady H. Monck.' William Smythe was convinced that inadequate steps had been taken either to detect the murderer of his sister-in-law, or to protect him from a renewed attack. On this subject he wrote angry letters to the Lord Lieutenant; the Chief Secretary; Mr. Gladstone and the editor of the *Freeman*. He published these, with the replies, in a second appendix to his pamphlet, under the heading: 'Put not your trust in princes, nor in any child of man'.

The fact that the victim of the Barbavilla murder was a woman, and that the intended victim was described as the most generous landlord in his county, gave rise to a great deal of publicity. This was followed by the 'universal horror'[4] caused by the tragedy known as 'The Phoenix Park Murders.'

The coercive measures had been stopped, the government having at last recognised that they were doing harm rather than good. Forster resigned, and was succeeded as Chief Secretary by Lord Frederick Cavendish, while Lord Spencer replaced Lord Cowper as Lord Lieutenant of Ireland. After taking part in Lord Spencer's state entry into Dublin, Cavendish walked across the Phoenix Park accompanied by Thomas Burke, the Under-Secretary. There they were set on by a band of assassins armed with knives, and stabbed to death.

The Phoenix Park murders caused horror and fury in Ireland as well as in England. The assassins were members of a small secret society, but millions of innocent people in Ireland suffered from the result, which was the passing in parliament of a Crimes Bill by which the country became, for a time, a police state.

In Ireland, during that summer of 1882, an insurrection in Egypt seemed remote and unimportant compared with events at home. An army officer, Arabi Pasha, led a rebellion against the Khedive with the object of freeing his country from European influence.[5] The British fleet bombarded and destroyed the rebels' fortifications at Alexandria, and Gladstone's cabinet decided to send out an army numbering over 16,000 under General Sir Garnet Wolseley.[6] Henry Monck's battalion, the 2nd Coldstream, had been sent over to Dublin where they were quartered at Richmond Barracks. Henry was on leave in July 1882, and he and Edith had taken the two children to Charleville before going on to the Shannon for a fishing holiday. Frank Cole had lately been widowed, and they persuaded him to join them in the little lakeside hotel at Killaloe. Late in the evening of 22 July, Henry received a telegram from his adjutant:

'You must return to duty on Monday. Battalion under orders to embark. Precise date not yet announced.' Charles and Elizabeth were still in London, and Henry wrote at once, begging them to come to Ireland before he embarked –

> I could not go without seeing you. Poor Frank! It must reopen an old wound seeing our distress, and it shows how self-denying my darling Edith is for one of her first thoughts was for him, and the distress our sorrow must cause him. I ought to be thankful to have lived so long without knowing sorrow. With the exception of your illness I have known none.

Another onset of Charles's illness prevented him and Elizabeth from reaching Ireland before the 2nd Battalion embarked from Kingstown on 1 August. When they finally joined Edith at Charleville, they were inundated by letters of sympathy, including one from Frank Cole to his 'Dearest Aunt', saying: 'Edith has behaved like a heroine; broken hearted, but thinking of everybody but herself.' In the present century, after two world wars, the grief caused by Henry's departure may appear excessive. At that time, however, it was unusual for soldiers to be called upon to fulfil the duties for which they had been trained. During their eight years of married life, Henry and Edith had not been separated for more than a few days; and in the unlikely event of his battalion being ordered abroad, she would normally have accompanied him. He had, too, particular reasons for not wishing to be far from home. He was desperately worried about his father's health and, in every letter he wrote from Egypt, implored him not to work too hard. And in all the letters of condolence to his parents, the anxious enquiries for Edith suggest that she may have recently had a miscarriage, possibly one of many, which would account for there having been no more children after the birth of Charlie in 1876.

Henry kept a brief journal describing the Egyptian campaign, beginning with the thirteen-day voyage to Alexandria: 'Many of the men sea-sick on parade, and the decks in a nice state of filth after.' After five days in the vicinity of Alexandria, the army re-embarked in fifty-two transport ships with a man-o'-war at the head of each of the five divisions; 'a very fine sight', Henry thought it. They arrived off Port Said on 20 August, then steamed up the Suez Canal to

Hon. Henry Monck in Wolseley's Army, Cairo. 1882.

Ismalia, where they landed on 22 August and 'bivouacked on the banks of the Sweet Water Canal – a misnomer, for it is the filthiest water imaginable.' From 24 August until 13 September, the entries in the diary contain little beyond accounts of long marches in pursuit of a retreating enemy. There was no transport owing to the railway line having been blocked and the engines taken away by Arabi's men. All baggage had to be left behind, supplies of food were very short, and for five nights there were no tents – 'not even a great-coat for covering.' By 29 August some sort of communications had been established, and 'light baggage' and tents arrived, the latter being very welcome as the nights were extremely cold. Henry entered in his diary: 'I ought to have mentioned before that H.R.H.[7] has undergone the same privations as anyone else. He is most energetic and has a kind word for everybody.' On 25 August there was an 'engagement' at Tel-el-Mahuta: 'We formed for attack, but beyond this we did nothing, as the cavalry had it all their own way.' There had been several casualties before ever they were under fire. At every pause in the march, they were allowed to drink canal water, and ordered to fill their water-bottles with it before proceeding. There had therefore been many cases of sickness, some of them fatal, among both officers and men, and nearly everyone had dysentry. At least two men in Henry's company had been drowned while bathing, and one stung by a scorpion. Yet Henry wrote to his father on 12 September:

> I think the newspapers seem to have exaggerated the amount of the sickness out here. I think that must have been the cause of your telegraphing to me to ask if I was suffering from illness... Now that he has got his troops up here, I think that Sir G. Wolseley is pretty certain to attack Tel-el-Kebir within the next few days.

The victory of Wolseley's army at the battle of Tel-el-Kebir went down in history as having been based 'on that rarest of military feats a long and completely successful night-march.'[8] Arabi was captured and his army destroyed. On the eve of the battle, Henry wrote to his father:

> If it should please God to take me in action, I am sure it will be a comfort to you and Mama to hear again from me, though I have told you before, that you have been model parents to me & everything in this world has been taught me by you both, & since my marriage my darling Edith has done her best to make me good & read the Scriptures,[9] and to keep up the good teaching you have given me.

In his diary Henry recorded:

> A quiet day. All the Generals were out between 3 and 7 this morning having a look at the ground in direction of Tel-el-Kebir. We got orders in the afternoon to strike tents at dusk & march... There was no moon but the stars were, as usual, very

bright. We were informed afterwards that we were steered by the stars. We halted several times during the night.

Sept. 13th: just before dawn . . . a tremendous firing in front of us and the whole of the sky in that direction lit up with flames. We had arrived at the right moment in the right place viz. in front of the works of Tel-el-Kebir. The shells began now to drop unpleasantly near us. They principally dropped behind us, on the very ground we had been halted on a few minutes previous, but some struck close in front of us.

Number 5 [Company] was now sent out in extended order, and remainder half of the battalion was deployed. The deployment was carried out as quietly as if we had been in the Barrack Square. We had now nothing to do but lie down & be shot at, the front line doing all the work, and we were not wanted in support. The behaviour of the men was very good under trying circumstances. There was a good deal of ducking at the noise of the shells whistling over our heads, but no confusion. The shell fire ceased after a short time, but a very heavy musketry fire was kept up and bullets were striking all round us in great quantities . . . Our men were very sore at not letting off a single round of ammunition after carrying their 100 rounds per man for so long. My section would, I think, have done well for we had some good shots in it . . . In the evening we heard that our loss was about 450 killed & wounded. Casualties in Battalion [2nd Coldstream] 1 officer & 7 men wounded.

The rest of the diary describes their journey to Cairo which they reached on the evening of 15 September, the railway having been repaired. From there he wrote a more detailed account of the battle to Charles – 'Certainly Wolseley is the right man in the right place . . . I hope I am thankful enough to Almighty God for all his mercies to me. I think you could have had no anxiety for me, as the papers must have had the list of killed & wounded.'

There was now little to do but hang about in Cairo waiting for the transport ships to take them home: 'It appeared in orders last night [October 1] that we go on or about Oct. 25th in the *Lusitania* which is a most beautiful ship. The Grenadiers go about 28th in the *Batavia,* their old ship & a very bad one! The Scots Gds. about 30th in the *Nevada,* also a bad one!'

Henry was the more impatient to get home through having received letters from friends of the family telling him that Edith had been quite ill with anxiety for his safety, and that his father had had another bad attack of 'rheumatism'. His letters from Cairo consisted mainly of enquiries for the health of his family, and comments on news from home, particularly of the farms. He wrote briefly of the day-to-day routine; of the many officers who had 'gone sick' and been sent home; of his having been on guard over Arabi Pasha; of expeditions to the pyramids and to see the 'Dancing Dervishes'; of the veiled women, donkey boys and running footmen. The war was over, except for an occasional minor skirmish with remnants of Arabi's army. He made light of an 'adventure with the Arabs', giving no details, but wrote later: 'I wonder who was fool enough to send that letter to *The Times* about my having been captured and beaten by Arabs.' His indignation was on Edith's account; her health and spirits had improved after learning that the fighting was over, but she had been greatly alarmed by the newspaper report of the 'adventure'.

Henry's parents were in Ireland when he landed during the second week in November, but Edith had come over to London to meet him. Charles had arranged for her to have 'a capital place' at the Admiralty from which to see the review on 17 November in celebration of the victory. The next day, Henry wrote an account of it to his parents:

> We marched from Chelsea to Wellington Barracks where our Brigade assembled under the D. of Connaught. We then marched inside the railings of Buckingham Palace and formed a hollow square of Quarter Columns, officers & colours in front & on either side. The Queen came out on the Balcony; we gave the Royal Salute, then Hats off & 3 cheers for the Queen. We then marched to the Mall, & the Queen with an enormous staff & escort drove down past us to Horse Guards Parade. Then we marched past & continued our march as per route in paper. I may safely say that I have never seen such a crowd before. Along the whole route it was the same, except that about Whitehall it was rather more dense than anywhere else... Our dinner to the Duke of Connaught last night was a great

success. Capital dinner & wine & everyone very glad at being home again.

Two years later, Henry was again in Egypt with his battalion which formed part of Wolseley's expedition to rescue General Gordon, the governor general of Khartoum. The garrison there had been besieged by an army raised by a fanatic calling himself the 'Mahdi' or Messiah. The insurrection had 'spread like wildfire', and Wolseley had long been urging the government to prepare an expedition. Delayed by the indecision of Gladstone and his cabinet, Wolseley did not reach Cairo till September 1884, and an ill-prepared expedition set out from Wady Halfa in October: 'For three months a most gallant army marched and fought its way against time up the uncharted Nile, while all England counted its daily steps.'[10] They reached Khartoum on 28 January 1885, but they were too late. Two days earlier, the garrison town had been stormed and General Gordon killed. Wolseley's army remained in Egypt while contradictory reports as to their future movements succeeded each other. A threat of war with Russia increased the vacillating attitude of the government but, when that subsided, they still could not make up their minds about the forces in Egypt. The 2nd Coldstream, with the Grenadier and Scots Guards battalions, were to go home; they were to be sent to Cyprus; they were to stay in the Sudan. The country being quiet, Henry – promoted captain since January – arranged for Edith to come out and join him, only to telegraph a cancellation on his battalion receiving orders to embark for England in S.S. *Deccan*. Again orders were changed and the ship entered the harbour at Alexandria, but the battalion was ordered to remain on board, and Henry considered this 'hopeful'. 'We are in a state of great uncertainty,' he wrote on 27 May, 'still not knowing in the least why we are stopped here.' The situation was exactly the same when he wrote a week later; but on 14 June they disembarked and encamped at Ramleh, as the *Deccan* was required to convey invalids home. In the meantime, the government at home had been defeated, Lord Salisbury was Prime Minister, and plans were again in the melting-pot.[11] Edith, who had been expecting every week to receive her own 'embarkation orders', was again told by Henry to stay where she was until further notice.

She could not, in any case, have left home at that time. She had taken the children over to Charleville and, in June, invited her cousin, Mrs. William Blacker, to stay with her. Mrs. Blacker had been Mary Lawless, and was a sister of Lord Cloncurry. One of her children had recently died, and it was through what Henry called 'Darling Edith's usual thoughtfulness' that the invitation had been given, Edith sharing the conviction of her husband's family, that a visit to Charleville was the perfect cure for all kinds of affliction. The Lawless family were appropriately named, and had a reputation for eccentricity. Although afterwards described as having been 'in a delicate state of health', Mary Blacker was in the habit of riding at dawn on Sugar Loaf Mountain. A few days after she arrived, she complained of feeling unwell; and on the following morning, 21 June, she was 'found lying in bed in an insensible condition. Everything possible was done to save her life, but without avail. In a wardrobe in her room a small phial labelled "Laudanum" was found, and on a glass under her bed were marks of the same fluid ... The jury returned a verdict that death resulted from an overdose of laudanum.'[12]

Henry had not yet heard of this tragedy when, driven nearly frantic by the news that his father had again become seriously ill, he asked his Colonel, also Generals Fremantle and Stephenson, if they saw any objection to his sending his papers in, giving 'family affairs' as the reason. He wished to know if his superior officers considered that there was 'anything dishonourable' in his leaving his battalion while it was overseas. 'They all said that I need have no scruples in doing so, as we are not on active service at all now,' he told his father. He despatched yet another telegram to Edith, warning her not to leave England, and arrived home before the end of the summer.

Notes to Chapter Twenty

1 Anthony Trollope, *The Landleaguers* (London, 1883).
2 Monck to Earl Spencer, 2 January 1886. (Copy in Monck's hand, Monck Papers.)
3 W. B. Smythe, *A Tale of Westmeath Wickedness and Woe,* Dublin, 1882.
4 From a manifesto issued by Parnell, Davitt and Dillon.
5 Egypt had been declared a bankrupt state and, to safeguard their interests in the Suez Canal, England and France had assumed dual control of the country. See G. Carter, *Outlines of Irish History.*
6 Sir Robert Ensor, *England, 1870-1914* (Oxford Press, 1936).
7 The Duke of Connaught, younger son of Queen Victoria, commanded the Brigade of Guards. He and his Duchess visited Henry at Charleville in 1900.
8 Sir R. Ensor, *op. cit.*
9 Edith's mother, Anne Countess of Clonmell, *née* Anne de Burgh, had been in the habit of holding 'bible readings' under a tree, which is still pointed out to visitors at Bishopscourt.
10 Sir. R. Ensor, *op. cit.*
11 Gladstone's government had never been strong and was further weakened by his failure to save Gordon at Khartoum, and by concessions made to Russia. Although they succeeded in passing the Third Reform Bill, they were finally defeated on 8 June 1885, on a scheme for local government in Ireland, involving county boards under a national council.
12 Report of inquest in *The Irish Times,* June 1885.

21

London and Charleville

In 1884, Charles had resigned from the Irish Land and Church Commissions. This sport-loving, outdoor man would never ride or shoot again and, with his great white beard, he looked considerably older than his age which was sixty-five. He had undergone more than one long course of treatment at Bath, when he and Elizabeth had stayed at Stead's Private Hotel, but this had not helped him as much as he had hoped. He was now hobbling about with the help of two sticks, and there were times when he could not walk at all. It was therefore impossible to carry out conscientiously the duties of a Land Commissioner. The loss of the salary further reduced his income which was already greatly diminished through reductions of rents, and for this reason he determined to retain for as long as possible his chairmanships of the National Bank and the Anglo-American Telegraph Company. Since he could no longer make the frequent journeys between Dublin and London, he and Elizabeth rented a furnished house in London for several months of the year. He continued to fulfil his commitments as Lord Lieutenant of County Dublin, though some of these were carried out by a Deputy Lieutenant when Charles was unable to travel. To Henry he wrote instructions regarding the celebrations for Queen Victoria's Jubilee in 1887, explaining that the Prince of Wales had asked him to support the project of the Imperial Institute.

When Henry resigned his army commission, his intention had been to relieve his father of some of the duties connected with the Irish estates, in addition to taking some kind of civilian employment which would enable him to contribute to the family exchequer. On returning to England, he immediately set about the business of job-

269

hunting. Privately, Charles had no illusions as to his son's earning capacity; he encouraged him, however, exerting his own influence in many directions. Letters were written, strings were pulled, but to no avail. Henry had quantities of friends, they all enjoyed his company and were delighted to ask him to shoot, but nobody wanted to employ him. An unusual situation then arose by which the young couple, Henry and Edith, took up permanent residence at Charleville, with Henry attending to estate business and those country duties expected of a land-owner; while Charles continued to be the bread-winner, taking over the house in Belgrave Road and spending long vacations at Charleville.

The arrangement was a sad one for Elizabeth. She had always greatly enjoyed her visits to London, but all her real interests lay in and around the home of her childhood. Following in her mother's footsteps, she had supervised the local schools, and was familiar with every detail in the lives of the families on the place. She had daily visited homes where there was sickness or bereavement, she knew where an extra supply of free milk was needed and in which families there was a delicate or handicapped child who would never be able to earn a living. She had run a Clothing and Blanket Club, started a lending library at Charleville, and supported charitable organisations in Dublin. The Reverend Charles McDonough had died in 1873. Elizabeth thought very highly of him, and is said to have laid him in his coffin 'with her own hands'. He had written a book which Elizabeth instructed Henry to read daily, while its author was preparing him for confirmation in 1865. The new rector of Powerscourt was the Reverend (later Canon) Galbraith. His parishioners included owners of small estates in the district, and many more who had built villas or small houses in or near Enniskerry. With their assistance, and with that of his young curate, Mr. Boyle, the Sunday schools and bible class were well staffed; and Elizabeth's allusions to 'my Sunday School' referred to the parish of Callary, a wild spot between Charleville and Glendalough, where in 1830 her father had given the land for, and contributed towards the building of, a church and adjoining school.

The division between 'high church' and 'low church' was not then so rigid as it became in later years. Elizabeth taught her Sunday school class to observe all the feasts of the Church's year, including Saints' days; yet some of the hymns she taught them would now be

called strictly 'Evangelical'. The *Sunday School Hymnary* contained
the first hymn that she and her sisters learnt:

> Now that my journey's just begun,
> My course so little trod,
> I'll stay before I further run,
> And give myself to God.

Also a small paper-bound book consisted entirely of hymns by Mrs.
Alexander.

While Henry was in Egypt and prayers for his safety were made in
Powerscourt Church, Elizabeth also asked the Roman Catholic
priest, Father O'Dwyer, to pray for her son at Mass. Catholic priests
as well as Protestant clergy were regularly invited to Charleville,
where they would be entertained by the witty conversation of Father
Healy.[1] Elizabeth kept in constant touch with her neighbours,
besides those who were tenants or employees. Among her closest
friends were Isabel Lady Carnwath, at Taney House, Dundrum; old
Miss Selina Crampton, livng alone at Bushey Park since inheriting it
from her father, the judge; and Meriel Hodson, the wife of Sir
George Hodson, at Hollybrooke House near Bray. These contacts,
with many others, were part of her life; her preoccupation with them
and with their interests never ceased, even when she spent the greater
part of each year in London.

It might be supposed that the establishment of Henry and Edith as
deputy squire and squire's wife, in the house which was still his
parents' home, might have led to awkward consequences causing
rivalries and disputes. That no such complications arose is due to the
fact that the young couple deferred in all matters to their elders, who
from London ruled the roost down to the last detail. Charles wrote
instructions regarding every tree, field and farm-building; the
frequent letters from him and from Elizabeth contained advice concerning Christmas meat for the men, warm petticoats for the older
women, the distribution of free milk, and which needy family was
sufficiently 'deserving' to be allowed to occupy a vacant lodge.
Henry took over the Callary Sunday school, assisted by written
directions from his mother:

> I had meant to read them 'the pink book' on the Sundays

after the Saints' days. If you do that, you will have to borrow Annette's, as I borrowed the one out of the box and forgot to replace it. I left some very nice books for you to lend them.

Both Henry and Edith were perfectly happy with the arrangement and took it completely for granted. In this family, the actual ownership of Charleville had never been an important matter to those who were fortunate enough to live there. It was a family house, and its technical head ran it as a sort of free hotel for any of the family who cared to make use of it. Edith adapted herself to this, as to everything connected with Charleville, as easily as if she had been born there. Accompanied by a large pack of dogs, she daily inspected the gardens, pleasure-grounds and home farm, calling at all the cottages where she would sit down and recount the latest news of her husband's family. Although not so well-read as her mother-in-law, she was perhaps more efficient than Elizabeth in domestic accomplishments. She was a great needlewoman and knitter, and kept neat and conscientious household accounts. The house ran on oiled wheels, and the food was so delicious that it was fortunate for Henry that he had the kind of small, spare figure which would never put on weight. Elizabeth was reputed to be extremely fond of flowers, her favourites being 'moss roses, violets and carnations', while she had shown signs of a more sophisticated taste in starting the cultivation of orchids in the 'stove house'. Edith's tastes were less conventional; twice a week she personally 'did the flowers', filling the rooms with bowls of informally arranged flowers, ornamental grasses, and variegated foliage, while she showed skill and knowledge in her supervision of the gardeners.

She and Henry entertained a succession of their friends and relations at Charleville, and in July 1886, they gave a large garden party, inviting all the neighbours including clergy of all denominations. 'I *hope* the day of your party turned out better than you expected,' Elizabeth wrote from London, referring to the uncertain weather. 'It was such a good thing to give it. Do you remember in old times, if it rained, we danced in the hall.' When Henry's parents were at Charleville, he and Edith would go off on fishing expeditions or to attend a round of shooting parties, leaving the children in the charge of their grand-parents. '*Never* think that it is a trouble to me to have the children. They give us so much pleasure,' wrote Elizabeth.

272

After returning to London, she and Charles did not confine their letters of instruction and advice to estate and county affairs. Constant letters were exchanged on the subject of the children's governess, and of when and where Charlie was to be sent to a preparatory school. Charles and Elizabeth disagreed on this point. Elizabeth wrote:

> I cannot but think you are right sending him early. I remember telling your father that you ought to be sent *earlier*, but he did not think so. I used to think *no school* was the least evil, but I have a good deal changed my opinion.

Charles thought that his grandson should be kept at home for another year –

> A boy learns many things at home better than he learns them at school, and some things which he will never learn at school at all. On the other hand, it sometimes happens that a boy gets *beyond* a governess, but I don't think that is the case with Charlie.

Henry and Edith had good reason to know that Charlie had long been 'beyond' the excellent governess whom he shared with his elder sister. More than thirty years afterwards, Annette delighted his children with stories of the mischievous pranks Charlie used to play on his cousins, the Royse girls; also of those Sunday afternoons when, unknown to his parents, he would go fishing with Norman Galbraith, the rector's son, instead of attending Mr. Boyle's bible class. Annette herself was no model child, but she was all for avoiding scenes and became very clever at 'covering up' for her brother. On the occasions when she had managed to persuade him to accompany her to the curate's class, he drove the pony while she coached him in the psalm which he should have committed to memory during the week. 'They came about me like wasps, and they stink even as the fire among the thorns,' he would recite triumphantly, grasping the general theme although never becoming word-perfect.

Elizabeth won her point, and Charlie was despatched to Mr. Nunn's preparatory school at Maidenhead in January 1887, two

Left to right: Annette Monck, Winifred Royse and Charlie Monck in front of the glass porch added to the front door of Charleville by their grandfather Charles, 4th Viscount Monck.

months after his tenth birthday. It would be uncharitable to suggest that Elizabeth's advice had been given from anything but disinterested motives, but there is no doubt that the sending of Charlie to a school near London brought her a source of great happiness. Crossing on the night ferry, he was able to spend the greater part of the day in London, before being taken to catch the school train in the evening. Any other boys who had crossed from Ireland with him would accompany Charlie to 78 Belgrave Road. The morning was spent in visiting relations: 'Aunt E.' and Feo, Edith's sister Maria, her unmarried aunts, the 'Ladies Scott', and, by far the most important, old Mrs. Scott, the widow of Edith's Uncle Charles, in whose house in Eaton Square Edith's wedding reception had been held. After luncheon, the boys would be escorted by Morris, the butler, to the hippodrome or the aquarium, or to Hegler's Circus. The small household included Mathilde, who had been Stanley's nursery-maid, while Fräulein Denneler was a more or less permanent inmate. These all took a hand in spoiling Charlie as he went

274

to or from school, and on his frequent visits to London during the term, for it was not long before Elizabeth held Mr. Nunn, the headmaster, in the hollow of her hand. 'I have asked for Charlie,' she would confess apologetically to Henry, going on to explain that, for one reason or another, it had been absolutely necessary to do so. It may have been a faint protest from Henry which caused her to write: 'My dear, *nothing* about Charlie *could* give me trouble. It is such pleasure to see him. He is a great darling.' Having 'asked for him' during the summer term – 'I said to Mathilde before him, to see if he would understand: "Il faut avoir des fraises pour le thé," and he jumped for joy.' She usually urged him to bring friends with him on these unlawful outings from school, but they were seldom allowed to come. A persistent cough, which Henry thought 'merely a trick', gave her an excuse to have Charlie examined by her own Doctor MacLagan each time he was in London, and the doctor's long-winded opinion and advice filled many pages written to Charleville. 'Denny thinks Charlie looking very ill,' she wrote, when he went home for Christmas.

> I think, and Feo, that he is thinner, but he is growing much taller as you will see . . . Mrs. Scott thought very badly of his going over with only a little boy – so do I. I am *much disquieted* about it. Mrs. Scott and I agreed that we are both very old fashioned, but all the same, I am sorry. Morris will ask the guard to look after them.

These fears were groundless, and in January Charlie was again in London on his way back to Maidenhead.

> How I feel for you without that *charming* boy . . . He is the most bright, good, and *charming* child. He landed in this morning looking so sweet and bright and cheery, and *trim* as if he were not come off a journey, just as Edith always looks after a journey, just as out of a band box . . . The care he took of me when we went out together. He is such a *thorough* gentleman.

Despite all this praise of Charlie, if Elizabeth had a favourite grand-child it was Annette, always referred to as 'my pet', or 'our dear *pretty* child', and many little notes and parcels were sent to her from London. In 1882 Annette received her first prayer-book from her grand-mother, the same small leather-bound volume also containing 'Hymns Ancient and Modern' and the New Testament. The latter section was divided into the daily morning and evening readings prescribed by the Church Calendar, by following which the New Testament was read through twice during the year. Charlie, however, had the advantage (to his grand-mother) of a real or imagined throat delicacy, necessitating a check-up by Doctor MacLagan several times during the school term. Charles might have called a halt to these goings on, even Henry might have put his foot down, had not Edith's tragic illness driven all other matters into the background.

In March 1887, Edith had been giving instructions to a gardener in the peach-house, when she suddenly collapsed, apparently in a dead faint. She remained unconscious until the next morning and Henry, convinced that she was dying, telegraphed to his parents asking them to inform the Scott relations. The telegram was followed by another to say that she had recovered consciousness but was still very weak. The local doctor diagnosed a stroke but, as Edith was only just past thirty, he held out hopes of a complete recovery. Daily bulletins were telegraphed to London, but these were replaced by letters as Edith gradually regained strength. 'I am so thankful that Puss is with you. I know what a comfort *she* can be,' wrote Elizabeth who had received an additional blow in the death, in Ireland, of her sister Georgina Croker, after a short illness. Elizabeth wrote of the 'sad, sad news' to Henry, telling him that 'Poor Fred was here before going to Euston, but he was late I grieve to say.' Fred was one of Georgina's six sons. Since he was supposed to be hurrying to his mother's death-bed, it might seem curious that he should have first paid a call on his uncle and aunt, thereby missing his train, had not a letter from his sister thrown light on the matter: 'I hope Fred has repaid you the money you kindly lent him for his fare. He was given money here for that purpose,' she wrote to her 'dearest Aunt Lizzie' after the funeral.

Edith made what appeared to be a complete recovery, but a second stroke in November and another in December left her with a very bad impediment in her speech which lasted for the rest of her life. It was tragic to hear her desperate attempts to express herself, only achieving an indistinguishable mumble from which an occasional word emerged clearly. A month after her third stroke she was up and going out, and it then appeared that she had a stiffness in her limbs which was always referred to as 'rheumatism'. For a time she suffered from deep depression, and Henry was over-whelmed with grief. Gradually, however, her cheerful and fun-loving nature proved to be stronger than her disabilities. Those who knew her well learnt to understand her garbled speech, though it was always to be a source of embarrassment to strangers. She and Henry courageously resumed their normal life, visiting and being visited by their friends, and the families on the place were soon able to interpret the peculiar sounds of Edith's speech as easily as they had learnt to 'talk on their fingers' to Fan.

Some of the family letters of the year 1888 are missing; and either for this reason, or because Charles and Elizabeth had begun to conform to contemporary prudery, the anxious enquiries for and advice about Edith give the impression that she had suffered a relapse or another stroke. All is explained, however, by the relieved and thankful letters following Henry's telegrams to his parents on 3 November announcing that Edith had been safely delivered of a second son, six days before Charlie's twelfth birthday. 'I am very glad you mean to "celebrate" the event,' Charles wrote two days later, referring to the proposed large party for the christening of George Stanley. 'I think it seems a good sign that Edith has been so much better lately.'

Charles had been less enthusiastic over another family event, for which he should have thanked Heaven fasting. In November 1887, he had told Henry that –

Mr. Pearce, the deaf and dumb clergyman who was at Charleville in the autumn, has proposed for Fan and she has accepted him. It is not a very eligible match in any way. His Father is Town Clerk of Southampton & they will be very poor, never have more than £700 a year, but on the whole I thought it better to give my consent. Fan had set her heart on it and would have been miserable if I had refused, and at her age she is not likely to have many children, and she is not at all expensive in her tastes or habits. It is proposed that they should be married about June or July next, before we go to Ireland for the summer.

It was a sign of Fan's popularity that she was seldom in London with her parents whose letters constantly referred to her as staying with relations or friends, sometimes accompanying them on tours on the continent or to seaside resorts on the south coast. Either during one of these visits, or through her family's connection with The Royal Association for the Deaf and Dumb,[2] she had made friends with the Reverend Richard Pearce and easily persuaded Henry and Edith to invite him to Charleville. Edith was particularly fond of Fan, who had often kept her company while Henry was away. Yet although she was a general favourite, no-one had expected her to marry; and Charles' attitude seems ungrateful, even if the '£700 a year' included the income from the capital he had already settled on Fan. Husbands for deaf-mutes of forty-three do not grow on every bush; Dick Pearce might have come from a humble background, but he was a fine man, well known in Hampshire for his 'wonderful ministry' among the deaf and dumb, and as merry and good-humoured as was Fan herself. He had been ordained by the Bishop of Winchester, and worked for the Winchester Mission to the Deaf. In 1886, being then the only deaf clergyman in the Church of England, he was presented to Queen Victoria who took a great interest in work for the deaf and dumb.[3] He and Fan were married on 26 April 1886, and died within two years of each other forty years later. In their house paper and pencils were always at hand for visitors who could not 'talk on their fingers', and those who knew the Pearces late in life agreed that it would be impossible to find a more cheerful and contented old couple.

Elizabeth was operated on for cataract in both eyes shortly after Fan's wedding, the date of which had probably been advanced for that reason. The operation was pronounced successful and she was thought to have made a remarkable recovery. She was able to write a cheerful letter to Henry from Folkstone, where Charles had taken her for a few days' 'change of air'. 'I wonder if it was you who sent me the bottle of delicious scent. If so, many *thanks.* I do love scent.' She and Harriet had always been physically tougher than their sisters, and would have scorned to be defeated by ill-health. Yet, when Elizabeth went to Ireland in August, her old friends saw a change in her and signs that she was beginning to feel her age, which was seventy-four. She was able to deceive her family, however: 'Mama is thank God *very* well,' Charles wrote from London in November. If she appeared so, it was because she could not afford to be otherwise. Charles was five years her junior, but owing to his frequent bouts of helplessness, he had become very dependent on her, while Henry depended on them both. All decisions regarding Charlie were now made by the grand-parents, who continued to run their home in Ireland from Belgrave Road.

Edith's general health was now excellent, but there had been no improvement in her speech nor in the 'stiffness' of her limbs. She had always been on affectionate terms with Henry's family; Charles, Elizabeth and Fan loved her and admired her courage, the Brooke cousins were fond of her, and Henry's 'Aunt Ha', who was often at Charleville, described her as 'dear kind Edith, always so kind to me.' The only fly in the ointment was Puss. This was perhaps inevitable, owing to her proximity to her old home. Although she was now Mrs. Royse and lived in the agent's cottage, to the people in and around Charleville she was still 'Miss Louise', the spoilt and petted daughter of the house. They liked her the least of Charles' and Elizabeth's children, but she was 'one of the family', and many of them had known her since her babyhood.

Who made the first suggestion that Puss should take up permanent residence at Charleville? Charles' letter of 9 March 1889, refers to plans, already submitted by Henry, for the conversion of the 'billiard room wing' for the Royse family. This consisted of three good rooms on the ground floor with several bedrooms above, and jutted out from the south side of the rectangle immediately behind the main building. 'I think your ideas on the subject are so good that I will leave it all to you,' Charles said, merely stipulating that the carpenter should first finish some estate work on which he was then engaged.

Edith must have concealed her dislike of the plan from Henry, who would not willingly have done anything to distress 'darling Edith'; and the plan exactly suited Puss, Dargle cottage being far too small for her large family. The necessary alterations were made, after which Puss moved in, presumably with Jack, and certainly with Joan, Winnie, Clare, Olive, Norah, Kathleen and Cecil. After having been the only girl at Charleville, fourteen-year-old Annette was now sharing her home with seven girl-cousins, all of whom were more intelligent and a great deal more talented than herself. Puss took care of her daughters' musical education and, later, they formed the nucleus of a Ladies' String Orchestra trained by herself, which became locally famous for their performances at charity concerts. It was owing to Puss that Annette and Charlie both learnt to play the violin, though they never reached the standard of their cousin Olive, who filled an album with local press notices of her amateur recitals.

The Royses' wing had a separate front door opening on to the pleasure grounds, and though attached to and communicating with the rest of the house, could be run as an entirely independent unit. This, however, was not what Puss intended. Meals were communal, and the scene in the dining room was reminiscent of the days when the Rathdownes and their nine daughters sat round the table. According to Annette, the cousins had 'great fun' together, but she and Charlie resented the presence of Aunt Puss who ordered them about and did her best to usurp Edith's position as mistress of the house.

Poor Edith was at a terrible disadvantage. It took her a long time to say anything, and though the servants understood her, it was easy for them to slip into the habit of taking orders from 'Miss Louise'; easier still for Henry, if he happened to be in a hurry, to transmit messages through his big sister who had ruled him since they had been children. The Royses had always been made free of the house and gardens; no-one can now remember for how long they actually lived at Charleville, before even the unimaginative Henry awoke to the fact that he had created an impossible situation, and transferred his sister and her family to a house belonging to George Brooke. Years afterwards, Edith stumblingly confided her side of the story to Frank Cole's daughter, showing her the meticulously-kept account books to prove the unfairness of implying that she had been incaable of running her own house.

Notes to Chapter Twenty-One

1 Father James Healy, 1824-1894. Curate, Bray, County Wicklow, 1858; administrator at Little Bray, 1867-1893; parish priest, Ballybrack and Killiney, County Dublin, 1893. *(Dictionary of National Biography).*
2 The records of The Royal Association for the Deaf and Dumb state that Charles and his family had given help and support to the Association since its early days, and that he had been chairman at their annual meeting in 1874.
3 From the records of The Royal Association for the Deaf and Dumb.

22

Back-seat Politician

Theoretically, Charles Monck's public career came to an end in 1884. In May 1887, writing instructions to Henry concerning the celebrations in Ireland on the occasion of Queen Victoria's Jubilee, he had added: 'Yesterday, for the first time for three years, I walked across the room without my sticks'; and six months later, 'I yesterday *walked* from the Achilles statue in Hyde Park to within a few paces of the Marble Arch. I never expected to be able to do this again.' During the past three years he had been driven each day to the City, where he had attended to his business until the evening; but in his helpless condition, he would not attend sessions in the House of Lords nor go to his club. To all appearances he had retired from political life; yet in fact he continued to exert 'back seat' influence on Irish affairs through correspondence with his many friends in the government who constantly wrote to consult him on the enactments of the Irish Land Bills, regarding him as the chief authority owing to his many years' experience as Land Commissioner. His correspondence increased as the result of his occasional letters to *The Times* in which he frankly expressed his views.

Among those who often sought his opinion was Lord Spencer, who was Lord Lieutenant of Ireland for the second time from 1882 to 1885, and became Lord President of the Council in 1886. When replying to his request for information on the landlord-tenant situation, Charles sent him detailed statistics to prove that 'the allegations of non-payment of rent – at least in Leinster – have been greatly exaggerated.'[1]

In December 1885, he privately confided to Henry an opinion he was soon to state openly:

> The situation in Ireland is most perplexing . . . The Crimes
> Act and measures of that sort dealt with crimes arising out of

Charles, 4th Viscount Monck, *c.* 1880.

the agitation, but they left the agitation itself untouched . . . I am very much inclined to think the best course would be to open negotiations with Parnell so as to ascertain clearly what it is he requires. He has never yet told us . . . I am sure that nothing effective can be done until communications are opened with him. You cannot leave a man who has 85 votes in his pocket out of account in settling the matter. Don't show this to *any* one.[2]

This was a reference to Parnell's powerful influence with the Irish electorate, the size of which had been greatly increased by the lowering of the franchise to include those who were not men of property. The object of the Ballot Act of 1872 was to secure secret voting, thus avoiding intimidation. Known as the 'Uncrowned King of Ireland', Parnell represented Cork city in parliament where he was leader of the Home Rule party, the term Home Rule being considered 'a more positive and less offensive version of the old demand for "Repeal" of the union.'[3] In the cause of Home Rule for Ireland he had played off one political party against the other, both Tories and Liberals being anxious to avoid having the whole weight of the Irish vote against them.[4] Largely owing to his influence, Gladstone and the Liberals were defeated in 1885, only to return to power, with a small majority, in February 1886. Gladstone was again Prime Minister, having pledged himself to bring in the Irish Home Rule Bill. 'I don't know what is to be the result of Gladstone's new govt,' Monck wrote to his son.

I think the general impression here is that it will not last long. Certainly no Govt has ever been started with so many first class men of its own side left out. Hartington, Goschen, Forster, James, Courtenay, almost enough to make a strong cabinet by themselves . . . I think Gladstone's *advertisement* for information on Irish affairs was great nonsense. He ought to know by this time where he can get trustworthy information if he wants it . . . My dear boy, you may say what you like about W.E.G. or any one else, so far as I am concerned. I should not like to think that you did not form and express your own opinions because they might not agree with mine.[5]

Henry's antipathy to 'W.E.G.' was shared by his mother, in spite of Gladstone's former admiration of her. In May 1886, she noted in her commonplace book:

> Mr. Gladstone (to his shame be it spoken) made a go-between of Labouchère to Chamberlain on the Home Rule Bill. He [Labouchère ?] delivered himself *thus:* 'Mr. Gladstone is a very clever man and a very pious man, but I should not like to play whist with him. He would have two or three aces in his sleeve, & say that Providence had put them there!'

In spite of Monck's incapacitated state, he was still regarded as a useful ally by Gladstone and his colleagues, who had counted on having his support for the Bill. He, however, refused to declare himself either for or against the measure, until he could learn what form it would take. 'Everyone here is in a state of expectation until Gladstone opens his hand,' he told Henry at the beginning of the session. 'I do not love Home Rule,' he wrote to Spencer, 'but I am brought to assent to it by the consideration that it is, in my opinion, the only possible policy. I expressed that opinion to you before Mr. Gladstone had declared himself in its favour.'[6]

Gladstone described Monck as being 'in essence a Home Ruler.'[7] It was well known that he had always upheld the principle of self-government for any country that was ready for it, and it was expected that he would have supported the Home Rule plan from its outset. He was, however, sufficiently well-informed to know that, though the British Parliament might concede a separate parliament in Dublin, the concession would be attended by restrictions and conditions that would be impossible for Irishmen to accept. Fearing possible complications in the event of war, the British government would never willingly agree to the complete independence of so near a neighbour. Parnell, as representing the Irish nationalists, might agree to Gladstone's terms as a beginning, as the 'thin end of the wedge'; but the nationalists would refuse to comply with them, and the result, Monck prophesied, would be 'anarchy', and eventually lead to the 'complete separation of Ireland from England'.

In common with Daniel O'Connell in 1843, and with Isaac Butt,[8] founder of the Home Rule League in 1873, Charles believed that complete severance of Ireland from Britain would be a calamity. His reluctance to contemplate such a severance might, to-day, be looked upon as unreasonable prejudice; but in the 1880's, citizenship within the British Empire entailed privileges the surrendering of which would have resulted in great hardship for those Irishmen who lived and worked in England or in other parts of the Empire. In spite of his severe indictments against British misrule, it was inconceivable to him that Ireland should be regarded by the British as a foreign land, and he and his countrymen as aliens. A further and even more serious reason against separation was the knowledge that it would certainly result in the division or 'partition' of Ireland, since the population of the province of Ulster was mainly Protestant, and these would refuse to accept a Dublin parliament, preferring to retain the British connection. An Ireland divided into two parts was a prospect too dreadful to contemplate, and there would be the added complication of the presence in the northern counties of a Catholic minority, and of a Protestant minority in the south.* Monck's years in pre-confederation Canada had shown him that hardship and bitter disputes were the certain consequences of a 'minority' being subject to one or the other government in a country with divided legislation.

He was made uneasy, too, by his awareness that the Irish nationalists themselves were not unanimous in their views. Even while they united to vote for home rule, there were already disagreements among them as to the exact meaning of the term and the degree to which Ireland was to become an independent nation. The Irish nationalists elected to the Westminster parliament were split into 'three separate groups, owing allegiance respectively to John Redmond . . . to T. M. Healy and to Justin McCarthy.'[9] Charles Monck repeatedly urged members of the government to open negotiations with Parnell, if only to learn how far his views on home rule coincided with Gladstone's.

It is a curious feature of Mr. Parnell's policy that, after five years of agitation for Home Rule, he appears never to have thought out, or if he has done so, has not communicated to his intimates in this enterprise, the most elementary details of his scheme. The latest utterances of Mr. Justin M'Carthy and Mr.

---

* There was at that time no frontier between the north and south of Ireland.

T. P. O'Connor show that no agreement has been come to among the Irish party as to what their place is to be.[10]

To some home rule implied the repeal of the Union and the re-establishment of 'Grattan's Parliament'; to others it stood for a Dublin parliament legislating for purely Irish affairs while sending representatives to Westminster; while there were many to whom it stood for complete separation from England. Few seemed prepared to look ahead to the future working-out of their respective schemes.

Charles greatly feared that Gladstone was drawing up a measure, the conditions of which could only be imposed by force – 'the country meanwhile being ruined by agitation,' in other words, by civil war.[11] When, in April 1886, Gladstone finally 'opened his hand', Monck's worst fears were realised. The Home Rule Bill proposed that a form of local government should be conceded to Ireland in a Dublin parliament, while the reins would still be in the hands of the 'Imperial Parliament' in which Ireland would not be represented. The parliament at Westminster would control foreign affairs, the army and navy, customs and excise duties, while Ireland would still contribute towards 'Imperial expenses'. Charles told Henry that his chief objection to the Bill was the exclusion of Irish representation at Westminster.

> I think Gladstone's plan is virtual separation between England and Ireland, and I don't think it will pass in its present shape, or in any shape this year, but the wretched thing is that the proposing of such a scheme makes government almost impossible except under a state of siege, which is no government at all. I don't in the least mind my opinions being known as far as I am individually concerned, but I have been in confidential communication with Spencer, and I should not like to have my views made public until I have explained them to him.[12]

Lord Spencer had written to Monck:

> I should greatly like to hear your views on the political situation in Ireland . . . You are a wise and unimpassioned observer of Irish Politics and thoroughly understand the

people. What is your view? Would it bore you to tell me?[13]

Spencer and Monck were on very friendly terms and this letter was only one of many in a long correspondence, during the course of which Gladstone used Spencer as a 'go-between'. Three months before the Home Rule Bill was laid before parliament, Charles had already been warned of what Gladstone was likely to propose. In January 1886, he wrote to Spencer:

> You will in future have the Parliament of Great Britain sitting at Westminster and the Irish Legislature sitting at Dublin . . . and yet it is proposed to retain to the Parliament of Great Britain, in which Ireland will not be represented, the sole right of dealing with some of the most important questions which can affect the interests of that country . . . The implication is that Irish members (if not excluded from Westminster) could misconduct themselves in reference to questions affecting Great Britain exclusively.[14] Are the Irish representatives the only portion of the community who have a 'double dose of original sin' that their country must be disenfranchised rather than that they should be trusted with powers which they may possibly misuse? Which is the greater anomaly, that Irish representatives should be trusted with the right of voting on questions in which they have no direct concern, or that they should be entirely excluded from the consideration of subjects in which they have a most obvious and palpable interest? I venture to submit that the proper mode of meeting this difficulty – if it was necessary to meet it – would be not by confiscating the rights of the Irish people, but by calling into existence for England and Scotland institutions similar to those which you are about to give to Ireland.[15]

The latter suggestion was his favourite solution, which he affirmed would get rid of the British government's 'vicious practice of exceptional legislation for Ireland'. He had been converted to Irish home rule, always providing that there was no rift in the United Kingdom. Let there be a Dublin parliament to deal with all Irish affairs; provide similar institutions for both England and Scotland; and let all three countries, on an equal basis, send representatives to a central parliament at Westminster. There is no record that his suggestion received any support. Spencer, in one of several letters to Monck in 1886, admitted that 'we may come to that. But,' he added, 'there is no demand for Federation or change in Wales, Scotland or England. We cannot propose what is not wanted.' He wrote that he was 'much concerned' to find Monck so strongly opposed to Gladstone's measure, referring to it as 'the local Government Bill', a term which would not have pleased the nationalists. 'From what you said to me some time ago, I hoped you would have been with us... I admit that logically your arguments as to taxation without representation are sound . . . Our plan will be no doubt much altered in Committee if it reaches that stage. Your views will be freely and fully discussed. I, for one, if a practical solution in your sense be found, will not object, but many competent men will.'[16]

In this, as in his other letters, Spencer made it clear that Monck's opinion was sought by, and carried weight with, the Liberal party. Spencer showed Monck's letters to Gladstone, who replied that Monck's argument was 'leaky in every point . . . But I contemplate with . . . satisfaction the likelihood that we may be able to frame proposals which will, in a considerable degree, remove his objections. For we should both, I am persuaded, greatly value his general support of a Bill which, as in essence a Home Ruler, he must be reluctant to condemn utterly.'[17] Spencer sent on Gladstone's letter to Monck who, though far from condemning the Bill 'utterly', reiterated his objection to taxation without representation which would, he said, degrade Ireland to the position of a vassal state. 'It is proposed to try a great constitutional experiment to which I, for one, most heartily wish success; do not let us begin by taking a step which is irretrievable, and disastrous should the plan fail.'[18]

Gladstone's and Spencer's anxiety to enlist Monck's support was due, at least in part, to a 'split' in the Liberal party. The dissentient Liberals, as they were called, were led by Hartington, Chamberlain and Goschen, who were in favour of a home rule scheme which would not exclude Irish representation at Westminster. Monck believed that they were 'on the right lines' and, in general, agreed with their policy.

In the meantime Parnell had declared in favour of Gladstone's original plan, which proved, Monck said, that the phrase '"Ireland a nation" means much less in the mouths of the Irish Nationalist

party than the ordinary signification of the words would imply.'[19]
'I do not think it will pass at all this year,' he had written to Henry,
and in this he was correct. The Bill was defeated on 6 June without
ever reaching the House of Lords. Gladstone dissolved parliament
but, in the ensuing election, received even less support for his Bill
from the electorate than he had done from the House of Commons.
'The elections have upset the notion of Gladstone's power, also his
theory of "masses against classes",' Charles wrote to Henry. 'It looks
at present very much as if Lord Salisbury would be strong enough to
form an administration.'[20]

The Tories returned to power; in August Lord Salisbury formed
his second cabinet; and still the subject of home rule was discussed at
meetings, in letters to the papers and in correspondence both official
and personal. All who had any knowledge of Ireland knew that
home rule must come; they only differed about the form it should
take. On 20 October 1886, *The Times* printed a letter from Charles
Monck which was intended to show that it was possible for a
common denominator of agreement to be reached by some of the
'several parties'. He dealt rather severely with Parnell's committal to
Gladstone's proposal to 'degrade Ireland to the *status* of a tributary
province', and recommended that the Hartington-Chamberlain
home rule plan should be considered. Since the latter scheme
included Irish representation at Westminster it had, he said, the
merit of proposing 'decentralisation' as opposed to Gladstone's plan
of 'disintegration'. He again pressed his own idea of an equal constitution 'for all sections of the United Kingdom', and ended with an
urgent plea that 'the administration of justice should be controlled at
Westminster . . . until some satisfactory arrangement of the land
question is obtained.'[21]

Though Monck was no longer officially a Land Commissioner, he
continued to nag at members of the government in an attempt to
bring about a revision of the 1881 Land Act. This had fixed Irish
rents, so that landlords could no longer force them up in order to
evict their tenants; but it had not provided for the subsequent drop
in prices which made it impossible for small-holders to pay even the
'fair rent' fixed in 1881. Evictions for non-payment were followed by
what Charles Monck called 'agitation' and less sympathetic people
'agrarian outrages'. Charles complained that such measures as the
Crimes Act and Coercion Bills struck at the agitation but did

nothing to remove its cause. 'I think Kavanagh[22] and others are taking a wrong line,' he had written to Henry, referring to those land-owners in parliament who objected to reducing their rents further than the reduction made compulsory in 1881:

> It appears to me that the tenants have never had so good a case for reduction [of rent] as they have this year, on account of the fall in the price of cattle, and the reductions of rent under the Land Act have really nothing to do with that. Royse quite agrees with my opinion, and he is making out a scale of reduction, 20 per cent to some & 15 per cent to others according to their circumstances. I think too our tenants deserve it, for they have always paid their rents well, and last year as well as ever. ['Last year' having been a particularly bad season.]

Having always believed that the small tenant-farmers had rights of their own with regard to the land they had worked, and which had been taken from their fore-fathers, the original owners, by force, he entered readily into the scheme for allowing them to avail themselves of the government loan in order to purchase their holdings. He pointed out to Henry, who held rigidly conservative views, that the sales of land also suited his personal convenience, as the proceeds would enable him to pay off some of his debts.

In 1887 a third Irish Land Act was passed, providing for 'judicial reduction of rents'. This was the 'arrangement' referred to by Charles in his letter to *The Times,* without which he saw a danger in leaving the landlord-tenant situation to the mercy of a Dublin parliament in the event of home rule being established. If there were to be no referee in the shape of a central government at Westminster, he feared for the fate of both landowners and tenants. The law to reduce all rents by a certain percentage was hard on those landlords who had already made reductions voluntarily, previous to the passing of the Land Acts.

Charles protested to Lord Spencer against a government scheme of 'expropriation', by which landowners were to be forced to sell their estates at a low price fixed by the government, even in those cases where there were satisfactory relations between landlords and tenants. He pointed out that most Irish properties were mortgaged, and that in the case of expropriation, a way must be found of settling with the landlord's creditors. There were extremists who were deter-mined to dispossess all landlords, including the good ones whose tenants wished for no change; while a Dublin parliament would include landowners who posed as nationalists, but were harsher and more unjust than any Anglo-Irish, non-resident landlord. Many of these had been land-agents and 'gombeen-men',* who, having made enough money on the side to purchase land of their own, were notorious for their inhuman treatment of their tenants.

Charles had drawn Henry's attention to a paragraph in *The Times* referring to the member for South Division, County Dublin, which illustrated the emptiness of promises made and opinions expressed during an election. 'While Sir T. Esmonde is abusing the landlords in Dublin, his agent in Wexford is calling on his tenants to pay up sharp!' [23]

There was solid ground for Monck's fears, but in the event they were proved unnessary for the immediate future. There was no ques-tion as to who should or should not control land legislation for the simple reason that there was as yet no Dublin parliament. The third Land Act was passed in 1887, but home rule seemed as far away as ever.

---

* Gombeen-men were shopkeepers who lent money to tenants who could not pay their rents.

Notes to Chapter Twenty-Two

1 Monck to Spencer, 19 February 1886. (Copy in Monck's hand, Monck Papers).
2 Monck to Henry Monck, December 1885. (Monck Papers).
3 Sir Robert Ensor, *op. cit.*
4 In 1885, when Gladstone's ministry fell, Parnell 'made clear to both Liberals and Conservatives that Home Rule was the price at which the votes of his supporters could be bought. Neither Conservatives nor Liberals, however, dared to risk the alienation of their constituents in England by an express promise. Parnell had, therefore, to decide between probabilities, and his ultimate choice was that the Irish support should be given to the Conservatives. Hayden and Moonan, *op. cit.*
5 Monck to Henry Monck, 20 February 1886.
6 Monck to Spencer, 8 May 1886. (Copy in Monck's hand, Monck Papers).
7 Gladstone to Spencer, May 1886. (Copy in Monck Papers).
8 Monck's connection with Butt, founder of the Home Rule Party, dated from his student days when Butt was professor of Political Economy at Trinity College, Dublin.
9 F. S. L. Lyons, *Ireland Since the Famine* (London, 1971).
10 Charles Monck to Henry Monck, (Monck Papers). Professor F. S. L. Lyons, *op. cit.*, describes Parnell as a 'genius . . . at not committing himself', when referring to his 'habitual ambiguities'.
11 Charles Monck to Henry Monck, 1886 (Monck Papers).
12 Charles Monck to Henry Monck, April 1886 (Private letter, Monck Papers).
13 Lord Spencer to Charles Monck, 17 December 1885 (Private letter, Monck Papers).
14 Monck knew that a large proportion of the English supporters of the proposed Home Rule Bill were motivated by their wish to rid Parliament of Irish members who, led by Parnell, had launched a campaign of obstruction. With the object of wearing down governmental opposition to home rule under their own terms, they held up debates on subjects unconnected with Irish affairs, so that parliament was frequently sitting all night.
15 Charles Monck to Lord Spencer, January 1886 (Private letter, copy in Monck Papers).
16 Spencer to Monck. Private letter (Monck Papers).
17 Copy in Monck's hand (Monck Papers).
18 Letter from Monck to *The Times*, 20 October 1886.
19 Monck to Spencer (Copy in Monck's hand, Monck Papers).
20 Charles to Henry Monck, 9 July 1886 (Monck Papers).
21 Letter from Charles Monck to *The Times*, 20 October 1886.
22 Arthur MacMorrough Kavanagh, 1831-1889. Member for County Wexford, 1866-1868, and for County Carlow, 1868-1880. He became Lord-Lieutenant of County Carlow in 1880. *Dictionary of National Biography*.
23 Charles to Henry Monck, 1885. Monck Papers.

23

'Not in my lifetime'

In 1890, Henry wrote to consult his father on his latest project – that he should stand for County Wicklow at the next election. 'I don't wish to say anything that might distress you,' Charles replied, 'but at my time of life, and in my present state of health, I don't think it would be wise of you to become a candidate for the county, which would certainly involve you in trouble and probably in expense.' This was intended as a delicate hint that Henry might at any moment succeed his father, in which case he would not be eligible for a seat in the House of Commons. The rest of the letter was concerned with arrangements to repay the thousand pounds which had been lent by Dick during the desperate situation caused by Stanley's debts.

His anxiety to wind up his affairs and the deterioration in his hand-writing were explained by the severe illness which occurred soon after he wrote. Less than two years later, he and Elizabeth crossed to Ireland for the last time, and it was obvious to all who saw him then, that he would never again leave his home. He was in great pain and shortly after he reached Charleville he became unconscious or nearly so. His family realised that this was his last illness, and that he had come home to die.

Elizabeth stole a march on him, however; taking her family so much by surprise that Fan, summoned from England by telegraph, did not arrive at Charleville until after her mother's death on 19 June. Her absence would not have distressed Elizabeth who was capricious in many ways but had no false sentimentality. There was no longer any need for her to worry about Fan who was in her element as parson's wife in a silent 'parish'. Among family problems which Elizabeth left unsolved was the tragedy of Edith, and all it meant in Henry's life; her dear Puss, headstrong, temperamental and totally unable to distinguish capital from income; and last but not least, Stanley,[1] estranged from his father but never out of his mother's thoughts. When her grandson Charlie first went to school Elizabeth had written, 'May God have him in His holy keeping,' and it was the same committal of all the 'loose ends' she was leaving behind, which caused her serenity during the last days.

After her death, Meriel Hodson wrote to Henry of her last visit to 'my best and dearest friend . . . the sweet face I loved so much. She said goodbye to me with such affection; she looked so lovely then. I like to think of the sweet smile and happy gentle face, which had lost all expression of anxiety.' Isabel Carnwath, too, had guessed what Henry was too inexperienced and Charles too ill to realise. 'I knew that your dear Mother was leaving us,' she wrote afterwards to Henry.

In the letters of condolence which he kept, there were many expressions of gratitude for Elizabeth's thoughtful kindness. 'No one was more tenderly sympathetic towards me in all my troubles than your dear Mother,' Lady Cloncurry wrote. 'I'll miss her kind little letters.' A summary of the many tributes to his mother was contained in a letter from his octogenarian neighbour at Bushey Park, signed, 'Ever yours affectionately, Selina Crampton.'

All the memories of so many years, all the kindnesses received rise up within me. Was she not the truest friend? So faithful, so warm, so true? Her heart was not only warm, it was *passionate* in its fidelity. I do not know anybody who resembles her! Her little peculiarities made me love her more, she was unlike anybody else. Who could describe her devotion to her husband, her children & her friends? . . .If there were no other reason for believing in a future state, I could not believe that warmth and energy and kindness were *extinct,* they must exist for ever. I think she had a very happy life, and though clouds gathered about her evening she looked through them all with wonderful courage and patience and spirit. Perhaps it is best she was the first to go, I often trembled for her future when she was to be left alone with all her work in the world done. But what a change it makes to me even when I look at the woods of Charleville from my windows and think – She is not there. But I do not forget [that] you and dear Lord Monck and Lady Edith and your dear children are there still, and perhaps Louise and others of your dear family . . . May the sun never set on

Charleville, that dear home which has been so long the light of our eyes and the joy of our hearts.

Nobody had expected that Elizabeth would be 'the first to go', still less that Charles would survive her by two years. All the letters of condolence written when he died in 1894, were destroyed with many other family papers after Henry's own death in 1927. The formal obituary notice in *The Times,* giving an account of his public career and praising his 'administrative qualities', ends by observing that 'he took no active interest in any recent political movement and enjoyed the respect and friendship of all parties.'

The 'recent political movements' had occurred during the four years before his death. The last of his own letters to survive was written in November 1890, and there are implications that he never fully recovered consciousness after that time, or that he was at least too ill to write. Otherwise he would have had plenty to say about the citing of Parnell as co-respondent in the O'Shea divorce case and the subsequent split in the Home Rule party, followed by riots during elections in Ireland. Still less could he have kept silent when Gladstone returned to power, and in 1893 presented the second Home Rule Bill which was passed, amid cheers, in the House of Commons, only to be rejected by the House of Lords. 'I fear its days are numbered,' Charles had said of the Upper House when it amended the second Land Act; and now the Lords had rejected a measure which, since his conversion to home rule, he had hoped for and worked for: an Irish parliament sending eighty representatives to Westminster.

Though in many ways in advance of his time, he was a product of the nineteenth century; and looking back, it is easy to criticise his views as having been too limited and too much influenced by the traditions of Daniel O'Connell and Isaac Butt. Had he lived long enough to see the British Commonwealth evolve out of the British Empire, and the change in the quality of Irish leaders, he would have kept in step with the modern world and recognised as inevitable, though perhaps regrettable, the conception of Ireland as a nation independent of Great Britain. 'It will not come in my lifetime, nor in yours,' John Robert Godley had written to Charles Monck, referring to the 'social revolution' as being the only remedy for the situation existing in Ireland in 1847; while Charles himself later declared, during a parliamentary debate, that it would take many years to repair the effects of 'centuries of neglect' by the British government. Neither he nor John Godley had visualised the precise form the 'social revolution' was to take; but in dedicating himself to Ireland's interests in general, and to tenants' rights and tenant-ownership in particular, he had known that each step forward helped to lay a foundation for reform on a national scale. Although he did not live to see the end for which he had worked, he believed that it was in sight and that Ireland was on the verge of self-government. 'I hope that dear Lord Monck may mercifully be hardly conscious of his loss,' a friend wrote when Elizabeth died; and the same merciful oblivion saved him from the fore-knowledge that twenty-seven troubled years were to pass before Ireland achieved home rule.[2]

The memory of him in his private capacity was kept alive by the personal testimony of the people of Charleville who, thirty years later, still spoke almost with adoration of his kindness, of his friendly, 'easy' ways, and of how greatly he and his wife were loved by their poorer neighbours. Henry was liked and respected, but never commanded the same, deep affection. He was considered just and conscientious, but praise of him was usually followed by – 'But you should have known the old lord!'

The downright manner for which Charles was criticised in his youth, had descended in full measure to Henry whose abrupt pronouncements were to become a standing joke and source of mimicry to a later generation. In spite of this, his cousins and nieces described him as 'very amusing and *so* kind', and he was never happier than when his house was filled with friends and relations. He always maintained that he could see an improvement in their health after a week at Charleville, and it was certainly the perfect place in which to spend a glorious holiday, or to recover from illness or any other kind of trouble.

The old traditions lived on, and in 1912, when Henry's son Charlie was a captain in the Coldstream and unable to go to Ireland for the funeral of his 'Aunt Puss', he wrote to his Royse cousins: 'Go to Charleville after the funeral; Charleville will do you good. It has always been as much your home as mine.'

Notes to Chapter Twenty-Three

1   Stanley survived his mother by six months. The cause of his death, in December 1892, is
    not known.
2   By the Treaty of 1921, the Irish Free State became a self-governing dominion within the
    British Commonwealth, pledging allegiance to the British Crown. Six counties of
    Northern Ireland separated from the Free State and remained an integral part of Great
    Britain. By the External Affairs Act of 1936, the Oath of Allegiance was abolished and
    Ireland became a republic. By the Ireland Act of 1949, the Irish Republic seceded from
    the British Commonwealth.

Index